Managing Knowledge

*To you, the reader,
and to middle managers,
who are an endangered species
in these challenging times.*

Managing Knowledge

David A. Wilson

*Published in association with
the Institute of Management*

*the Institute
of Management*

FOUNDATION

Butterworth-Heinemann
Linacre House, Jordan Hill, Oxford OX2 8DP
A division of Reed Educational and Professional Publishing Ltd

ℝ A member of the Reed Elsevier plc group

OXFORD   BOSTON   JOHANNESBURG
MELBOURNE   NEW DELHI   SINGAPORE

First published 1996

British Library Cataloguing in Publication Data
Wilson, David A., 1939–
  Managing Knowledge
  1 Management   2 Knowledge, theory of
  3 Information resources management
  I Title   II Institute of Management
  658.4

ISBN 0 7506 2054 4

Typesetting and artwork origination by David Gregson Associates, Beccles, Suffolk
Printed and bound in Great Britain by Clays Ltd, St Ives plc

Contents

Series adviser's preface

This book is one of a series designed for people wanting to develop their capabilities as managers. You might think that there isn't anything very new in that. In one way you would be right. The fact that very many people want to learn to become better managers is not new, and for many years a wide range of approaches to such learning and development has been available. These have included courses leading to formal qualifications, organizationally-based management development programmes and a whole variety of self-study materials. A copious literature, extending from academic textbooks to sometimes idiosyncratic prescriptions from successful managers and consultants, has existed to aid – or perhaps confuse – the potential seeker after managerial truth and enlightenment.

So what is new about this series? In fact, a great deal – marking in some ways a revolution in our thinking both about the art of managing and also the process of developing managers.

Where did it all begin? Like most revolutions, although there may be a single, identifiable act that precipitated the uprising, the roots of discontent are many and long-established. The debate about the performance of British managers, the way managers are educated and trained, and the extent to which shortcomings in both these areas have contributed to our economic decline, has been running for several decades.

Until recently, this debate has been marked by periods of frenetic activity – stimulated by some report or enquiry and perhaps ending in some new initiatives or policy changes – followed by relatively long periods of comparative calm. But the underlying causes for concern persisted. Basically, the majority of managers in the UK appeared to have little or no training for their role, certainly far less than their counterparts in our major competitor nations. And there was concern about the nature, style and appropriateness of the management education and training that were available.

The catalyst for this latest revolution came in late 1986 and early 1987, when three major reports reopened the whole issue. The 1987 reports were *The Making of British Managers* by John Constable and Roger McCormick, carried out for the British Institute of Management and the CBI, and *The Making of Managers* by Charles Handy, carried out for the (then) Manpower Services Commission, National Economic Development Office and British Institute of Management. The 1986 report, which often receives less recognition than it deserves as a key contribution to the recent changes, was *Management Training: context and process* by Iain Mangham and Mick Silver, carried out for the Economic and Social Research Council and the Department of Trade and Industry.

It is not the place to review in detail what the reports said. Indeed, they and their consequences are discussed in several places in this series of books. But essentially they confirmed that:

● British managers were undertrained by comparison with their counterparts internationally.
● The majority of employers invested far too little in training and developing their managers.
● Many employers found it difficult to specify with any degree of detail just what it was that they required successful managers to be able to do.

The Constable/McCormick and Handy reports advanced various recommendations for addressing these problems, involving an expansion of management education and development, a reformed structure of qualifications and a commitment from employers to a code of practice for management development. While this analysis was not new, and had echoes of much that had been said in earlier debates, this time a few leading individuals determined that the response should be both radical and permanent. The response was coordinated by the newly-established Council for Management Education and Development (now the National Forum for Management Education and Development (NFMED)) under the energetic and visionary leadership of Bob (now Sir Bob) Reid of Shell UK (now chairman of the British Railways Board).

Under the umbrella of NFMED a series of employer-led working parties tackled the problem of defining what it was that managers should be able to do, and how this differed for people at different levels in their organizations; how this satisfactory ability to perform might be verified; and how an appropriate structure of management qualifications could be put in place. This work drew upon the methods used to specify vocational standards in industry and commerce, and led to the development and introduction of competence-based management standards and qualifications. In this context, competence is defined as the ability to perform the activities within an occupation or function to the standards expected in employment.

It is this competence-based approach that is new in our thinking about the manager's capabilities. It is also what is new about this series of books, in that they are designed to support both this new structure of management standards, and of development activities based on it. The series was originally commissioned to support the Institute of Management's Certificate and Diploma qualifications, which were one of the first to be based on the new standards. However, these books are equally appropriate to any university, college or indeed company course leading to a certificate in management or diploma in management studies.

The standards were specified through an extensive process of consultation with a large number of managers in organizations of many different types and sizes. They are therefore employment based and employer-supported. And they fill the gap that Mangham and Silver identified – now we do have a language to describe what it is employers want their managers to be able to do – at least in part.

If you are engaged in any form of management development leading to a certificate or diploma qualification conforming to the national management standards, then you are probably already familiar with most of the key ideas on which the standards are based. To achieve this key purpose, which is defined as achieving the organization's objectives and continuously improving its performance, managers need to perform four key roles: managing operations, managing finance, managing people and managing information. Each of these key roles has a sub-structure of units and elements, each with associated performance and assessment criteria.

The reason for the qualification 'in part' is that organizations are different, and jobs within them are different. Thus the generic management standards probably do not cover all the management competences that you may need to possess in your job. There are almost certainly additional things, specific to your own situation in your own organization, that you need to be able to do. The standards are necessary, but almost certainly not sufficient. Only you, in discussion with your boss, will be able to decide what other capabilities you need to possess. But the standards are a place to start, a basis on which to build. Once you have demonstrated your proficiency against the standards, it will stand you in good stead as you progress through your organization, or change jobs.

So how do the new standards change the process by which you develop yourself as a manager? They change the process of development, or of gaining a management qualification, quite a lot. It is no longer a question of acquiring information and facts, perhaps by being 'taught' in some classroom environment, and then being tested to see what you can recall. It involves demonstrating, in a quite specific way, that you can do certain things to a particular standard of performance. And because of this, it puts a much greater onus on you to manage your own development, to decide how you can demonstrate any particular competence, what evidence you need to present, and how you can collect it. Of course, there will always be people to advise and guide you in this, if you need help.

But there is another dimension, and it is to this that this series of books is addressed. While the standards stress ability to perform, they do not ignore the traditional knowledge base that has been associated with 'management studies'. Rather, they set this in a different context. The standards are supported by 'underpinning knowledge and understanding' which has three components:

● Purpose and context, which is knowledge and understanding of the manager's objectives, and of the relevant organizational and environmental influences, opportunities and values.
● Principles and methods, which is knowledge and understanding of

the theories, models, principles, methods and techniques that provide the basis of competent managerial performance.
● Data, which is knowledge and understanding of specific facts likely to be important to meeting the standards.

Possession of the relevant knowledge and understanding underpinning the standards is needed to support competent managerial performance as specified in the standards. It also has an important role in supporting the transferability of management capabilities. It helps to ensure that you have done more than learned 'the way we do things around here' in your own organization. It indicates a recognition of the wider things which underpin competence, and that you will be able to change jobs or organizations and still be able to perform effectively.

These books cover the knowledge and understanding underpinning the management standards, most specifically in the category of principles and methods. But their coverage is not limited to the minimum required by the standards, and extends in both depth and breadth in many areas. The authors have tried to approach these underlying principles and methods in a practical way. They use many short cases and examples which we hope will demonstrate how, in practice, the principles and methods, and knowledge of purpose and context plus data, support the ability to perform as required by the management standards. In particular we hope that this type of presentation will enable you to identify and learn from similar examples in your own managerial work.

You will already have noticed that one consequence of this new focus on the standards is that the traditional 'functional' packages of knowledge and theory do not appear. The standard textbook titles such as 'quantitative methods', 'production management', 'organizational behaviour' etc. disappear. Instead, principles and methods have been collected together in clusters that more closely match the key roles within the standards. You will also find a small degree of overlap in some of the volumes, because some principles and methods support several of the individual units within the standards. We hope you will find this useful reinforcement.

Having described the positive aspects of standards-based management development, it would be wrong to finish without a few cautionary remarks. The developments described above may seem simple, logical and uncontroversial. It did not always seem that way in the years of work which led up to the introduction of the standards. To revert to the revolution analogy, the process has been marked by ideological conflict and battles over sovereignty and territory. It has sometimes been unclear which side various parties are on – and indeed how many sides there are! The revolution, if well advanced, is not at an end. Guerrilla warfare continues in parts of the territory.

Perhaps the best way of describing this is to say that, while competence-based standards are widely recognized as at least a major part of the answer to improving managerial performance, they are not the whole answer. There is still some debate about the way competences are defined, and whether those in the standards are the most appropriate on which to base assessment of managerial performance. There are other models of management competences than those in the standards.

There is also a danger in separating management performance into a set of discrete components. The whole is, and needs to be, more than the sum of the parts. Just like bowling an off-break in cricket, practising a golf swing or forehand drive in tennis, you have to combine all the separate movements into a smooth, flowing action. How you combine the competences, and build on them, will mark your own individual style as a manager.

We should also be careful not to see the standards as set in stone. They determine what today's managers need to be able to do. As the arena in which managers operate changes, then so will the standards. The lesson for all of us as managers is that we need to go on learning and developing, acquiring new skills or refining existing ones. Obtaining your certificate or diploma is like passing a mile post, not crossing the finishing line.

All the changes and developments of recent years have brought management qualifications, and the process by which they are gained, much closer to your job as a manager. We hope these books support this process by providing bridges between your own experience and the underlying principles and methods which will help you to demonstrate your competence. Already, there is a lot of evidence that managers enjoy the challenge of demonstrating competence, and find immediate benefits in their jobs from the programmes based on these new-style qualifications. We hope you do too. Good luck in your career development.

Paul Jervis

Preface

Knowledge is not a finite, visible resource, and cannot therefore be managed by traditional methods – yet it is the key to success in today's business environment.

Knowledge is the common factor that links all business improvement techniques, from work study and systems analysis to total quality management and business process re-engineering. They all depend on people using their knowledge to develop new processes – and they all result in people's jobs being changed or eliminated. People at work may not show it, but they are always suspicious of business improvement projects, and will use their knowledge to protect their positions rather than to sacrifice themselves on the altar of shareholder profit. And that is why work study was abandoned, why TQM is falling from favour, and why BPR will go the same way too, unless everyone at work can be sure they personally will not be disadvantaged.

Knowledge is the link – the neglected resource which your organization must manage if it is to improve and compete effectively in world markets. Knowledge has fuelled all human progress in the past, and has virtually unlimited potential to continue doing so in the future. To manage knowledge means to exploit it to the full, without exploiting the people who possess it. Knowledge is the ultimate resource to be managed for continuing survival and prosperity, but your organization cannot possess and control it like other resources. The old assumptions and methods designed for the physical resources of previous eras are not effective and a new approach is needed.

Two hundred and fifty years ago the agricultural age ended and the industrial age began. Our economy became based on manufacturing, and working life changed so radically we refer to the change as the Industrial Revolution. Now as we move into the information age, our economy is becoming based on knowledge, and working life is changing again – and not just in the UK but throughout the developed world. Global, buyers' markets are typified by surpluses of many agricultural and manufactured products, and global communications mean that discriminating buyers can choose on the basis of quality and value and buy from the best in the world. The information age is bringing with it a greatly intensified competitive environment for organizations of all kinds.

But in the UK we feel we are being swept along rather than leading the way in this new revolution. One of the reasons may be that we are still clinging to the methods and beliefs which brought us success before. We are still managing the traditional factors of production at a time when knowledge is the most important resource. Michael Porter, in *The Competitive Advantage of Nations* (1990) observed, 'It is how factors of production are deployed, more than the factors themselves which determines success ...' And Peter Drucker, in *Post Capitalist Society* (1993) comments that 'Knowledge is the only meaningful resource today. The traditional factors of production ... have become secondary. They can be obtained ... easily, provided there is knowledge.' And yet most managers still focus on the traditional factors of production. Knowledge is not a balance sheet item, and so most managers do not even recognize it as a resource. However, some principles are beginning to emerge about how best to manage this most important resource, and some methods and tools are available.

One of the reasons for our unexceptional economic performance in the UK may be because our whole set of management methods and beliefs – our management paradigm – is no longer serving us well. It was developed in the industrial age, and now in the information age it has become inappropriate and an impediment to national progress. The industrial paradigm is based on the principle of command-and-control, and depends heavily on the hierarchical organization structure. It is supported by Adam Smith's division of labour, and F. W. Taylor's scientific management, both of which tend to destroy the knowledge resource rather than help create and husband it.

For instance, as products or processes are divided up into component parts, understanding becomes impossible. Understanding this sentence is impossible if the words are examined separately – just as understanding is impossible for separated tasks on an assembly line. Also separation of the managing from the doing breaks the learning cycle, thus impeding the creation of knowledge. For knowledge to flourish, we need a principle which encourages us to bring tasks together, not split them apart.

Scientific management is founded on time study, in which an observer measures process times, and counts the output of a worker with the intention of improving the methods and efficiency of the process. Time study is impossible with knowledge products which are intangible, and knowledge processes which are invisible inside people's heads. As separate, supervisory management of knowledge is impossible, we should apply principles that encourage self-management, and develop principles that value effective thinking more highly than efficient thinking.

Hamstrung by the industrial paradigm, managers initially responded to the increasingly competitive business environment by applying ever more sophisticated technology in their attempts to regain control. In manufacturing for instance, MRP computer systems were replaced by highly complex MRP 2 systems, but with disappointing results. Meanwhile in Japan, the less technical, employee-oriented approaches of quality circles, kanban and kaizen brought quality and value to world markets and continued to win market share.

In the 1980s total quality management, the Western version of kaizen was being hailed as the ultimate solution, but enthusiasm waned as early promise did not convert into long-term fulfilment. Many enthusiastic quality teams gradually lost their empowerment as the dead hand of hierarchical control re-asserted itself. And now disappointed managers are turning to the latest fashionable approach, business process re-engineering, which for many organizations will prove to be just as disappointing as previous fashions. Why? Not because the technique is unsound, but because of the industrial paradigm and the adverse effects of hierarchical command-and-control on the knowledge resource. However, in the few learning organizations where knowledge is valued, both of these techniques will yield continuing benefits.

Organizations which value the knowledge resource do not have a culture which reinforces the belief that managers have all the answers, and workers are untrustworthy idiots who must be watched and told what to do every step of the way. Knowledge-based organizations are at last accepting the evidence from fifty years of research into how people behave in organizations. It all points to the same conclusion: people's judgement and behaviour are seriously impaired by the situational pressures of top-down command and control. Good people behave badly, energetic people behave lazily and intelligent people behave stupidly. Some progressive organizations are moving away from the command-and-control culture, towards one which can best be described as inform-and-entrust – and the results are astonishing. Such organizations are typified by a non-hierarchical, team-of-teams structure. Work is organized around value-adding processes, or as projects, and carried out by small, empowered, multi-skilled, self-managed teams. Teams co-ordinate their efforts through exceptionally free and open communication, nourished by trust and shared values, enabled by frequent meetings and supported by digital networks. Ideas and creativity are valued, and routine work is extensively supported by automation. Personal and organizational learning is valued above all things.

Examples of organizations which conform to this pattern include many small, high-tech start-up companies which have not yet organized along hierarchical lines. Also, there is a growing band of larger organizations at the leading edge which includes IBM(UK) Ltd, that are abandoning the hierarchy in favour of a federation of small, multi-skilled teams.

Networks, teams, projects, computers, TQM, BPR, HRM, empowerment: how do they all fit together in the management jigsaw? They do all fit together with an undeniable logic, to form a fascinating picture, as we shall see when we examine them through a new lens – the new paradigm for managing knowledge.

Why read this book?

This book is for you and for me. I want you to gain from reading it, by improving your understanding and perhaps gaining a management qualification. I also want the book actually to make a difference and change things, and these twin purposes have influenced the way the book is written. When you are asked to write a dissertation on teamwork for instance, you must quote relevant research and the source text, such as the books of Belbin or Tuckman perhaps. But knowing information is not the same as having knowledge. Library shelves are stacked with the findings of management researchers. Their work may be interesting, their methodology rigorous and their logic impeccable – but most of it is ignored by practising managers. Why? Because most of us make decisions at work and at home on the basis of personal values and what we feel is right for us, not on logic. Knowledge comes when information combines with other information which perhaps you already know at some level deep down. When this happens, it can create a new insight – profound knowledge which changes the way you view the world and behave as a manager.

The book is in four parts. Part I examines today's business environment, and recounts the shortcomings of 'traditional management'. Part II puts forward an alternative management approach based upon knowledge and learning. Part III offers practical help with the new approach, and Part IV is an attempt to divine possible outcomes of this period of change, and examine what choices may be open to us.

I have worked hard at making this book easy to understand by adopting an informal style, and using everyday language which you may think strange for an academic text. As usual you will find logic, references to the work of management researchers and commercial examples from around the world. But perhaps more important, I hope you will also find parallels with what you already know to be true from your own experience of people and organizations. The purpose of the book is to reframe the theory and your practical experience of the world, to produce something which I hope fits with your personal values as a human being, and feels right for you as a manager. If it is successful no one will be able to stop you trying out your new ideas just as soon as you have the opportunity – and that is when we will all start to benefit from managing knowledge.

David Wilson
E-mail: dawilson@brookes.ac.uk

Acknowledgements

If this book has value, it is because of the spadework done by other researchers and authors. Most of the knowledge in it has been around on library shelves and in people's minds for many years. At one level I feel like Isaac Newton must have done when he wrote to Robert Hooke: 'If I have seen further it is by standing on the shoulders of giants.' But unlike Newton, I am not on my own – we are all trying to find a clear path through the whirlwind of change engulfing us at present. The book, along with others of its genre, is an attempt to assemble from a number of incomplete perspectives a clearer view of what to do next – a view which many managers may already have begun to construct for themselves. So my role has been that of scribe, capturing and clarifying on paper what seems to be an emerging consensus – the belief that in the right circumstances, knowledge can solve any business problem.

Thank you to my colleagues in the School of Business at Oxford Brookes University who have supported me, in particular Dr Nelarine Cornelius and Michael Mitchell who read the first drafts and whose comments and moral support where invaluable. Thanks also to my wife Ann, and children Daniel and Claire who have endured my keyboard fixation over the last nineteen months.

Part I: Problems with command-and-control – an outdated management model?

'I wonder if anyone is born to obey,' said Isobel. 'That may be why people command rather badly, that they have no suitable material to work on.'

Ivy Compton-Burnett (1941)

Part I of this book sets the scene by describing the new economic conditions we are now experiencing as we leave behind the old industrial age and move further into the information age. We all pause from time to time, to comment on the remarkable changes that have taken place in recent years, and Part I refers more to the real world we experience directly every day, than to the logic of theory and research.

Chapter 1 compares the business environment of today with that of the 1970s, to highlight the growth of global markets, the intensified competition which has arisen from information technology and the over-supply of most commodities and manufactured products.

Chapter 2 outlines the shortcomings of the command-and-control style of management, which encourages dull and slow ways of working that are not competitive in today's markets. Again the chapter starts by referring to our own experience of organizations, before examining the origins of the command-and-control approach.

1 Realities of the 1990s – the customer in the driving seat

Why read this chapter?

Your future as a manager will be influenced by the environment in which you work – and that is changing fast. In fact, so much has already changed in the business world that some of our deeply held convictions about how to manage may now be inappropriate. The simple truths that worked in the slow-moving 1970s no longer work so well today, and may already be overdue for revision before they become dangerously misleading.

This chapter sets the scene for the book, by reviewing some of the changes over the last couple of decades, the effects of which we can see all around us now. So much has changed that we may instinctively feel the need for a radically new approach. Organizations are changing. Just to survive they are learning to adapt – and keep on adapting – to constantly changing market requirements. But to thrive in future, organizations will need to get ahead of the game and participate in creating opportunities, rather than just reacting to threats. And this will require smarter, more flexible responses than can be achieved by traditional methods.

A changing world order – greater diversity and more complexity

You are a manager. You are also a consumer, but how much does your experience as a consumer influence your decisions as a manager? Perhaps not enough. We are all so busy at work today, addressing the urgent problems that we seldom have the opportunity to reflect on the important problems: we keep on running, and can't find the time to wonder if we are still running in the right direction. One of the objectives of this book is to give you the chance to question what you are doing, and develop a personal strategy for survival in the new world order which is emerging in the 1990s. We are living through a period of transition between the industrial age and the information age. You may be working for an organization which is still clinging to the old certainties – ever more precariously as they crumble away – or you may be working for a more progressive organization, but either way, you will probably be dealing with customers and suppliers from both these camps. It would be simpler if we were all working for, and with organizations committed to changing their structure and processes to suit the new world order. In fact the most likely scenario is that you presently work for an organization which is organized along traditional lines, but which has become aware recently of the need for reduced costs and increased flexibility, and so has responded by making some moves towards a flatter organizational structure, and perhaps embarking upon a total quality management (TQM) programme. If so, well and good, as these are steps in the right direction. The TQM organization is a half-way house from the industrial age organization to the information age organization. The gulf between the two is so great it is unlikely an organization could leap directly from one state to the other without using the stepping-stone of TQM in between.

So what does your experience as a consumer and customer tell you? To spot the trends, let us cast our minds back a couple of decades, and ask what changes have taken place in products and services since then. To help you get in the mood of the mid-1970s, remember Watergate and the impeachment of President Nixon in 1974? It was the year of oil shortages, the films *The Sting* and *A Touch of Class*. Patricia Hearst was kidnapped, Jimmy Connors won at Wimbledon, and the Three Degrees had a hit with 'When will I see you again?' In 1975 the Vietnam War ended, Rod Stewart sang 'Sailing', digital watches with liquid crystal displays were first available in the UK, Billy Jean King won at Wimbledon for the sixth time and the first personal computer was launched in the USA: the Altair 8800, equipped with just a quarter of a kilobyte of memory.

More products and better quality

The first point to note is that most of the products which were around then are still around today – in fact many products started much earlier than the 1970s and still haven't disappeared. Take Camp coffee and Birds Custard for instance. On the other hand we have lost Surprise dried peas – and good riddance to them. We have also lost the Altair 8800 and vinyl 33rpm records which have been swept away and replaced by far superior descendants based upon microprocessor technology, which continues to advance at blinding speed. On balance though, what seems to have happened is that we have gained an astonishing added range of choice in products without many of the original products disappearing. We now have balsamic vinegar, tarragon vinegar, red and white wine vinegar ... but good old malt vinegar still remains. This can only mean that the golden oldies must have lost market share, from 100 per cent for Camp coffee during the war years, to a tiny percentage now. So companies must have diversified by launching new products in order to maintain cash flow. Thus instead of making a small range of products in large quantities, companies have been forced to produce a wide range of products, each in relatively small quantities. This of course takes more managing, adding to the information processing and decision-making overhead, which in traditional organizations is likely to add to costs and put pressure on margins. The challenge which a few progressive organizations are finding answers to, is how to handle the increasing intellectual workload arising from complex and diverse customer requirements, while at the same time cutting net costs.

A similar effect is now taking place in the service sector. In 1975 the telephone network was a state-owned monopoly offering a very limited range of telephone services and equipment. For instance your choice of telephone handsets was limited to table-top or wall-mounted, available in three or four different colours. The unspoken and unquestioned assumption was that the public wanted a basic service at the cheapest possible price. Now British Telecom is a privately owned company exposed to competition from Mercury, Vodafone and others. Its market share and earnings are dependent on how well the company serves its customers, compared to Mercury for instance. Result? – we now have an organization which offers a very wide range of services and equipment, and which responds to customer complaints and anticipates their needs. In fact the industry as a whole offers a bewildering range of products and services, including retail outlets that specialize in selling just telephones. Now you can buy Mickey Mouse telephones, transparent ones with neon lights inside, cordless phones, cellular phones, answer-phones, fax-phones ... and the list continues to grow. A far cry from the old telephone service which took months to install a line, and billed its customers with few details of how calls were charged, other than splitting the total into two figures, one for direct-dialled calls and one for operator-connected. How has all this happened? Clearly privatization and deregulation have played a big part, but so too have advances in information technology and British Telecom's TQM programme.

We can begin to see the same effects starting in the public sector. If the dustmen dropped rubbish on your doorstep in the year when President Nixon's expletives were being deleted from the White House tapes, there was little you could do other than reserve a few of your own choice expletives for the apparently uncaring local council officials. They often appeared uncaring but individually I'm sure the officials did care really, though they felt – and were – powerless to do much about the situation. Their attitude was their defence in a situation most of us at one time or another have experienced: a customer complains and you are unable to respond in a satisfactory way because your job description or position in the organization does not allow it. Now though, following citizen's charters, compulsory competitive tendering (CCT) and various TQM-like initiatives in councils around the country, local officials respond to our communications in a more obviously caring way. Local councils have learned to react to their 'customers' when they complain, but have yet to learn to take a proactive approach. How long before we get a daily refuse collection service to our homes, as occurs elsewhere in Europe? When will we have a collection service which allows us to sort our collected refuse for re-cycling, as happens in parts of the USA? It will take a change in mindset, but I suspect these and other improvements will not be long in coming, – in fact some may already have arrived by the time you read these words, and it shouldn't surprise you if they are accompanied by savings in net costs. Such is the pace of change today.

So what should we make of all this? Can you develop a new perspective – a long view of trends – one based on your own personal experience, which of course is being added to day by day? If you can, you may see something tomorrow or next week on TV, in your newspaper or in a shop window which will help you refine your view. 'Hmm,' you'll think, 'that seems to fit in with what I've been reading.' Or perhaps a news item will cause you to think, 'That's odd. That doesn't fit with the mindset I'm developing. Are the trends beginning to reverse?' We should be highly suspicious of the future: it has a track record of making fools of forecasters. A trend is a trend, when will it bend? We all need to keep an eye on what's happening, but right now the trends to greater diversity and complexity seem set to continue, and with good reason: we as customers love choice.

Over-supply in world markets

We have been living for decades with butter mountains and wine lakes, and in recent years world markets have experienced over-capacity in basic industries such as steel, coal and oil. Now the same problem is beginning to arise in the manufacturing sector of world markets. It appears for instance that the world has too much ship-building and car manufacturing capacity, and soon if this is not already the case, we will have more capacity than the world needs for producing passenger aircraft and machine-tools.

So what's going on? Can we make sense of what is happening here? It seems the products of the industrial age helped to make the products of the previous age – agricultural products – too plentiful, so that we ended up with surpluses of agricultural products at about the time the industrial age reached its peak. And what's more, the same effect is happening again, with the products of the information age helping to make the products of the previous age – industrial products – too plentiful, with surplus capacity in the manufacturing sector.

Let's start by looking at how people have used their time at work over the ages. Long ago in the middle ages when the great cathedrals and castles were being built in England, everyone depended on the land, and their lives were governed by the seasons. Towns were small, and most of the population was dispersed across the countryside in small, mostly self-sufficient rural communities. Apart from a few churchmen, craftsmen, merchants and soldiers, nearly everyone worked from dawn to dusk on what they could win from the fields, just to feed and clothe themselves. Then in the eighteenth century the Industrial Revolution started gathering momentum. People left the countryside to live in towns and work in factories, where they produced, amongst other things, farm implements to make the agricultural sector more efficient, which in turn meant more farm workers could be released to work in the factories. A self-sustaining cycle of change was under way. By the time traction engines and threshing machines were being used in the late nineteenth century, the numbers of people working in agriculture had fallen to less than half the population, but the change cycle had further to run before slowing down. A flood of products from the industrial sector continued to improve yields and reduce costs in the agricultural sector. By early this century for the first time ever, more people were employed in industry than in agriculture, and today industrial products such as artificial fertilizers, insecticides, combine harvesters and milking parlours – to name just a few – have reduced the numbers directly employed in agriculture to less than one in twenty of the population. This is a remarkable achievement, when you consider that only 200 years ago, most people spent most of their daylight hours just trying to scratch a living from the soil. No one then could possibly have imagined that in the future, less than 5 per cent of the population would be producing more than enough food for everyone.

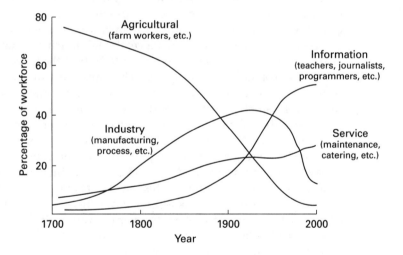

Figure 1.1   *Growth and decline of different sectors in the workforce over the years*

Figure 1.1 shows the estimated percentages of the UK population working in agriculture, industry and in the information sector. It is a simplified version of a chart which appears in Dizard's book *The Coming Information Age*. It shows that the numbers working in industry peaked in the 1950s – around the time prime minister Harold Macmillan was telling us 'You've never had it so good' – and then began to decline. Since then, the numbers of people working in the information sector have overtaken the numbers working directly on manufactured goods. It seems the pattern of change is repeating itself, with people transferring from the manufacturing sector to the information sector, and producing information products which help to make the business of manufacturing much more efficient. Robots, computer numerical control (CNC) machines and other products of the information age have, in the space of a decade or two, reduced the average cost of direct labour in manufacturing to less than ten per cent of total costs. And this is why we are beginning to see over-capacity and surpluses occurring in a growing range of manufactured products, even as opportunities for jobs in manufacturing continue to contract. How long before less than one in twenty workers in developed countries are employed in manufacturing?

Changing priorities: quality, service, delivery, design, price

What is your long view on finance? What trends can you spot that might affect you as a manager? Changes are happening all around us but which changes will persist as trends, and which will reverse in a few months time? It is easier to detect trends over two decades than it is over two years, because the slower, long-term underlying trends tend to be obscured by a confusing array of rapid, short-term, transient effects. If we can spot the trends and understand the underlying causes, we can have more confidence in our predictions.

Take the UK economy for instance, though much of what follows is also relevant to most Western economies. In 1975 the Government was able to control the money supply much more tightly than it can now. A company seeking finance at that time could either raise money through the stock markets or borrow from the bank. But both sources were strictly regulated and unsatisfactory for most business borrowers. The Stock Exchange had strict rules which made it difficult and expensive to get access to equity funding, and the banks did not always have funds to lend, and even when they did, sometimes recalled loans at short notice. This was because the UK banks had to place deposits with the Bank of England, which restricted the amount of money they had for lending to their customers. If the Government felt that inflation was getting out of control, the Chancellor of the Exchequer would require the banks to add to their deposits with the Bank of England, thus taking money out of the economy and putting the brakes on spending. It was a crude, indiscriminate control which did rein-in profligate home spending, but it also crippled efficient exporters.

Before the 1970s it was also difficult for individuals to borrow money. Hire purchase was the main form of consumer credit. There were no credit cards, and mortgages were quite difficult to get: you had to be a regular monthly saver with a building society before you could even apply for a mortgage. Up to this time the UK economy could still be regarded as separate from Europe and the rest of the world. The Government could control the flow of goods, services and cash into and out of the economy through controls, tariffs and barriers of various types and within this ring-fence the Government could control directly the amount of money in circulation. But now the ring-fence is breached and funds can move freely and rapidly into and out of the country. International fund managers can switch funds electronically around the globe, the transfers taking place almost instantaneously as managers chase transient opportunities of marginally improved risk and return. The net result is that anyone can borrow money anytime – provided they can pay the interest rates being charged. This has led to greater volatility in financial markets, with interest rates and exchange rates between currencies swinging faster and further in each direction. It affects mortgage rates and consumer confidence which in turn causes high-street spending to spill over or dry up without warning.

So what are the implications for you at work, and your organization? Perhaps all we can say about the future is that it appears to be getting more uncertain and less predictable. Back in 1975 most big companies had well-paid economists and mathematicians at headquarters who specialized in forecasting and corporate planning. Big companies accepted that they were bureaucratic and inflexible, and thus rationalized the need to look ahead and plan well in advance. But the corporate planning departments have largely disappeared now, as their forecasts often proved to be 50 per cent or 100 per cent off the mark, or predicted the opposite of what actually happened. Companies are now trying to reduce bureaucracy and become more responsive: instead of trying to predict and plan for future opportunities, they are trying to spot and catch present opportunities as they arise. In these turbulent times centralized planning and control do not seem to work, either for companies or for countries. At both levels for the time being, it seems we prefer to live with the processes of the free market and democracy – despite their imperfections.

For you back at work all this means that when the economy suddenly turns from boom to bust, or vice versa, you and the rest of your organization must be ready to respond. It may mean for instance that quality and reliability become less important and the lowest price becomes more important, or vice versa. When people have money and feel confident about the future, they will invest in quality, reliability and good design. They are prepared to pay for fast delivery and good service. But when people lack confidence in the future, are short of money and have time on their hands, they can do things for themselves and will pay only for their short-term needs. You and your organization must be ready to meet the shifting needs of your customers, because if you don't, someone else will.

To summarize then, I hope you agree that the business world seems to have got less predictable over the last couple of decades: it is difficult to know what the market will be demanding next year – and virtually impossible to guess five years hence. There are few barriers to trade, our cosy protected home markets have merged into a single global market where competition is fierce, and where there is no hiding place for inefficient suppliers of poor-value services or products. The message is clear: organizations must learn to be fast, flexible and responsive, able to adapt to the changing business environment, and to continue to delight their customers.

How then, can we teach an old dog these new tricks? That is the subject of the next chapter but first you may find it useful to respond to the questions below. They are an opportunity for you to stop and reflect for a moment, and perhaps learn something about yourself.

Pause for thought

These questions are designed to help you bring your preconceptions to the surface, to help you decide what your opinion is about the issues covered in this chapter, and to see if there are any inconsistencies in your mental model of the world. As a manager you probably have few opportunities to reflect on what your beliefs are: it is not until you have cause to commit yourself that you ever need to examine that deeply buried set of assumptions which you use to support your decision-making at work. This set of assumptions – your mindset – can have a hidden but profound influence on your decisions and actions, and it is important that they form an accurate mental model of your working environment.

There are no officially correct responses. But think carefully before answering and you may become more aware of the values and beliefs which control your decision-making. Next to each statement below, there is a spectrum between two opposing points of view. It's simple to respond: just put a mark on the line at the point which most accurately reflects your feelings on the statement. In each case, before answering think of a couple of practical illustrations that you could use to justify your response.

1 The organization I work for needs to be more adaptable.

Agree |_____| Disagree

2 The organization I work for is prepared for the information age.

Agree |_____| Disagree

3 The organization I work for started into TQM over a year ago.

Agree |_____| Disagree

4 The range of products/services we offer is bigger now than it was a year ago.

Agree |_____| Disagree

5   I know who my customers are.

Agree |_____| Disagree

---

6   I expect we will have to reduce our costs or prices next year.

Agree |_____| Disagree

---

7   I expect our customers will require us to produce to a higher quality next year.

Agree |_____| Disagree

---

8   I expect our markets to be over-supplied within the next five years.

Agree |_____| Disagree

---

9   The organization I work for has policies in place which will allow us eventually to beat our competitors.

Agree |_____| Disagree

---

10   I would bet £1000 that I can say what the bank interest rate will be this time next year.

Agree |_____| Disagree

---

11   I would bet £1000 that I can predict which of our products/services will be in heavier demand next year.

Agree |_____| Disagree

---

12   As the management role becomes more demanding, I expect to have to delegate more responsibilities in future.

Agree |_____| Disagree

References and further reading

Dizard, W. P. (1985) *The Coming Information Age. An overview of technology, economics and politics.* Longman.

2 Organizing to control and organizing to survive

Why read this chapter?

The dinosaurs with their large size and small brains, were once the world's most successful species. Now they are extinct because they couldn't adapt to a new environment. The biggest organizations – like the biggest animals – are never the most nimble-footed, but size is not the only factor, or the koala bear would out-manoeuvre the panther. In a fiercely competitive environment, a small brain and slow reactions can also be fatal.

The dinosaurs dominated a stable world for millennia. When the environment changed they were wiped out within the space of a few years, but as we know, some species survived and thrived. Today the business environment has changed, and some once-dominant organizations are down-sizing, de-layering and clutching at the latest business fad as they wither in the heat of global competition. But at the same time other organizations are thriving, so what is it, apart from size, that stops some organizations from reacting and adapting to change? Not exactly small brain perhaps, but dozy thinking can be as bad as ponderous movement. Either way, it is to do with how information is handled and decisions are made, and the way people behave and relate to each other. And central to all these issues is the organizational structure.

In this chapter we will see that the traditional hierarchical structure has become outmoded, as it assumes conditions which are no longer true. This is disconcerting, but it is not just theory: there are major companies which have re-structured so fast and so fundamentally as to cast doubt on nearly everything we thought we knew about management. Two case studies will suggest alternative ways of organizing, but we will leave the characteristics needed by today's organization until the next chapter where you can think about the guiding principles for an appropriate design.

Organizing for control

Until recently, organization has almost always been achieved through a hierarchical structure, designed to allow centralized command, with jobs and responsibilities divided up and defined in greater and greater detail as they are delegated down through the levels of the hierarchy. It operates on the Daddy Knows Best principle, with the 'chain of command' shown on the organization chart as lines of communication through which authority is delegated, Figure 2.1.

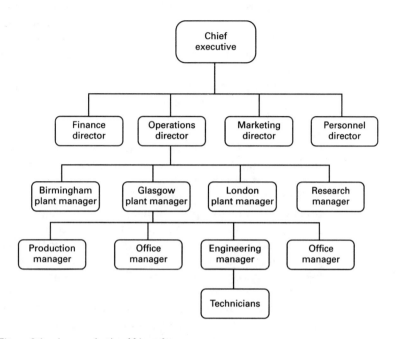

Figure 2.1 *An organizational hierarchy*

These lines extend from the chief executive at the top, down through the layers to every person on the lowest layer of the hierarchy. The number of people reporting directly to the chief executive – usually between six and ten – is known as the 'span of control'. It is not possible to supervise closely more than this small number of subordinates, who in turn have a limited number of people reporting to them. Everyone in the hierarchy has a span of control, and everyone has their place in the chain of command. This is how the 'command-and-control' model operates.

But the word 'organization' should not be synonymous with 'hierarchy': it is becoming clear there are other ways of organizing, for which we have not yet developed a comfortable vocabulary. For instance some ways of organizing are more akin to a federation than a hierarchy. So from now on, let us reserve the noun 'organization' to describe any working group held together by communications and a common purpose. But before we look at alternatives, let us first take a closer look at the hierarchy to see why an alternative might be necessary. The whole purpose of the hierarchy is to enable one person at the top to be in charge – to have ultimate authority and exercise overall control. Naturally this appeals to entrepreneurs and proprietors risking their own money; it also suits governments and shareholders who can then hold one person – the chief executive –

responsible for the actions of the whole organization. But it does not suit the needs of today's highly competitive global markets.

The hierarchy is so familiar to us that we have deeply ingrained preconceptions about it, some of which are paradoxical. For instance, we assume that it is the only feasible way of organizing, and we expect that as we gain in ability and experience we will rise up through the layers. On the way up we expect our pay, power and access to information all to increase in recompense for the extra responsibility. We expect life to get more rewarding in a variety of ways when we get promoted, but the pyramid shape means that on each promotion there are fewer opportunities left. Thus most people's expectations are bound to be frustrated as their career paths grind to a halt somewhere in middle management, at which point two personality types emerge: the resigned and the ruthless.

Competition for promotion should be on the basis of ability, but in practice other factors predominate. One way of getting promotion is to job-hop. Take your know-how and experience away to a better job in another organization. Another way is to play the company politics game, and make sure you always look good to people above you, because they control your future. Don't argue with your bosses, even if you disagree. Be enthusiastic about their ideas. Take every opportunity to flatter – by being available to them instead of to your staff and customers. To progress beyond the ranks of middle management you must not only be (perhaps not even be) good at your job, but you must be self-interested and politically skilled. You must stand out from your peers – not only by enhancing your own apparent performance but also by casting doubt on that of your peers. We may not care to admit it, but from our experience of hierarchies and the command-and-control model we all know they do produce this type of dysfunctional behaviour. You may feel this is a caricature of organizational life, for despite the pressures many people do manage to behave honourably most of the time, but the hierarchy is hardly a recipe for co-operation and it is not for nothing that we call our life at work a rat race when it is the rats that often win.

We have learnt to live with these undesirable characteristics by regarding them as inevitable side effects of any organization and part of human nature. Until recently we have never seriously considered any other form of organization because of our unshakeable belief in control from the top. But in addition to encouraging politics and discouraging constructive, goal-oriented debate, it seems the hierarchy may actually be fatally flawed by our expectation that one person with absolute authority should be in control at the top. In business today it is already obvious that the command-and-control organization in its purest form cannot remain competitive for long with the chief executive insisting on approving every decision directly, or indirectly through policies and procedures. Even with the ablest of chief executives, the command-and-control model just does not work any longer: the business world is moving too fast. There are still a few organizations – mostly in the public sector – which in principle operate strictly by command-and-control. From these we can see the result is always a decision-making bottleneck at the top and a bureaucracy that is inflexible, unresponsive and too slow in responding to their 'customers'. That is why organizations are showing so much interest in 'empowerment' just now. It is a fashionable buzz word that sells short courses and conferences for managers, but it is debatable whether sufficient real empowerment can ever be achieved within the framework of a hierarchical organization because empowerment and control are opposites. To be empowered is to be free to act – free from the rules and authoritarian dictate which are the very substance of hierarchy.

Empowerment

What is empowerment? Is it just the modern, fashionable word for delegation? Are you empowered if your boss writes more responsibility into your job description? Probably not – unless others in the organization are also told that you have new power to act. You must be given new authority along with your new responsibility, and even that may not be enough for genuine empowerment. You also need the desire, the information and the ability to exercise your new authority.

Your desire to act will depend on what you feel will be the result of your actions. You may feel that your suggestions will be met with passive resistance, and active discouragement; your actions may be seen as 'rocking the boat', or threatening to some people. The resistance to change may be enough for you to doubt whether the advantages are worth the personal risks and effort required. If your boss feels threatened by your initiatives, your actions may jeopardize your promotion prospects – especially if they don't work out as well as expected. The organizational culture must be right for you to feel motivated to exercise your new authority: there must be little personal risk, and there must be real rewards for working to improve things.

Access to information is essential for empowerment. It is not possible to make reasoned suggestions for improvement without access to costings, budgets, financial analyses and other performance indicators. In theory anyone who can show a need for this type of information should be allowed access to it, but in practice it is most unusual for approval to be given to anyone outside the upper levels of a hierarchical organization. I know of a private company not far from Oxford where the production manager was censured by his managing director for using financial information from annual reports made public in compliance with company law. This attitude wipes out any prospect of empowerment. Empowerment is only possible when the relevant information is freely available.

> What abilities do you need to be empowered? Empowerment should mean something more than just being authorized to give a refund to a dissatisfied customer, or deal with other situations which can be expected to arise from time to time. Genuine empowerment should give you the power to improve the way things are done – and that requires initiative, imagination and a proactive approach to your job. So, given the authority, the motivation and the information, have you the analytical and communication skills to convince your colleagues of the need for change? Perhaps you have, but if you haven't had to act in this way before, there is a fair chance some of your skills will need polishing up. Can you analyse for cause and effect? Can you prepare a cash-flow forecast, or calculate an internal rate of return? Can you give a convincing presentation and write an effective report? These factors are bound to have an influence on how truly empowered you are. We will return to these skill areas in later chapters of the book.
>
> Empowerment requires fundamental changes in people's values, beliefs and practices. It requires more than word processing skills to change a few job descriptions: it requires leadership, perseverance and time. It is not a quick fix which can be activated overnight.

To summarize then, most Western organizations are still structured as hierarchies so that, in theory, one person can be responsible for everything the organization does. However despite the theory, in practice most organizations implicitly concede that in its purest form the command-and-control model is unworkable: they would grind to a halt without the goodwill of employees who are prepared to bend the rules a bit and do things which strictly speaking are beyond their authority. Trade unions know that job descriptions and rules are mostly unworkable, which is why demarcation disputes and the work to rule are so effective. The problem is that command-and-control seems sensible and seems to work, just as the sun seems to rotate about the earth. But in fact the work we do nowadays is changing: indeed what we do now is already so different from what people did at work only a couple of decades ago, that for some workers the whole idea of command-and-control may already be a complete illusion. We are stuck with an outmoded form of organization which was conceived in a previous age, and a growing band of chief executives know it: hence their interest in empowerment and the 'flat organization', but tinkering in this way may not be enough. Later in this chapter we will look at some startling success stories of organizations which have abandoned the command-and-control model in favour of non-hierarchical methods of organizing. But first, let us take a look at how the hierarchical organization originally came into being.

De-layering and the flat organization

Some chief executives have restructured their organizations with far fewer levels – moving to a 'flatter' organization. It is said this has two immediate effects. First, it shortens the chain of command so that a report has fewer levels to go through as it passes up to a manager with the authority to decide, and then down again to employees with the duty to act. The report is delayed at each level as each manager reads it, takes what action is appropriate to her or his authority at that level, and then passes on a filtered version of it to the next level. Thus, with fewer levels to pass through, there should be fewer delays; decision-making should be quicker and the organization should become more responsive.

The second effect is that managers have to work with much wider spans of control, which forces them to delegate more responsibility. If you squash the same number of employees into a structure of fewer levels, each level must be wider, which stops managers breathing down the necks of their subordinates. Close supervision is possible with ten people reporting to you – you could spend half a day a week on the details of each person's problems. With thirty, it is no longer possible: if each of your subordinates only has five problems they want to discuss, that makes 150 for you, and your mental capacity is limited. You can only keep close tabs on a few of these and so your subordinates have to take on more responsibility.

In practice, de-layering is usually accompanied by a reduction in the head-count. It is suddenly found that much of the filtering and passing on of messages which middle managers do, is simply unnecessary and a broad band of middle managers is let go, out-placed, retired early or whatever the current euphemism for depriving people of their jobs happens to be. However there may be no alternative: the sick patient may need surgery to survive the fierce competition of the single global market.

The origins of command-and-control

The classical hierarchy was developed during the Industrial Revolution by the owners of the new mines, mills and factories which were growing in size and complexity. They needed to deploy labour efficiently as a factor of production in order to maximize profits, so they adopted the command-and-control model used by the armed forces. This approach was effective then because industrial workers had low education and expectations, the work was observable, and the outputs were tangible. Today however these conditions seldom apply: workers and the work they do have both changed and the command-

and-control approach is no longer effective. Indeed for some, it is already just an illusion.

So what's wrong with hierarchy? Perhaps we should now be asking what's right with it, for it is based on a set of assumptions about the business world which were developed during the industrial age and are no longer appropriate. Management is about achieving results through people, and many of our assumptions about how to manage people date back to a time when results meant output in the form of yards of cotton or barrows of coal – tangible products from the manual workers who worked in the mills and mines of the Industrial Revolution. Circumstances are very different now in this so-called information age. More and more repetitive tasks are being automated and most people are now employed as knowledge workers, using critical or creative intellectual processes which are impossible to observe – to produce outputs such as words spoken to a customer, or lines of computer code which are mostly intangible, difficult to measure, and beyond the reach of conventional management control.

The desire for control

The profit motive and the desire for control were the elemental driving forces which powered the Industrial Revolution, and they still remain deeply embedded in our preconceptions about how businesses should be run. Prior to the Industrial Revolution, most people worked on the land and there was great variety in what they did. The types and quantity of work they did were constantly changing, driven by the seasons and the weather. There was little to do in the winter, but come the summer, fifteen-hour days of labour from dawn to dusk were just accepted as part of the normal pattern. And the results were unpredictable: a poor harvest one year might be followed by a glut the next – and complete crop failure was common, resulting in real hardship. As late as 1846 the potato famine in Ireland resulted in a million people dying from starvation, and another million leaving their country. It is not surprising therefore that people sought greater control over their lives and greater predictability.

During the eighteenth century, country folk were attracted by the regular work and better wages available in the towns. They began to move out of the fields and into the factories, and as they did so, their work changed: it was less dependent on the seasons and the weather, and became more repetitive as the owners sought the most efficient ways of doing things to achieve consistently high output and maximum profits. The workers were not required to think or decide how to do their jobs. They just had to do as they were told by the owners. The owners were supported by contemporary writers such as Adam Smith, the Scottish economist who in 1776 used pin-making as an example of the economies to be gained through specialization and division of labour. He showed that six workers working together, one doing nothing but cutting off lengths of wire, one just forming the pinhead ... and so on, could produce far more in a day than six workers working separately, each completing one pin before starting on the next. So that is what happened for the next 135 years: Adam Smith's ideas reigned supreme until early this century by which time some very large organizations had developed. Then in 1911 Frederick Winslow Taylor, the father of work study, developed this line of reasoning into the scientific management school of thought, a mechanistic approach which emphasized analysing and planning in detail the narrow tasks of each worker, providing the right physical conditions and then timing the work and controlling the workers to see that they did it as planned by the managers. Most of the thinking required for the job done by the worker was thus extracted and given to the managers.

Up to this point, labour was thought of as a largely brainless factor of production, similar to land, capital, materials and machines, to be exploited by the entrepreneur in the pursuit of profit. For a time, the trade unions were the only counterbalance to the power of the owners. Eventually however, this exclusive focus on the owner's desire for control was moderated somewhat by the behaviourist school which took some account of the needs of the people working in these organizations. Elton Mayo with his famous Hawthorne experiments was the first to show that people cannot be controlled like machines, and have feelings which affect their output. Initially Mayo followed Taylor's mechanistic approach and assumed that if the best physical conditions could be found, people's output could be maximized. He measured the effects on the output of a team of women assembling telephone relays when he added and took away rest breaks, some with free hot meals, in an attempt to find the optimum pattern. However, to his amazement, almost every change he made, whether positive or negative, resulted in increased output, and at the end of the five-year experiment when the original unimproved conditions were restored, output was 25 per cent up and remained that way for twelve weeks. Obviously an uncontrolled variable was influencing the results. For the first time it became clear that people's feelings are important, and people must be supplied with more than just the right physical conditions if output is to be maximized.

Subsequently Abraham Maslow in 1943 drew up a Hierarchy of Needs, and Frederick Herzberg in 1959 wrote of Hygiene Factors, which added to our understanding of what motivates people at work, but Chris Argyris in 1957 and Douglas McGregor in 1960 were critical of the influence of organizations on the human spirit, in requiring people to be dependent, passive and to use few of their abilities. McGregor put forward his Theories X and Y which presupposed that people were passive, lazy and unimaginative at work, but just the reverse when outside their organizations. Argyris went so far as to say that organizations are not suited to the needs of psychologically healthy people. However, despite these charges, the profit motive and the hierarchical command-and-control structure of organizations has, until recently, remained unchallenged at the centre of our beliefs about how work and business should be managed.

New types of worker, new types of work

Now, as we move into the information age, the nature of work has changed again, just as it did 200 years ago when we moved into the industrial age. Automation and computer control have gradually removed the need for people to do much mindless repetitive work, as machines can do this class of work faster, cheaper and more reliably. More and more jobs now require mental, not manual skills, involving the processing of information and the creation of knowledge. In other words, the thinking element, which was extracted from the job and given to the managers by F. W. Taylor and the Scientific Management school, has been creeping imperceptibly back into people's jobs until it now forms the most important part of the work. The mindless tasks – the flypress operator on the shop floor, the tracer in the drawing office, the comptometer operator in the accounts department – have gone. They have been replaced by rather fewer jobs such as the circuit board rectifier, the telephone sales caller and the photocopy machine repairer, in which the workers must use their brains more than their hands. The managers of these jobs cannot directly observe the mental activity going on inside a worker's head, and they certainly cannot measure it in the same way that F.W. Taylor measured the manual activities of labourers loading pig iron into railway trucks at the Bethlehem Steel Company. Is it therefore possible for them to plan it or control it directly?

Work measurement is done by an external observer, watching the work being done. It is founded on the principle of time study in which a routine manual operation is broken down into small elements which are timed by stopwatch several times, to establish a basic time for each element. The basic element times are adjusted for the rate at which the worker is working and a rest allowance added before they are added up to give the standard time for the operation. But mental work takes place out of sight, entirely inside the head of the worker and a work study specialist cannot therefore observe and analyse it.

Managers may be able to estimate overall times for some routine mental tasks of the type which should be automated anyway, but non-routine mental work is not open to analysis by the techniques of work study and scientific management. You could never establish the standard time for deciding how to deal with a customer complaint, or the standard cost of a process improvement idea. The principle of a normal rate of working – so fundamental to the science of work study – just cannot be conceived for mental work. Working hard at a physical task always results in the job getting done quicker, but thinking hard is often counter-productive; it can cause the flow of ideas to dry up. The gestalt processes of the mind take their own time, and cannot be switched on at nine in the morning and switched off at five in the evening. How long should it take for a copywriter to produce 50 words of advertising copy? Demanding that it be done quicker, or right first time will clearly result in poorer quality.

The productivity of workers' minds and the quality of mental work therefore lies quite beyond the direct control of managers – and yet most senior managers still cling to the illusion of control and remain committed to the hierarchical approach. Companies and nations now compete on the basis of knowledge and mental work: it is now urgent that we find more effective ways of managing these resources. In this era of de-regulation and globalization of markets, it is no longer possible to compete on the basis of access to any of the traditional factors of production – land, labour, materials and capital – these can be attracted by anyone with a good idea. Michael Porter explains: 'It is how factors of production are deployed, more than the factors themselves, which determines success.' Also: 'Firms will not ultimately succeed unless they base their strategies on improvement and innovation ...' (1990). Some senior managers understand this and are looking for ways of tapping into that boundless source of value – the potential of the human minds in their organizations.

Hierarchy abandoned at Semco – prototype for success in a changing world

Curt Semler, a plant manager at Du Pont, threw in his job in the 1950s to start his own business building industrial centrifuges. He set up in Sao Paulo, Brazil, and by the late 1960s over 100 people worked for Semco, earning revenues of around $2 million a year. In 1980 Curt passed control of Semco, by now a conventional 12-layer hierarchical engineering company to his son Ricardo Semler as chief executive and major shareholder. In his book, Ricardo describes how he began by firing 60 per cent of the top managers – and thus started the remarkable 12-year series of events which produced 'the world's most unusual workplace.'

By 1992 Semco was six times bigger, but Ricardo had reduced the levels of management from twelve to three, thought of as three concentric circles rather than layers, with no managers and employees. Instead, there are six Counsellors at the centre, surrounded by a ring of up to ten Partners, in turn surrounded by everyone else in a large circle of Associates. The six Counsellors are roughly equivalent to vice presidents, and the ten Partners are the leaders of Semco's business units. And within this large outer circle, people are arranged in teams of five to twenty, each with an elected Co-ordinator.

And that's not all that's unusual: if you think your organization values and empowers workers, compare it with this. Workers at Semco decorate their own workplaces, arrange their own work-flows, set and monitor their own production goals, and decide for themselves when they start and finish work each day. They also help redesign products, formulate marketing plans, hire new colleagues, and appraise their bosses twice a year. All workers are free to dress as they please, join unions, participate in strikes and do as they please away from work so long as it does not interfere with work. There is no rule book, but workers must take their 30 days of holiday each year, and there are special initiatives to combat discrimination against women and people over 50. The financial books are open to all workers, who are encouraged to take classes on how to read balance sheets and other financial statements. Executives set their own salaries and 23 per cent of all profits are distributed as bonus equally amongst all workers. All workers are expected to use their brains as well as their hands, and so naturally Semco does not give special prizes for employee suggestions.

Does it work or does it work! Productivity is up sevenfold, profits are up fivefold and there are periods of 14 months in which not one worker has left the company. There is a backlog of 2000 job applications and in a poll of recent college graduates in Brazil, Semco was voted the company most of them wanted to work for – by 25 per cent of the men and 13 per cent of the women. And we are talking here about an engineering company operating in the harshest of economic conditions, during a period when inflation in Brazil ranged between 100 and 1600 per cent per annum. Semco puts quality of life first, and trusts its destiny to its employees. 'Do this,' says Semler, 'and the rest – quality of product, productivity of workers, profits for all – will follow.'

Semler has proved truthfulness, openness and trust works at Semco. Is there a chance it could work at your organization too?

The management response – new ways of organizing

Many companies around the world are now competing in over-supplied markets. Unwilling to compete on price because of their higher fixed costs which arise from investment in computer technology, their response has been to compete on quality, flexibility, speed of response to customer requirements, and service. The machinery – that is, the computer technology which caused the over-supply by massive increases in productivity – is inherently flexible, far more than the old mechanical methods, and is well suited to this response. It is ironic therefore that it is the people in organizations who are now finding it difficult to respond flexibly – not because they are inflexible individually, but because they are made inflexible by the rules and secrecy of the hierarchical organization structure, which was designed to control people, not to empower them, and is definitely not suited to such a response.

As discussed earlier, organizations which try to hold on to centralized command-and-control soon find the intellectual bottleneck at the top causes them to stagnate, making them unable to cope with the increased decision-making and higher mental workload required for flexibility. Progressive companies have therefore restructured as 'flatter' organizations, spreading the decision-making load throughout an empowered work force of quality circles and self-managing small teams trained to use scientific problem-solving methods. But a few truly innovative companies have completely abandoned the hierarchy and the whole concept of command-and-control. You have read about Semco with its three-level circular organization and you may have heard of the giant industrial company ABB, Asea Brown Boveri which reported revenues of nearly $30 billion in 1991 with 215,000 people working in 140 countries – also with just three levels of management. Tom Peters (1992) writes about ABB and lots of other companies that operate 'beyond hierarchy'. And everyone has heard of IBM: even they have abandoned their 14-layer structure, as described at the end of this chapter. These practical examples show beyond doubt that there are other effective ways of organizing, but we have not yet examined why a company should be willing to take the enormous risk of re-structuring so radically when improvements in quality, flexibility and customer service can be achieved by other means, such as de-layering, Total Quality Management, and Business Process Re-engineering. That is the next task.

Business process re-engineering

Question: why is BPR causing so much interest in the business world?

Answer: Because it promises spectacular improvements in customer service, responsiveness and quality, coupled with dramatic cost savings and improved sales. And what's more, it promises quick results and has actually delivered all these benefits in several well publicized cases. For instance, IBM has a credit facility to help customers pay for purchases of IBM products. Each credit request used to pass through six stages in three departments and took between six and ten days to process. The actual processing work only took 90 minutes: the rest of the time the request was just sitting in someone's in-tray or out-tray. Since re-engineering, a single generalist processes requests over the phone, and turns them around in four hours.

Question: So what exactly is BPR? It sounds like a magic wand – a bit too good to be true.

Answer: It does sound that way, and turns out that way too for many organizations. Dr Mike Hammer, the guy who coined the term BPR – a former computer science professor at MIT and now president of Hammer and Co. Inc. – estimates that as many as seven out of ten so-called re-engineering projects fail (1993). But he has done all right out of it, and the concept has been around since the late 1980s, so there must be something behind all the hype. And of course there is, but so many people have jumped onto the bandwagon that the term BPR now seems to be used for almost any approach to process improvement.

The basic idea is that to survive, any business must consist of processes that convert inputs such as labour, materials and information, into outputs in the form of goods and services which offer the highest possible value to the customer. These central processes must be efficient in maximizing quality and service, while minimizing costs and response times. But older, larger organizations tend to be sluggish in responding to change, and some now have business processes which are looking inefficient in comparison with those of their competitors. Their chief executives know that something is very wrong. They try the usual approaches to improve efficiency to no avail, and sense the need to take radical action to stem the inexorable drift into uncompetitiveness, loss of markets and oblivion. And BPR promises a solution.

BPR has the potential to put businesses back on course again, by ignoring what is done now, starting from scratch and re-designing the processes to produce the outputs the customer wants. It is a dramatic, revolutionary, high-risk, high-reward strategy which contrasts with Total Quality Management which has similar goals but adopts the less risky strategy of gradually but continually improving existing processes.

BPR requires far better use of information technology, may involve major restructuring of the organization, results in far fewer jobs in the re-engineered areas, and usually leads to redundancies.

Question: So who stands to gain from BPR?

Answer: Three influential groups, apart from the owners of the businesses and their customers of course. The first group is computer hardware and software suppliers, who know that information technology plays a central role in BPR. Some of the most successful examples of BPR are in the financial services sector, where processing of mortgage applications, insurance claims, and loan requests often involve long, frustrating delays for the customer, while paperwork gets passed on from department to department. New computer systems can now handle document images, thus cutting out the need for keyboard entry of information from customers' application forms. Also, new software can automate the work flow, eliminating the in-tray, and even allowing multiple images of the same document to be processed in parallel by different people in different places. Thus the re-engineered process is captured within the system, which automates routine tasks, eliminates delays, and controls the whole procedure. Leading edge gear of this type is expensive of course, but dramatic savings in direct labour still produce short pay-back periods. BPR sells computers – no wonder the suppliers have latched on to the concept.

The second group is the consultants who go in to businesses to solve problems. The consultant, like a fairy godmother, needs a magic wand to wave, and BPR fills the bill perfectly. It requires specialist expertise which the business is unlikely to have internally, and it generates big savings which justify big fees. What more could a consultant wish for?

And the third group is the academic community who see it as a new offering to add to their product range. They do research and write books and journal articles on BPR. They also prepare case studies, run courses and arrange conferences to spread the gospel, and for all of these there is a ready market. Business audiences need to keep up with the latest methods, especially those which have a reputation for quick results and the potential for delivering a competitive advantage.

These three groups circle round in mutual support, like three vultures circling above a weakening animal. But ask yourself this: how do organizations get to be so unfit as to require such traumatic surgery and transplant? How do the remaining employees feel about their employer who cuts people from the payroll in large numbers at short notice for no fault other than doing as they were told? And can you think of any reason why the same organization will not need the same treatment again in a few years' time?

Question: Is BPR a desperate act of last resort – or a smart thing to do?

Organizing for survival

Let's not beat about the bush: the case for the prosecution is this. The hierarchy has outlived its span, and should be replaced. The idea of one person controlling everything and everyone in an organization is unworkable. Any successful hierarchical organization achieves its success despite the hierarchy and not because of it. And the business environment is so competitive that we can no longer afford to be hamstrung by rules and unnecessary authorizations.

Daddy no longer knows best: just to survive, too many initiatives are needed on too many fronts for it all to be controlled – let alone driven – by one person. I have friends who run businesses which have pulled out all the stops to add a bonus feature at no extra cost to their consumers – only to be beaten to the market by two competitors who have both added three bonus features. This feeds down the supplier chain where the message is 'We want a product or service specifically tailored to meet our needs, at higher quality than you've supplied in the past – and by the way, we need it at a price 10 per cent less than last year.' So the suppliers tighten their belts and do what's necessary to win the business: they follow the advice of the management gurus, and listen to the Department of Trade and Industry. They get close to their customer to discover their detailed needs, by arranging exchange visits between their designers and operations personnel. They cut back on all expenses, tighten up on quality, and somehow come through, albeit with reduced margins, but with a tender which meets the customer's requirements – only to be told the order will go to another supplier offering even better value. They are at their wit's end – literally. They have run out of ideas and don't know what to do next. On their own, the few people at the top just do not have enough brain power to get enough balls in the air and keep them there for a satisfactory performance. They have to get more brains working on the problem. Organizations survive now by outsmarting the competition and success depends on the ability to marshal the critical resources of brain power and knowledge. And the sad irony is that many chief executives don't believe it possible to ask for help with brainwork from their employees, where virtually unlimited reserves of potential capacity remain untapped.

Don't delegate – federate! IBM shows the way

In 1991 IBM had 14 layers in their world-wide hierarchy. By 1994 in the UK they had abandoned hierarchy (except in the factory) in favour of a federation of 32 small self-managing businesses, free to act however they wish but accountable to a UK board, Figure 2.2.

Each of the four board members acts as mentor to eight of the small business heads – but only when asked to do so. And to underline the fundamental change in culture, the IBM rule book

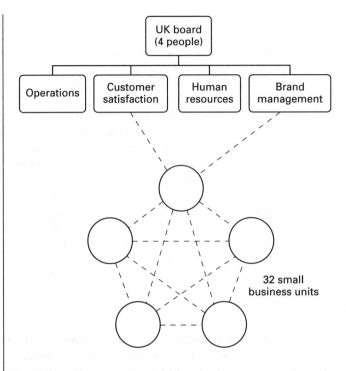

Figure 2.2 *Organization structure for IBM (UK)*

has been scrapped. Even the rigid, buttoned-down IBM dress code has been swept away: it's OK to wear brown shoes and a colourful tie now. It underlines the empowerment message: anyone can wear anything they feel is appropriate to the circumstances.

Simon Dyson, personnel director for IBM UK, is currently (June 1994) working on the UK human resources policy. It will consist of federal policies concerned with matters such as disability, maternity, etc. which must be adhered to by all business units. On other matters, business units will decide for themselves what policies they operate. At a time of drastic change Simon feels it is important to guarantee commitment to some aspects of IBM's traditions, such as RFI – respect for the individual – and this will be enshrined in federal policy.

Although the change process is not yet complete, the new approach seems to be paying off: after three years of restructuring costs and reporting losses IBM UK is back in profit again – albeit with only about 10,000 employees, the same level as 1969, and gross margins about half what they were then.

If IBM can abandon centralized planning and control, any organization can.

This irony points to the conclusion we have been converging on. For an organization to survive in today's over-supplied and intensively competitive global markets, it must manage all its knowledge resources effectively so as to out-think, out-smart and out-perform its competitors. But the hierarchical organization provides exactly the wrong environment for this to happen. There must be some form of control, but in its futile pursuit of detailed centralized control, the hierarchy encourages just the wrong types of behaviour: rule-following instead of initiative, in-fighting instead of co-operation, secrecy instead of openness, compliance instead of empowerment, and politics instead of performance. The conclusion is obvious: to survive, organizations must abandon their obsession with centralized control, and replace it with a new obsession for managing knowledge.

So, having knocked down the hierarchy, the problem is what should we put in its place? Some answers are emerging, and to find out about these, turn to the next chapter.

Pause for thought

Now this is pretty revolutionary talk, and unless you have previously had the chance to think about issues such as these, I expect after a lifetime of indoctrination in the virtues of the hierarchy, you may be feeling uncomfortable about some of it, to say the least. If this is the case, take time out to reflect on these issues. It may help if you dip into some of the titles at the end of this and the next chapter. Semler's book is easy reading to start with – more like a novel. Peters' book is better treated as a reference book to sample from. Reading and pondering will give you time to adjust your preconceptions.

Organizations determine how people behave and relate to each other and how they feel about their jobs. So put theory aside for a moment, and search your feelings and instincts before you respond to the following questions.

1   Write down the best thing about working in a hierarchy – something which makes you feel good about your colleagues, and motivated to do your job.

2   Has there been any occasion when the rules at work have impaired your ability to do what was right and necessary at the time? If so, jot down two or three words to describe any such occasions, and how you felt then.

3   Can you think of any occasions when in-fighting has wasted energy on unfruitful behaviour? If you can, jot down two or three words to remind you of that.

4   Can you think of any political situation in your organization which permanently impairs its performance? If you can, jot it down.

5   How far are you trusted with information by your superiors? How does this affect the way you feel about your work and your organization?

6   Are your own personal interests entirely the same as those of your organization? Jot down one or two issues over which they diverge, and how these affect you at work.

References and further reading

Argyris, C. (1957) *Personality and Organisation: The conflict between system and the individual.*

Hammer, M. and Champy, J. (1993) *Reengineering the Corporation.* Nicholas Brealey.

Maslow, A. H. (1943) *Motivation and Personality.* Harper and Row.

McGrgegor, D. (1960) *The Human Side of Enterprise.*

Peters, T. (1992) *Liberation Management – Necessary disorganisation for the nanosecond nineties.* Macmillan.

Porter, M. E. (1990) *The Competitive Advantage of Nations.* Macmillan.

Semler, R. (1993) *Maverick! The success story behind the world's most unusual workplace.* Century.

Smith, A. (1776) *Treatise on the Wealth of Nations.*

Taylor, F. W. (1911) *Principles of Scientific Management.* Harper.

Part II: An emerging management model for the information age

These things shall be! A loftier race
Than e'er the world hath known shall rise,
With flame of freedom in their souls,
And light of knowledge in their eyes.
                    Hymn by J. A. Symmonds (1840–1893)

Having discussed in Part I the shortcomings of traditional methods of managing, Part II sketches the emergence of an alternative to the command-and-control approach. This alternative recognizes that the abilities and aspirations of workers have changed, and so too has the nature of the work they do. It accepts that, at a time when all other resources are in abundant supply, knowledge is now the most important basis for competition.

Chapter 3 describes different types of knowledge which have been identified, and shows that prior to embarking on Total Quality initiatives, traditional organizations seldom even acknowledge its existence as a resource.

Chapter 4 builds on the bridgeheads created by the Learning Organization and TQM, to propose an improved inform-and-entrust model, designed to exploit the knowledge resource to the full.

3 Managing knowledge – creating the right environment

Why read this chapter?

You will work for several organizations in your lifetime – that's inevitable in a world of global markets and constant change. Also, your present employers may be obliged to re-structure soon if they haven't already done so recently. In changing organizations you have choice, and naturally you should favour a form which is likely to be successful; one which can deliver exceptional value to its customers, and at the same time if possible, one which can deliver improved personal satisfaction and financial rewards to its employees. Competitive organizations which set out to manage their knowledge resources effectively will meet both these challenges by valuing their people, who jointly hold the knowledge and use it to outsmart the competition.

In this chapter we will discuss the knowledge-intensive organization. What types of knowledge are there? What is the best environment for knowledge to flourish? What prevents an organization transforming itself from a traditional command-and-control orientation, to one which values knowledge above everything? And what are the implications for you, in a world where knowledge will be the only basis for sustainable competitive advantage?

We will look at the theories of academics and writers to see what guidance they can offer. We will examine the paths trodden by some of the growing band of organizations which have explored this territory. And finally we will use our common sense and experience of life, to put it all into perspective and derive some general principles for the design of tomorrow's knowledge-intensive organization.

What is knowledge?

At the most basic level, knowledge is that which is known, and so it is an essentially human form of information. The words data, information and knowledge are poorly defined and used interchangeably to some extent, so let us agree some definitions. By selecting and analysing data, we can produce information, and by selecting and combining information we can generate knowledge. Using the analogy of the physical world, data forms the atoms of the knowledge world, information the molecules, and knowledge the materials from which everything is constructed.

The processing hierarchy

Figure 3.1   *The processing hierarchy*

Another way of looking at it is that knowledge is a link in the processing chain from data to action, Figure 3.1. We process data to produce information, then information to produce knowledge. Then we use knowledge to produce decisions, and finally, action. This is true whether or not computers are involved in the processing. For instance, if you are standing on the platform at Paddington Station, wanting to get to Oxford, you may consult a timetable (data) to look up the departure time of the next train (information). Then you may look at your watch to see what time it is (more information) and subtract this from the departure time so that you can know how long you have to wait (knowledge). Along with other knowledge of the options open to you, you can then decide what there is time for: enough only to board the train? ... or to buy a newspaper first? ... or to sit down and wait with newspaper, coffee and bun? (decision and action).

In this example, note that you selected a single time from the timetable – a single data item from a larger body of data, which becomes information because of its relevance. Then by considering two sources of information, knowledge of the waiting time was produced. And knowledge of several options was required for a decision and action. Thus the processing chain is more akin to a hierarchy in which large, simple, lower, more atomistic layers are progressively refined to produce at the top just one, or a few complex decisions and actions (Wilson, 1991). Before leaving this simple example, it is worth noting that a business may sometimes have the choice of either working through the processing hierarchy, or buying-in knowledge in the form of professional expertise – rather like having a colleague with you on Paddington Station, who has made the journey before and already knows the best course of action.

Computer-held knowledge

People generally are not good at handling more than small amounts of data, but computers excel in this area. People are much better at the top of the processing hierarchy, where computers are almost useless except in some very narrow, specialized domains of knowledge, such as buying and selling in the financial markets. The computer experts are pushing the use of computers higher and higher up the processing hierarchy, and have developed expert systems, or knowledge-based systems as they are known, which contain expert knowledge and can help specialists make decisions in a particular situation. An expert system consists of a situation model, a knowledge base, and an inference engine. The software can be bought as an empty shell which must then have its knowledge base filled with the knowledge of one or more human experts in a particular field before it can be used by lesser experts in the same field. An oft-quoted example from the 1970s is the Mycin system which contains the knowledge of expert haematologists, and was designed to be used by doctors in general practice whenever they faced a problem of diagnosing disorders of the blood. Mycin is a rule-based system, the knowledge base consisting of thousands of 'if ... then ...' type rules. Mycin asks the GP some basic questions about the symptoms of the patient, and then depending on the answers to these questions, asks further questions, recommends blood tests, and eventually gives a diagnosis.

Explicit and tacit knowledge

There are two classes of problem in constructing expert systems: the technological and the human. The technological problems will eventually yield to increases in computer power, but the human problems are likely to be more intractable. They are to do with the apparent inability of human experts to explain all they know. The usual procedure in building an expert system is for a knowledge engineer to elicit the knowledge of experts by questioning them, and then make it explicit by coding it in the form of a set of rules to put in the knowledge base. But some of what human experts know, is known at a deeper level and the human experts are unable to explain how they know it. It appears to be at the level of an instinct, a gut-feeling, an intuition which the expert has developed through years of experience and which he or she has come to trust. Perhaps as a manager that kind of feeling will be familiar to you. Ikujiro Nonaka, professor of management at Hitotsubashi University in Tokyo, refers to this as 'tacit' knowledge – a term originally coined by Michael Polanyi of Chicago University in 1948 – in contrast to the 'explicit' knowledge which managers are easily able to communicate and share (Nonaka, 1991).

Personal and organizational knowledge

Tacit knowledge is developed and owned by individuals throughout an organization, not just managers. It is personal knowledge, consisting of highly subjective insights, intuitions and hunches, rooted more in action than in reflection, which means that some of it can never be made explicit and instantly available for anyone else in the organization to use – and that is why empowerment is so important. The skills of a chef can only be developed slowly through practice and apprenticeship to a master chef, just as the instincts of an auditor – the nose to sniff out malpractice that tells when and where to dig deeper – can only be developed by practice and working alongside others with more experience. Recipes and procedures can help of course, but ultimately it is personal, tacit knowledge which really makes the difference.

Where tacit knowledge can be made explicit however, by codifying it as a computer program, a recipe, a formula or even a product specification, then personal knowledge becomes organizational knowledge which can be shared and stored so that it will not be lost when the individual eventually leaves the organization. Where tacit knowledge cannot be made explicit, the organization can only hold on to it by encouraging holders to pass on their knowledge by apprenticing others and making sure that it is held by several people. But either way, people will not pass on their tacit knowledge within the organization if it means losing their bargaining power and control of their work, or if they believe it may endanger their own job security.

Migratory and embedded knowledge

Joseph Badaracco (1991), speaking from the perspective of the organization, uses another term to describe explicit knowledge when it is captured as formulae, designs, manuals or books, or in pieces of machinery. He calls it migratory knowledge, because it can move out of the organization very quickly. When knowledge migrates to other organizations, the originating organization does not lose the knowledge itself, but may lose the value of the knowledge when sole possession of it is the basis for competitive advantage.

In contrast to migratory knowledge which can move so fast, Badaracco also draws attention to knowledge which is 'embedded' in the organization, and thus can only move very slowly, even when its commercial value is high and firms have strong incentives to gain access to it. Embedded knowledge is organizational knowledge which cannot be owned and used in isolation by an individual. It is more akin to the soul or culture of an organization, in that it exists as norms, attitudes, relationships among individuals and groups, and ways of making decisions. When Honda formed a strategic alliance with Rover in the early 1980s, Rover gained immediately by receiving migratory knowledge in the form of the Honda engine which was installed in the first Rover car to be produced by the alliance. Then, over the next ten years or so, Rover slowly acquired embedded knowledge from Honda, in the form of working practices which, through empowerment, just-in-time techniques, multi-skilling, quality circles and a whole raft of TQM-like initiatives, generated a culture of continual improvement. As a result, Rover was transformed from a loss-making dog with a reputation for poor quality, into a profitable world-class star performer which British Aerospace, who had acquired a majority share holding in the 1980s, were able to sell in 1994 to BMW. Bernd Pischetsrieder, boss of the German car maker, was quick to note that BMW does not invest abroad for reasons of cheap labour: 'You can't just replace one staff with another ... that is where the corporate knowledge is.' Pischetsrieder clearly recognized the value of the embedded knowledge at Rover. Did British Aerospace appreciate that they were trading access to this knowledge – a source of long-term profitability – in exchange for a one-off cash settlement?

Accounting for knowledge as an organizational asset

At present, few people consider knowledge to be an asset of an organization, which is hardly surprising, as it is not shown as such in annual reports and statements of accounts. This situation will have to change before we can believe in the knowledge-intensive organization: how can we truly claim that knowledge is valued above all things if no mention of it is made in the balance sheet or profit and loss account?

Changes needed in management accounting practice

The accounting profession is very conservative: it has developed slowly over centuries. It has not changed much at all since the 1930s and so we should not expect it suddenly to change now. However, as well as financial accounting, Robin Cooper and Robert Kaplan (1984) point out that much management accounting information is now obsolete and due for an overhaul. Much of it is at best irrelevant to managers, and it can be positively harmful to companies, in encouraging managers to work with high levels of work-in-process, maximizing their own local throughput without regard to the needs of other managers or customers. For instance, management accounts often set a standard scrap allowance of, say 8 per cent in manufacturing, and if the manager responsible comes in on target then that is fine as far as the accounting system is concerned. But it certainly is not fine for the customer, who suffers long lead-times, poor delivery, higher costs and variable quality – resulting in lost markets for the company concerned. Good accounting measures for today's markets should monitor the performance of the organization as a whole, not that of individual departments. One such example is the ratio of processing time to lead-time, i.e. the time the value-adding processes take, expressed as a percentage of the total time from receipt of order until delivery to the customer. Ideally this should be close to 100 per cent, showing there is little time wasted on non value-adding activities such as storing and inspecting between processes, but usually it is much less than 5 per cent – which is not surprising when it is not even measurable by normal cost accounting methods.

You probably have your own examples of madness caused by chasing accounting targets. The end-of-month scramble to rush work out of the door regardless of quality is a favourite. Another is described by Brian Joiner (1994): an engineer brings a significant cost-saving idea to his boss, who turns it down because the costs would impact on his budget, while the savings would arrive in another manager's cost centre. And Thomas Johnson (1992) argues that to survive, top-down managing by remote control through budgets and accounting targets must stop. He shows that each department achieving their separate cost targets actually impairs the company's overall ability to compete. 'People left to their own devices produce better results.' You should not be surprised by any of this: budgets and financial targets are the flawed and self-defeating devices of the command-and-control approach. Sooner or later they must be scrapped, along with the hierarchical organization structure. Financial targets should not be used to control what people do, though overall figures for the whole organization must of course be checked from time to time.

Changes needed on the balance sheet

Let us return now to the balance sheet, and see how knowledge is handled, compared with tangible fixed assets, such as office equipment. If you buy a new computer and add to fixed assets, total assets on the balance sheet are not affected as cash is reduced by the same amount as fixed assets are increased. Then through depreciation, the effect on profits is spread over several years. However when the computer operator goes on a word processing course, the organization gains knowledge in exchange for the cost of the course, and total assets should not be affected. But at present total assets are reduced by the full cost of the course, the whole of which is charged against profits in the year of purchase. The acquisition of the knowledge is not recognized in the balance sheet, even though the value of the knowledge, like that of the computer, will last for several years.

But knowledge is different from fixed assets which can be locked up and insured, and which can be sold for some residual value if they are no longer required. Knowledge can walk away with the holder – and how can its value to the organization be established? Once acquired, its value may be many times more than what was paid for it, or less, or even negative. By passing on the knowledge so others can use it too, its value may be more than what was paid to bring it into the organization. And if applying the knowledge reduces the competitiveness of the organization, as may be the case with some management accounting techniques, the value to the organization may actually be negative. A further complication is that the value of explicit knowledge depends upon the embedded knowledge of the organization which determines if and how the explicit knowledge of individuals gets used.

However despite these difficulties, knowledge should be recognized as an asset, even though like work (as we saw in Chapter 2), it cannot be observed and measured. Knowledge is built into the product or service sold to the customer, in much the same way as tangible materials are. Wilkstrom, Normann et al. (1994) use the examples of a twist drill and a headache tablet to show that it is this 'manifest' knowledge which is important and delivers value to the customer, not just the materials. So, like materials, knowledge costs money to acquire and forms part of the value of a product or service, but unlike materials, the organization's store of knowledge is not diminished with each delivery to the customer – on the contrary, if the organization learns how to deliver more value through contact with the customer, the deliverer's knowledge may actually be increased with each delivery. Thus, an important component of product or service has a cost which is impossible to measure directly. Clearly, the idea of a standard product cost composed of a standard knowledge cost, along with standard materials cost, standard labour cost, and an overhead allocation is out of the question. What is the point in going through the increasingly complex and costly procedure of establishing standard product cost, when only the two smallest components – direct labour and direct materials – can be established with any degree of accuracy? And why do we employ 120,000 accountants in the UK when Japan with twice our gross domestic product and twice our population, gets by with only 6,000? If these figures are to be believed, we in effect employ forty accountants where they employ one! The answer to both these questions once again is that we are obsessed with the concept of detailed, top-down control of people through financial targets.

Obviously there are fundamental differences between Western and Japanese approaches to running an organization.

The need for a new paradigm

Michael Porter (1990), in examining the competitive advantage of nations, finds no single cause entirely satisfactory in explaining the differences that exist in national competitiveness. His stated aim is to help firms and governments choose better strategies, but he cannot accept that differences in competitiveness are caused entirely by differences in management practices, because 'What is celebrated as good management practice in one industry would be disastrous in another.' However, I believe there must be a few common principles at the core of good management practice which apply in all industries and all nations. Porter does make improvement and innovation a central part of his study, and notes that 'As more and more industries have become knowledge-intensive in the post-World War II period, the role of factor [of production] costs has weakened even further.' So if there is some part of good management practice which applies across all types of competitive activity, it is no longer to do with the traditional factors of production, and is more to do with how knowledge is managed.

I expect by now you may be feeling some mental discomfort. Although you can see the sense in many of the ideas put forward, and you agree with the diagnosis, the treatment seems too radical to contemplate. Scrapping the hierarchy and taking away control is a bit like the driver letting go of the steering wheel: won't the organizational bus veer off the road and into the ditch? And what role is left for you as a manager?

Certainly a bus with no one at the wheel will not get far, but that is not what is being proposed. A better analogy for the new alternative is a fleet of smaller vehicles in unknown territory, all bound for the same destination, and in touch by CB radio. By co-operating and trying out different routes they will get round obstacles and arrive much quicker than the bus. And your role as a manager, far from being diminished, will be enhanced. It will require you to take a new, more proactive approach: to help your team find new ways and to focus on managing the knowledge of the team instead of managing by remote control the money and the people and the other traditional factors of production. And it will require you to adopt a new style: coaching, co-ordinating and supporting the overall effort, instead of planning from your limited perspective, issuing instructions and setting individual targets.

What is required is so radically in conflict with our experience, that the foundations of our beliefs about management – our old mental model of the world, or 'paradigm' – must go, along with its associated vocabulary, and be replaced by a new paradigm with new words and new values.

What is a paradigm?

A paradigm is a set of beliefs, theories and methods which are held to be true by a community of practitioners in a particular field of expertise. It consists of a 'mindset' of mental models or preconceptions which are learnt as part of preparation for membership of that community.

Paradigms, once learnt, remain at subconscious level, seldom to surface for re-examination and questioning. They have a profound influence on how practitioners perceive their world, usually helping them to predict it and guide their decisions, but occasionally leading them to misinterpret observations which are anomalous or unexpected.

Thomas Kuhn (1970) describes an experiment which showed how we tend to see only what we expect to see. Playing cards were flashed to subjects to identify, but they did not know the pack contained some anomalous cards such as a black four of hearts for instance. The subjects correctly identified the normal cards, but they also unhesitatingly identified the anomalous cards as normal – the black four of hearts sometimes as the four of hearts and sometimes as the four of spades. The subjects were not aware of any trouble, and immediately fitted the odd cards to one of the conceptual categories of their experience.

Sometimes practitioners will cling to a particular paradigm for many years after evidence to disprove it has been uncovered. As more and more anomalous observations accumulate, pressure builds for the paradigm to be modified to take account of them. When this is no longer possible, a 'paradigm shift' eventually occurs, in which the old paradigm is abandoned and replaced by a completely new one. For instance in 1543 Copernicus showed that the earth revolved round the sun, his work causing a paradigm shift from the previously held belief that the sun revolved round the earth. However the old geocentric model, refined fourteen centuries earlier by Ptolemy, took another 100 years to be abandoned entirely and for the shift to be completed, even though the heliocentric model explained much more satisfactorily the regular, apparent backward motion of the planets.

Such a paradigm shift is bound to be disorienting. Our instincts rebel: we cling to the language which helped define the old paradigm, and we look for reasons not to change. Is this new thinking dangerous – a wolf in sheep's clothing? It sounds subversive: power to the people – is it a left-wing plot? Is it a threat to the establishment, to the nation? It is such a leap into the unknown. It must be risky.

You may have come across calls for a paradigm shift before, but anyway keep an open mind: suspend disbelief while we take a trip around the newly emerging paradigm. The theories may not be entirely new to you, but the practice may be so different from anything you have experienced before in organizations of any size, that the gulf looks too wide to leap. And indeed it probably is, but there are stepping stones. First though, let us take a look at life on the other side; later we can find ways of getting there.

There is a quiet revolution going on. Some people are giving up power to others, and some losing their jobs. What will be the effect on you and your job? Can you stop it, and if not what should you do to prepare yourself? The answer is no, you cannot stop it, for this is an international revolution which you, along with millions of others like you around the developed world – called customers – are causing. The long-term shortages and sellers markets which existed until after World War II are gone. It was these conditions which allowed centrally planned, dictatorially managed organizations to exploit customers (and employees) in pursuit of shareholder profit.

In a world of efficient communications and surpluses, customers have choice, and they are exercising it to deprive any organization of revenue if it does not serve them well by offering them high value and responding to their changing needs. The customer revolution is inevitable, especially if you sell in world markets. And you should prepare yourself by looking ahead, knowing what changes are likely to be necessary, and helping to facilitate them. You may not approve of all the results of the market economy, but if you fight it by resisting changes at work, your job and your employer could cease to exist. Or you could just be deemed too inflexible for employment in the new environment.

There are parallels with the revolution which brought the USSR to an end. Previously, the few Russians lucky enough to visit Western countries were amazed at the volume, choice and quality of products available in our supermarkets. At home their experience was entirely one of shortages, queues, lack of choice and poor quality, which they accepted because they knew no better. The free market economy in the West is certainly not without its faults, but compared to the planned economy of the USSR it is a paragon. The reason for the collapse of the communist regime was that despite their secret police, censorship and control of the media, they were eventually unable to prevent the ordinary Russian people from finding out what life was like elsewhere in the world. Access to information through satellite TV and videos must have contributed to the downfall of central planning in the USSR. Russia's 80-year experiment with communism proved that central planning and totalitarianism is less durable and less efficient at meeting the needs of people than democracy and market forces. This is true within nations, and some companies are now showing it to be true within business organizations too. Some at the top will fight to hold on to the absolute power they enjoy, but customers and the new imperatives of the market will prevail. Hard-liners of the old guard who resist the revolution will find it difficult to play a role in the new regime.

Beyond command-and-control – the knowledge-intensive organization

What then, will the post-revolution, new-paradigm organization look like? Let us start with what the academics have to say – and there seems to be some agreement across their various views. In his 1990 book Peter Senge (1990) of MIT describes what he believes we should aim for, and calls it the 'Learning Organization'. Ikujiro Nonaka of Hitotsubashi University, Tokyo, whom we referred to earlier in this chapter, calls it the 'Knowledge-Creating Company'. Peter Drucker in 1989 however, speaks of the 'Information-based Organization', and later, in 1993, proposes the 'Responsibility-based Organization', while Tom Peters (1992) writes about 'Knowledge Management Structures and the New Organizing Logic'. There is a common philosophy and some common themes across all these perspectives, which you can see listed (see box). This new philosophy may make more sense if you can dip into some of the books referenced at the end of the chapter.

New philosophy, new themes

The new philosophy is that information and knowledge will soon be, if they are not already, the only basis for competition between organizations in world markets. This requires a radically new type of organization, with new structures, values, methods and objectives.

There is much theory around, and a few practical examples, but we still need a prototype for the new organization, to replace the old command-and-control prototype. A new prototype should embody the important common themes from theoretical studies and practical examples.

The common themes are:

● Market competition.
● Non-hierarchical, fluid organizational structures.
● Openness, freedom of information, self-management.
● Networks and excellent communications.
● Teams, mutuality, alliances and co-operation.
● Leadership, coaching and co-ordination.
● Shared vision and values, metaphors and ambiguity.
● Knowledge, learning, understanding.
● People orientation, respect for the individual, ethics.
● Commitment, involvement, responsibility, trust.
● Enthusiasm, fun, fulfilment, personal growth.
● Truth, facts, methods, techniques.
● Value and quality determined by the customer.
● Organizational learning and continual improvement of product and service.
● Broader, more complex, more worthy goals.

This is quite a long list, but in Chapter 4 we will see how all the elements fit together.

For a few progressive companies, information is now their most valuable work-in-process and knowledge their most useful tool; learning and creativity are replacing manual skills and long hours as their basis for adding value now. They understand that the old command-and-control approach – with a brainy few at the top trying to do all the thinking for their brawny workers – will increasingly be outsmarted by organizations which expect all workers at every level to think and to make their full knowledge contribution. For instance at Semco (the Brazilian company mentioned in Chapter 2) they have already dismantled their command-and-control structures. They have replaced them with an alternative model which contrasts so strongly with the old model, that I can best describe it as an 'inform-and-entrust' model. It is one which gives back to all employees something taken away from them during the Industrial Revolution – the responsibility for planning, controlling and improving their own actions. It trusts and encourages employees at all levels to learn, to create and use knowledge, to be flexible and to act according to the situation – in other words, to be self-managing.

As a new prototype, inform-and-entrust sounds fine in theory – there can be few chief executives now who do not at least pay lip-service to the concept of empowerment. Make information freely available, and provide employees with knowledge of how to interpret and use it – then trust them to make their own decisions. The 'law of the situation' as described by Mary Parker Follett in her paper given in 1925, can make commands unnecessary: give people the facts and they don't need to be told to do what any sensible person would agree is required (Follett, 1941). This assumes however, that employees will stop behaving in the passive, lazy, and unimaginative way that McGregor's Theory X presupposes – and which practical experience confirms. No doubt that is why many chief executives of hierarchical organizations are scared witless at the idea of going beyond the rhetoric of empowerment – with good cause because within the existing context, it really is unrealistic to expect employees to start behaving differently overnight, just because they have been told they are now empowered.

The hierarchy, as Gerald Fairtlough points out (1994), is a means of executing the wishes of the people at its head, and so other people's views become irrelevant. Thus empowerment within the hierarchy becomes a guessing game: if you can guess what is on your boss's mind, you are empowered to get on and do it. Hierarchies are 'blankets' which 'stifle initiative' and 'inhibit commitment to the goals of the organization as a whole'. Viewed from this perspective, it is not surprising then, that quality circles, Total Quality Management and other programmes to empower employees only bring temporary improvement, and the blanket of hierarchy soon reasserts itself.

However, if you look at the list of common themes for the new organization prototype, you will see that many of them are also common to Total Quality Management. Our prototype for the new organization may therefore be constructed around TQM combined with a non-hierarchical structure and some alternative form of control in place of budgets and management accounting figures.

Total Quality Management

TQM has a long pedigree, dating back to the work of William Edwards Deming (1986) who helped the Japanese shed their reputation for poor quality in the 1950s. They used his ideas – and those of another American, Joseph Juran, to shed their poor quality image by adopting a scientific approach to continually improve their processes. This 'kaizen' (continual improvement) approach has allowed them to catch up, overtake and build an increasing lead over the rest of the world in industry after industry. But Western companies were too busy focusing on profits to notice the effectiveness of Japanese management. For 30 years Deming tried to make himself heard in the West, but kaizen – or TQM as we call it – has only generated widespread interest since the 1980s. Almost too late, and only after losing several key industries it is now actively promoted by the DTI and well over half of the FTSE 100 companies have investigated it, or are actively using it. The public sector has also shown interest, with several county councils applying some, but not usually all aspects of TQM.

In fact, TQM is more than just a scientific approach: it also requires a new philosophy which knocks from the top of the agenda the self-defeating goal of maximizing profits, and replaces it with maximizing customer-perceived quality. And there is a third important element: teamwork – multi-skilled groups of employees working together to solve company problems, instead of individuals competing to maximize their own narrow targets.

Thus the whole TQM package presents a fundamentally new approach to management, which is quite difficult to communicate, yet must be passed on in a way which is not too radical for most managers to stomach (Wilson, 1993). Brian Joiner is a TQM consultant, and in his book referred to earlier in this chapter, he uses a neat device for summarizing the main features of TQM – the Joiner triangle, shown in Figure 3.2.

Although at the beginning most people assume TQM is about the management of quality, it actually turns out to be more about quality of management, addressing many of the defects of the Western command-and-control style of managing, but only within the framework of the hierarchy and top-down control.

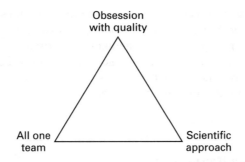

Figure 3.2   *The Joiner triangle*

Obsession with quality

Of the three corners of the triangle, this is the one which is fundamentally new, and marks out TQM as a radical departure from the classical management mould. By identifying quality, even above profit, as the prime objective, and focusing on process rather than product, TQM marks the beginning of a new paradigm. The new, customer orientation is reinforced by insisting that quality can only be defined by the customer. Rigid, internal specifications make improvement impossible: the aim is to exceed constantly rising expectations and continue to delight the customer.

Scientific approach

To improve, you must change something, and change always imposes an extra load. We must therefore change only on real evidence, quickly abandon changes which bring no improvement, and hold on to previous improvements when new changes are made. The key words are 'evidence' and 'improvement': without them we end up with the extra load but with no benefit. The scientific approach requires us to measure, monitor and analyse, using a range of statistical techniques to determine cause and effect, and distinguish between common and special causes of variation. Intuition and small, trial-and-error tests also have their place, as sometimes despite the analysis, the most important factors may not be measurable, or may even, according to Deming, remain 'unknown and unknowable'.

Scientific approaches to management have had a bad press in the West for nearly half a century, really since the Hawthorne experiments brought to an end the era of F. W. Taylor's scientific management. However, there is nothing wrong with the scientific method, even when humans are the subject of study. The method was first developed by Francis Bacon in the sixteenth century, and has formed the basis for advancing our understanding in virtually every field of study – including the study of management by academics. So why have managers ignored such a powerful method and preferred instead to concentrate on politics?

All one team

This message addresses some of the problems outlined earlier, of managers working to achieve their own financial targets, even at the expense of other managers and the organization as a whole. The organization as a whole must pull together, and one way of trying to achieve this, according to Richard Schonberger, is to encourage everyone to regard whoever they pass on work to, whether inside or outside the organization, as their customer, who should be listened to and accorded due respect. Similarly, they should think of themselves as an internal customer of whoever they receive work from inside the organization. Thus communication and co-operation between departments is encouraged by building a chain of customers through the organization.

Other initiatives to build a single team, focus on improving communications vertically as well as horizontally. Managers are encouraged to listen and enable, rather than instruct and supervise. And when quality failures happen, as they always will from time to time, the process should be criticized, not the employee. Then, an atmosphere of trust rather than fear can develop in the team, in which it becomes possible for people to be honest about how the failure occurred, and for appropriate changes to be made to the process so that the same failure can never happen again.

The acid test – does TQM work?

There is a basic problem: TQM requires everyone to be empowered to make hundreds of small improvements, as a normal part of their jobs. Where employees need special problem-solving techniques, or statistical knowledge, they are supported in acquiring these new skills. Workers are empowered and expected to use their brains – in other words, this is a knowledge-intensive approach to management. But giving knowledge and power to low-level operations workers upsets the hierarchy and undermines the authority of middle managers. So whereas kaizen takes root and flourishes in Japan's less control-oriented companies, in the West, TQM needs constant effort to keep it going. Typically the first flush of enthusiasm carries it through for about the first two years, but it never gains its own momentum. Enthusiasm is relentlessly smothered by the all-pervading blanket of hierarchy, and without some new impetus this effective long-term solution stalls – often to be replaced by the latest quick-fix flavour of the year. When TQM fails in the West, it is usually because the organizational context is wrong, and certainly not because the method itself is unsound. Knowledge stops flowing: TQM turns the taps full on, but the hierarchy puts too many kinks in the hose.

Inform-and-entrust: from principles to practice

Where do we go from here? We have a mess of problems associated with the old paradigm, and a bunch of theories and principles for making better use of knowledge. And we have some practical examples of organizations that have made progress towards the new paradigm. What we need now is a clearer view of what the knowledge-intensive organization should look like, and some idea of how to get to that state.

We have some clues: TQM seems to be the best pointer to the type of approach needed. It is a widely practised technique which is founded upon continual improvement, and therefore depends on learning and development of knowledge. Even though TQM is limited in its applicability, it can form a stepping stone which organizations can use in crossing the gulf from command-and-control to inform-and-entrust.

In the next chapter we will examine how the principles we have discussed may be brought together in an integrated way to form self-reinforcing virtuous circles of great power and effectiveness. We will use an adaptation of TQM as an effective prototype for the knowledge-intensive organization.

Pause for thought

The hierarchy is particularly bad at encouraging us to share and use information. It is highly likely that you know something which could be valuable to your organization, but you do not share this personal knowledge because of a variety of 'blocks'. Which of the following blocks, if any, have you experienced? Jot down a word or two to remind yourself of the circumstances of each.

1   You are holding on to the knowledge until you can trade the knowledge for something in return.

2   Your boss should really know what you know, but doesn't, and would feel threatened by your greater knowledge.

3   Your boss doesn't believe that you are in a position to know anything of value, and therefore won't listen to you.

4   Your knowledge conflicts with the rules or culture of the organization, and you know it would be pointless to put it forward.

5   If you reveal your knowledge, you will pick up extra work, but with no extra reward.

6   Once you share your knowledge with others, your own position may be weakened.

Can you think of any other blocks preventing personal knowledge from becoming organizational knowledge? If so, jot them down.

We can all imagine the characteristics of the perfect marital partner, but what about the perfect organization to work for? What would be its characteristics? Look again at the list of common themes for the new philosophy given earlier in this chapter, and then list the characteristics you would choose.

References and further reading

Badaracco, J. L. (1991) *The Knowledge Link – How firms compete through strategic alliances.* Harvard Business School Press.

Cooper, R. and Kaplan, R. (1984) Yesterday's accounting undermines production. *Harvard Business Review*, July/August.

Deming, W. E. (1986) *Out of the Crisis.* Cambridge University Press.

Department of Trade and Industry. *The Route Ahead* (a directory of publications and videos available under the Managing into the 90s programme). DTI London.

Department of Trade and Industry. *The Quality Gurus – What can they do for your company?* Managing into the 90s. DTI. London.

Drucker, P. (1989) *The New Realities.* Butterworth-Heinemann.

Drucker, P. (1993) *Post-Capitalist Society.* Butterworth-Heinemann.

Fairtlough, G. (1994) *Creative Compartments – A design for future organisation.* Adamantine Press.

Follett, M. P. (1941) *Dynamic Administration.*

Johnson, H. T. (1992) *Relevance Regained – From top-down control to bottom-up empowerment.* The Free Press.

Joiner, B. L. (1994) *Fourth Generation Management – The new business consciousness.* McGraw Hill.

Kuhn, T. S. (1970) *The Structure of Scientific Revolutions* (2nd edn). Chicago University Press.

Nonaka, I. (1991) The knowledge-creating company. *Harvard Business Review*, November/Decemeber.

Peters, T. (1992) *Liberation Management.* Macmillan.

Porter, M. E. (1990) *The Competitive Advantage of Nations.* Macmillan.

Schonberger, R. J. (1990) *Building a Chain of Customers: Linking business functions to create the world class company.* The Free Press.

Senge, P. M. (1990) *The Fifth Discipline - The art and practice of the learning organisation.* Doubleday.

Wilkstrom, S., Normann, R. et al. (1994) *Knowledge and Value – A new perspective on corporate transformation.* Routledge.

Wilson, D. A. (1991) *Business Information Systems.* Wolsey Hall Oxford Ltd.

Wilson, D. A. (1993) *Managing Information – For continual improvement.* Butterworth-Heinemann.

4 Inform-and-entrust: a model for the knowledge-intensive organization

Why read this chapter?

This is where we put together some general principles for the knowledge-intensive organization.

The earlier chapters showed how the old command-and-control approach disempowers people and thus creates exactly the wrong environment for knowledge management and the organizational learning which is needed to allow responsiveness and flexibility. The need for change is urgent, but our current management paradigm freezes us in old ways of thinking. It is a dead weight which constantly reasserts itself to prevent permanent change, and if we are to progress, eventually it will have to go. But what will replace it?

The purpose of the chapter is to present the ideas covered so far as an integrated, credible alternative to the command-and-control paradigm, but not to be prescriptive about the details of the redesigned organization. Knowledge as a resource needs managing – or to use a farming metaphor – husbanding. Like a cereal crop, the ground must be prepared for it to grow; the right conditions must be provided for it to be stored; and it must be used and sold to provide an income. This alternative approach was referred to at the end of Chapter 3 as the inform-and-entrust paradigm. It has a new feeling of rightness and common sense, and offers a truly convincing, much more powerful alternative to the command-and-control paradigm – one which re-unites the functions of planning and doing, and thus allows learning to occur and knowledge to thrive.

At the heart of the new paradigm lies a set of methods and values which are described here through the device of the inform-and-entrust triangle. This is my way of presenting the paradigm as an updated version of TQM, adapted to suit the knowledge-based organization – that is any organization, not just manufacturing companies in the private sector where TQM was born. The paradigm empowers people, but at the same time allows co-ordination and control through people's desire to subscribe to a shared vision, and enjoy the benefits of federation. It offers a credible alternative to top-down, centralized control through budgets and management accounting figures.

Rolls-Royce Motors leaves behind craft demarcations and hierarchy to win flexibility with small, multi-skilled teams

After accumulating multi-million pound loses, in 1990 Rolls faced closure and Peter Ward the chairman and CEO took drastic action: within two years he cut both the break-even level of production and the employee numbers by more than half (Griffiths, 1993).

But this was no crude down-sizing – it was a fundamental re-design of the whole organization based upon Japanese-style working teams which respond to each other as internal customers. The remaining 2,500 employees were organized in 16 zones, each with its own manager operating as a business within the business, responsible for cost, quality, delivery and even materials purchased. Within these sub-businesses are multi-skilled teams of six to ten members who operate with total flexibility, regardless of craft backgrounds. The new multi-skilled teams are becoming empowered, responsible and self-managing: commitment and proprietorship are heightened, with shop-floor employees attending product events so they can appreciate customer reaction at first hand. Needless to say this radical approach provoked great scepticism, and resistance from middle managers trying to protect the status quo, but the system is now gaining its own momentum, with the remaining managers no longer having to push.

And the results? Massive improvements in quality as well as productivity. By early 1993 the number of rectifications needed per car had gone from 150 to 47, clearly boosted by re-combining meaningless short tasks back into meaningful work. For instance, each assembly team worker takes three hours to assemble a complete engine now. It becomes 'his' engine whereas before, the job was divided up into specific short tasks spread across several workers, none of whom felt responsible for the whole engine.

The story is still unfolding: in January 1995 the operations MD for Rolls-Royce Motors, Charles Matthews, reported Rolls back in the black with a positive cash-flow (Matthews, 1995). On-time delivery to dealers had risen from 50 per cent to virtually 100 per cent. The time to make a car had fallen from 70 days to 28 days and WIP had fallen from 600 to 200 partly finished cars. However, the writing is on the wall for engine making at Derby, as Rolls do not have the financial clout to develop a new engine for the next century, and have forged a supply agreement with BMW. Watch the press for further developments.

Preparing the ground for knowledge to grow

Knowledge is the result of learning. If we want individual and organizational knowledge to grow, we must provide the right environment for learning to occur. And in theory we know a great deal about learning: scientists and educators have been writing about the subject ever since Socrates put quill to parchment. However learning by, and within organizations has only recently created much interest.

Learning – the traditional approach

Historically the Church always took the lead in education. Then during the Industrial Revolution, the State began to take an interest. Schools were founded, and laws were passed to restrict the exploitation of children and allow them time off work to attend school. These initiatives in the nineteenth century came from members of parliament and industrialists who were concerned for the welfare of young people. In 1902 the Local Education Authorities took over the voluntary schools, and education up to the age of 14 was eventually made compulsory in 1918.

A top-down approach to primary and secondary education is clearly appropriate. The State as the main provider of education, broadly determines through the National Curriculum what is taught in schools. But businesses also use top-down 'training needs analysis' to establish what training they should provide for their employees. This 'mugs and jugs' approach, with the mugs waiting passively for the jugs to fill them, may work in primary and secondary schools, but it scarcely works at all in adult education and training. As an educator I know that if you do not want to learn something, I am powerless to make you – but if you do want to learn something, I am equally powerless to stop you. Clearly, your own internal motivation is absolutely essential if learning is to be effective. Learning can be hard work and painful, so you must have a strong, personal reason to sustain your motivation. You will only remain truly committed if you help decide what you are to learn, and believe the effort will be worthwhile in the end.

Training needs analysis can become a tool of top-down control, with managers sending their staff on courses for the wrong reasons. It looks good for managers to take a systematic approach to developing their staff – but only in the context of the old command-and-control paradigm. From the earlier chapters we know knowledge work is different: how can a training needs specialist know what training you need – in other words, what your weaknesses are? The answer is, if at all, only through your co-operation, which you may be unwilling to risk. In the old paradigm, training is for the lower levels, not for those at, or on the way to the top – and it can be unwise to reveal weakness when promotion depends on perceived strength and competence. You are the one who knows best what training would be most relevant to your present and future roles in the organization. Would it not be more sensible to provide an environment of trust and encouragement and then offer all employees a wide range of training options to choose from? We can anticipate the traditional response to such advice: 'You must be crazy! My training budget would go through the roof, and my staff would use their new training to get better jobs elsewhere.' But Nissan has shown this need not be the case. The company values the knowledge resource, links pay and promotion to the learning of skills, and has a permanent commitment to training. Their staff realize they would be crazy to leave just to stagnate in a slightly better job elsewhere.

A huge amount has been written on the subject of learning, and how to facilitate it for individuals and organizations. Learning is fundamental to knowledge, and if you want to know more about learning, the work of Ronnie Lessem (1993) is a good place to start: he has written an excellent review of the gurus and their different perspectives. There is one principle which should be emphasized however, because it keeps recurring throughout the literature: the linking of thought and action. Genuine learning which results in changed performance certainly cannot be demonstrated without action, and without action, probably no permanent learning occurs.

It all started with Francis Bacon, the sixteenth-century Chancellor of the Exchequer and founder member of the Royal Society who first proposed the Scientific Method as a basis for adding to knowledge and enabling understanding. Briefly, the method consists of five steps:

- Observe (some effect or phenomenon).
- Define (it, precisely in words).
- Hypothesize (or guess the cause).
- Experiment (by designing and running a test, in order to ...).
- Prove (and thereby construct a theory relating cause and effect).

Bacon, who was a contemporary of Sir Francis Drake and Sir Walter Raleigh, proposed the method in his book *The Advancement of Learning* in 1605, and although learning is now seen to be more of a cyclic process, the basic theory is too fundamental to be bettered. It reappears in David Kolb's learning cycle (1984), which is concerned with learning by management, Figure 4.1.

It also appears in Deming's Plan-Do-Check-Act cycle, Figure 4.2, which allows learning and improvement within quality circles, so fundamental to kaizen and TQM.

In fact you won't find any expert who suggests that learning can be achieved by separating thinking from doing, or planning from executing in the way that happens in the classical command-and-control organization. It seems to be an unavoidable requirement for learning to take place: the thinking and planning must be carried out by the same people who are doing or executing the task to be learned about.

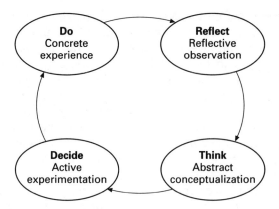

Figure 4.1   *The Kolb learning cycle*

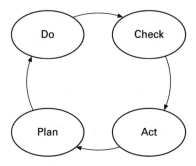

Figure 4.2   *The Deming PDCA cycle*

Learning – the need for a new approach

By now you probably agree that knowledge is a most valuable – if not the most valuable – asset of an organization. And assets should be secure but accessible – not kept in a storehouse with holes in the walls and uncooperative storekeepers. Remember, knowledge is that which is known – by people. Knowledge is stored in people's heads – and of all knowledge, it is the tacit and embedded knowledge which is the most valuable in building a sustainable competitive edge. Unlike the explicit and migratory knowledge which can be bought and sold in much the same way as other factors of production, tacit and embedded knowledge is controlled by those who 'know' it. It can of course be passed on to others in the organization, but only slowly and only if the people holding the knowledge are prepared to make the effort to pass it on. This realization should cause us to think again about the value of the people in our organizations, and in particular the bad effects of a high staff turnover.

How to assess your organization's approach to learning

What do you call your people?

The way we think about things is inextricably tied up with the words we use. Revolutionaries know this, and so do spin-doctors, advertisers and advocates of political correctness. For our new paradigm we too need to be careful about the words we use.

How do you describe your people? Are they workers, or direct labour, or employees, or staff, or managers, or executives, or associates? Each of these terms has dictionary definitions which you can look up, and political or emotive connotations which you cannot look up so easily, but which nevertheless have a powerful influence on how we think. You work for your organization: you are therefore a worker. But you probably feel the word is not very appropriate to describe you, because it conjures up images of sweat and toil, horny hands, dirty coats and lunch boxes.

In the knowledge-intensive organization where the functions of thinking and doing are combined, the distinctions between managers and workers, between line and staff, and between direct and indirect, disappear or become irrelevant. Let us therefore use the word 'staff' or even just 'people' to describe those who are members of an organization. These words are widely understood and have fairly neutral connotations.

Do your people stay, or do they go?

First, a high staff turnover will not allow time for embedded knowledge to be passed on, and it will therefore be swept away by the current of people passing through the organization. Second, a high staff turnover often indicates high dissatisfaction and feelings of resentment and alienation amongst staff, which will make them less likely to use and pass on their knowledge. We have always known that there are direct costs associated with a turnover rate which is greater than can be accounted for by natural wastage – the costs of attracting, selecting, recruiting and training extra new staff. A high annual percentage staff turnover was thought of as inefficient – wasteful but offset by savings on, say, the lower pay or conditions which are said to cause the high turnover. But a high staff turnover is much more serious than that: it indicates the invisible but calamitous wasting away of organizational knowledge – the source of value to its customers, and its competitive edge. So what should be done to avoid a high staff turnover?

Are your people valued?

If you want your staff to stay with you and feel involved and committed, then value your staff – and show that you value them. But you know how some managers would react to this advice: 'If I do that, they will ask for a pay rise.' Theirs is a natural response, and a predictable one from the old command-and-control mentality in which managers and workers face each other adversarially across a deep philosophical divide. But it does show that managers appreciate that there are few, simple decisions in their job: an organization is a very complex system in which a decision can have direct desired results, but will usually have other indirect effects as well. Peter Senge (1990) refers to this 'systems-thinking' as the Fifth Discipline, an essential skill in the learning organization. Perhaps staff will ask for a pay rise, but in the new inform-and-entrust environment it will not just be a manager's job to resist demands for increased pay; there will be other market-driven, team-centred mechanisms which will moderate pay demands. All members of a team which charges for its services will question whether they can afford someone who demands too high a price. The knowledge-intensive organization should be thought of as a completely different system from the old command-and-control system; in the new system, the motivating forces and control mechanisms will work in entirely new ways.

Do your people understand the power of 'systems thinking'?

Senge describes how cause and effect are not usually related in a simple, once-off type of way, but often form a circle of causality which either reinforces the effect or stabilizes the effect at some level. Engineers may recognize these as descriptions of positive and negative feedback, but we are all familiar with the concept of the vicious circle and its twin, the virtuous circle, which are both examples of self-reinforcing circular causality. Here are some examples:

- I meet friends regularly for a drink after work. I am under stress at work, so I drink a bit more to relieve the stress. It affects my work the next day, and I experience more stress. I drink even more to relieve the extra stress and it affects my work even more ... a vicious circle.
- I am overweight. I do some jogging and lose a little weight. I feel a bit better, so I step up the exercise and lose more weight. I feel even better still, so do even more exercise ... a virtuous circle.

Eventually if I lose too much weight, I will begin to feel worse after exercise, and this is an example of the stabilizing effect of negative results.

Senge gives a much fuller explanation, with lots of examples which operate in organizations. He explains how in some cases, effects are separated from their causes by space and time, which can make it difficult for staff to learn and understand the results of their actions. Organizations are full of these circular causal relationships, and there are some virtuous circles which only operate in the inform-and-entrust environment. Here are two examples, taken from Fairtlough (1994).

Are your people empowered and committed?

If you empower someone by giving them responsibility for a particular task, you are in effect telling them you believe they are capable of doing it. The task becomes that person's 'baby', and he or she is likely to want to fulfil your expectations of their ability. Think about the last time you were given extra responsibility. You were flattered, your reputation was at stake and you became committed to the task. It is a natural, human response, and it is natural too that if you did a good job, you should be considered again for extra responsibility. Empowerment breeds commitment, which makes further empowerment likely. A virtuous circle.

Is there an atmosphere of openness and trust?

Openness requires you to be honest about difficulties, telling the whole truth and not just the bits which reflect well on you. It requires managers to make information freely available so that everyone can learn from it. But being open in this way is risky: people feel exposed and threatened when mistakes are made public. But as Deming points out, nearly all errors are caused at least in part by the system, not just by the individual closest to the scene. However, in the old command-and-control environment, errors are covered up where possible to avoid blame, and no one learns from them. When errors cannot be hidden, someone is made the scapegoat so that the rest can keep their promotion prospects intact.

In the inform-and-entrust environment, openness and trust can grow together in the same way it does socially when two people get to know each other intimately: the relationship depends on a mutual exchange of confidences. It works the same way in organizations: trust builds as people discover it is OK to be open with small errors, and gradually they feel able to be more and more open.

It is not easy for anyone in the organization to develop the habit of openness, least of all the leaders. Suppose there is a potential quality problem; should everyone know about it? Leaders constantly worry that if too many people in the organization have sensitive information, it will get out to customers or competitors. Such risks are usually very small in comparison to the enormous – though difficult to quantify – benefits of openness and trust. Some quality problems are notoriously difficult to tackle. The original cause of the problem may be separated in time and space from the bad effect – for instance a buyer purchasing less than ideal material may be contributing to production problems later – and if it cannot be admitted widely that a problem exists, the problem is unlikely ever to be satisfactorily resolved.

Do your leaders lead by coaching?

The leaders at the centre of the concentric circle, Semco-style organization are the custodians of the new environment, with the authority to maintain an appropriate organizational structure and communicate the all-important values we have just been discussing, which are essential if knowledge is to be accumulated and managed. It goes without saying that the type of leader needed for the knowledge-intensive organization is a very different animal from the old command-and-control leader. In place of the charismatic master who has all the good ideas and expects all the glory, we need the modest patron who can build and support worthy visions, and for whom reflected glory is often sufficient. Less of a brigadier and more of a football coach perhaps? It is difficult to capture these ideas and communicate them efficiently, and indeed the new leaders must be excellent communicators who, like politicians, understand how to use words, metaphors and analogies in building consensus, creating worthy visions and setting complex goals.

It is difficult to be prescriptive, but we can be certain of some fundamentals. Leaders must have genuine respect for all individuals, and must create an environment in which everyone will be treated in a fair and dignified manner. This can only be achieved if, as far as possible, everyone has job security, and is encouraged to grow and develop through learning new abilities.

Leaders must not only be good communicators in their own right, but must also strive for excellent communications throughout the organization. If leaders are to build values, create visions and ensure they are shared widely, there must be lots of opportunities for communication, and media channels must allow rich and complex messages. When it comes to communicating visions and values, plenty of face-to-face communication is essential.

Is communication free and unconstrained?

Learning is impossible without free communication, and even the use of existing personal knowledge is restricted without it. In fact everything we have talked about depends on excellent communication – and yet the scope of this book means we can only refer to it briefly here. Get hold of some of the references at the end of Chapters 3 and 4 if you can, in particular Fairtlough (1994), who devotes a chapter to the subject. He distinguishes between codified and uncodified communication, constrained and unconstrained communication, directed and broadcast communication. Codified information is stripped of any irrelevancies to give a precise and concise message which can be understood widely by people from all sorts of backgrounds. Uncodified information however, is used by people within a close-knit group, and depends heavily on shared values and experience. It includes body language. It is rich, personal, non-standard, indirect, and capable of conveying perceptions and emotions that cannot easily be codified. It is essential for communicating the tacit, implicit, embedded knowledge which is the basis for team learning.

Constrained communication carries information which is distorted by the influence of power. Dissent makes the job more difficult for people in authority. They can use their power to suppress dissent through fear without questioning whether it is based on a better argument. People in hierarchical organizations know it is dangerous to say what they think, and so communication is constrained. For unconstrained communication, people must know the power of the better argument will prevail.

Through broadcast communication, everyone in the organization receives the same message at the same time. For instance, this could be by open, face-to-face meeting, by a memo to all staff, or by electronic conferencing. Directed communication on the other hand, goes only to a limited number of people, and often just to a single person. Clearly, some types of information are only of interest to a few people, and to broadcast such information would just contribute to the information overload we all suffer from. But organizations dedicated to openness must use broadcast communication as freely as possible.

Fairtlough (1994) uses the term 'communicative competence' to describe the unconstrained, open, codified, broadcast communication which is the norm within a group of people who have learned to operate efficiently as a team. He concludes from his experience as chief executive of Shell Chemicals UK Ltd, and founder chief executive of Celltech Ltd, that communicative competence should give rise to a virtuous circle in which this skill and confidence generates success in solving problems and this success leads in turn to a greater commitment to open communication. Working in such a team is deeply satisfying: in a meeting the germ of an idea may be put forward by one person, picked up and added to by another, discussed and developed by others, eventually to be tested and applied. An idea is valued on its merits, not on who put it forward. Contrast this with the situation we all experience far too often: the meeting in which you put forward an idea to solve a problem, someone else puts forward another idea, a third person yet another idea... In command-and-control hierarchies lots of ideas may get put forward, but none get developed by the group. It is more important that your idea is the one adopted, regardless of the relative merits of the other ideas put forward. Teamwork is destroyed: people instead of ideas compete, and the net result is poor decisions, zero learning, and no chance of continual improvement. It explains all too clearly how, in Senge's words, 'a team of committed managers with individual IQs above 120 can have a collective IQ of 63' (Senge, 1990).

Are you feeling you have been here before? Is this talk of quality, teamwork and continual improvement bringing on a sense of deja vu? If so, it is not surprising, because the fundamentals of managing knowledge are the same as the fundamentals of TQM. The difference is that TQM focuses on delighting the customer, and continually improving the quality of product and process, whereas in managing knowledge we must take a more comprehensive view which has more worthy goals and includes other stake-holders, in particular the employees. However, as most people have had some exposure to the principles of TQM, it can be helpful to view the knowledge-intensive organization as an evolutionary descendant of TQM.

Building on TQM

There is nothing wrong with TQM – as far as it goes – but in some situations its bias towards manufacturing and its focus on the needs of the customer can raise awkward questions for which it provides no satisfactory answers. TQM was developed in the West as a response to problems of mediocre quality in manufacturing companies in the private sector. Japanese manufacturers had demonstrated that it was possible to offer customers high quality products at reasonable prices, and so TQM focused on customer-defined quality of manufactured products. Some of the principles of TQM have been applied in the public and service sectors, but private companies in the manufacturing sector are still where TQM is easiest to apply. There are two reasons.

First, in manufacturing there is (as discussed earlier) an observable process and a tangible product which can be inspected and stored if necessary before being delivered to the customer. Both the product and the process can be studied objectively – analysed, measured and counted. Tangible products and observable processes respond well to the scientific approach. But in the service sector where knowledge work determines the quality of an intangible product, observing, measuring and analysing may be impossible.

And second, in the private sector the roles of the customer – those of paying for, receiving, and benefiting from the product or service – are usually enacted by a single person or group. But in the public sector these roles may be split across several people or groups. For instance, who are the customers of a school? The government pays for, society benefits from, and pupils receive the educational service the school provides. These different groups will all have different values and quality expectations which confuse the central motivating force of TQM – the obsession with quality. This is nearly always the case in the public sector. Who should define quality in the social services, the armed forces, or the Crown Prosecution Service? In these examples the people on the receiving end of the service are seldom paying for it directly, and the people benefiting from the service may not be receiving it directly. Consequently there is considerable scope for disagreement over what constitutes quality of service, as any villain having his collar felt by the local policeman could tell you.

Thus TQM is best suited to a sector in Western economies in which the prospects for employment are small and declining – the manufacturing sector. TQM in its present form is not nearly so well-suited to the public sector and the burgeoning service and information sectors where most employed people now work. By contrast, the new inform-and-entrust paradigm, which is just TQM developed to suit the knowledge-based organization, is appropriate for any organization in any sector.

The inform-and-entrust paradigm – a simple model

New paradigms need a new vocabulary and new mental models. One of the best ways of helping people develop these is by communicating with mental images: metaphors, analogies and simple diagrams. We need a simple model of the inform-and-entrust paradigm, one which will make clear its rationale and help to lead us forward. The model I have derived is a modified version of the Joiner triangle. This shows that TQM is in itself a big step towards what is required – in effect a stepping stone between the old classical approach, and the new knowledge-intensive approach. It also makes it possible to integrate the common themes of the various references quoted. All that is necessary is for the three cornerstones of the Joiner triangle to be expanded – redefined to encompass the wider perspectives now required, Figure 4.3.

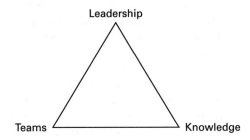

Figure 4.3   *The inform-and-entrust triangle*

Leadership

At the peak of the inform-and-entrust triangle, 'Leadership' replaces 'Obsession with quality' in its parent, the Joiner triangle. Quality of product or service as the supreme goal instead of profit is fundamental to the TQM philosophy, but it can make TQM difficult to apply in the public sector, and it ignores the needs of those other key stake-holders in the organization, the employees, who will eventually come to see the quality motive as just as exploitative as the profit motive. It is almost as unrealistic to expect employees to sacrifice heart and soul for maximum customer quality as it is for maximum shareholder profit. A wider cause, encompassing quality, but more worthy than quality alone is required to fire the imagination and energy of employees and gain their wholehearted commitment.

Leaders will be needed at various times and places in every process throughout the knowledge-intensive organization, but the type of leader required will not normally be the charismatic, forceful personality who drives his or her people onward towards goals not necessarily of their own choosing. In the knowledge-intensive organization, the leader will be the type of person who listens, informs and interacts – and provides representative leadership, a bit like a member of parliament who sets worthy goals which people might not think up on their own, but to which they are nevertheless prepared to commit themselves.

Senior managers should provide overall leadership through a vision of service to a wider group than just the customers, to include employees, perhaps also the local community, the nation, or even all mankind. This may sound like the king providing leadership by jumping on his horse and galloping off in all directions, but far from diluting commitment to customer quality, it actually works to the benefit of customers. Knowledge is not like other resources which get thinner the wider they are spread: it seems to get thicker and richer. Like a muscle, the more it's used the more it develops. We know for instance that employees tend to treat their customers in much the same way that they in turn are treated by their managers. When employees are treated badly, they treat their customers badly, but when they are treated well, those attitudes too are passed on to the customer. It seems so obvious: the quality of the total customer experience depends on the quality of employees' total working life.

Leadership should therefore include the concept of responsibility – a duty of care beyond the minimum required by law, owed by individuals, teams and managers to their internal and external customers. One example of this is the responsibility that senior managers should have for all their employees, to help them acquire new skills and develop themselves through learning and education so that they grow to fulfil their potential as employees and as human beings. The word 'training' is perhaps best left behind with the old paradigm. It has the wrong implications: that a trainer determines what is to be learned, thus separating planning from doing; and that the emphasis is on manual skills and repetition, rather than mental exercises to develop understanding.

The new leaders should therefore behave more like football coaches than sergeant majors, and their most important tasks are:

● communicating worthy goals via metaphors and visions which allow some freedom of interpretation, and thus build commitment,
● developing and communicating shared values to channel and support commitment to the goals,
● setting up and maintaining a non-hierarchical structure, to remove fear and allow trust and co-operation to develop, and then,
● nurturing knowledge by ensuring full and free opportunities to all for communication of, and access to information.

Teams

The inform-and-entrust triangle has 'Teams' in place of Joiner's 'All one team'. TQM, remember, is designed to suit the classical organization structure in which most horizontal communications between departments are not formally recognized – hence the one team idea to improve internal co-operation. The inform-and-entrust organization however is better restructured along less rigid lines, consisting of multi-disciplinary semi-permanent groups of people, subdivided into teams. These according to Quinn Mills (1993), may be 30 to 50 people, further sub-divided into self-directed teams of 5 to 7 people. Or they may be groups of about 100, divided into teams of between 5 and 20, as described by Semler (1993). Fairtlough (1994), refers to 'creative compartments' of 'a few hundreds of people', and later gives examples of groupings within compartments of 'teams of six to ten' people. So teams are very important – not just the one whole-organization team, but teams within a team – bonded together by a common mission and shared values. New companies often operate for years without ever getting round to drawing up a formal organization tree, but once put in place, dismantling it seems to suggest foolhardy recklessness. The tree is designed to enable centralized control, and shows permitted channels of communication. But as we have seen, centralized control is impossible in today's fast-moving business environment, and free communication is required in abundance, which is just what the tree is designed to restrict.

Teams should be where everything comes together – they should be the focus for organizational learning. They should be guided by values shared across the whole organization. They should be responsible to and for their own members and to and for other teams. It should be within and between teams that information is shared and where embedded knowledge resides. Senge (1990) describes team learning in detail, and Semler (1993) has shown how to abandon the hierarchy and as a result allow everyone to look forward to coming to work in the morning.

Knowledge

This slogan replaces what lay at the third corner of the Joiner triangle – the 'Scientific approach'. Again, it is meant to encompass all the process improvement techniques that were included in the Scientific approach, but makes clear that knowledge workers should use the right-hand side of their brains as well as the left – emphasizing the need for imagination, creativity and intuition as well as science. It also suggests that learning and improvement should be a fundamental part of knowledge work, and not something which takes place only within the confines of the quality improvement group or quality circle.

Knowledge is the product of learning on the part of individuals and organizations. To quote Badaracco (1991): knowledge '... takes many forms: technology, innovation, science, know-how, creativity, information.' He makes the distinction between migratory knowledge

– which can spread quickly because it exists in books, formulae and designs – and embedded knowledge, which cannot slip away so easily because it resides primarily in organizational relationships, attitudes, values and ways of working. There are many parallels between Badaracco's migratory/embedded categorization and Nonaka's explicit/tacit categorization, and it seems that an organization's tacit, embedded knowledge is the key to releasing potential, adding value and gaining competitive edge. For example, often individuals in classical organizations own much explicit knowledge which never gets used by the organization. One very pertinent example is the knowledge owned by lecturers in business schools, which is often ignored in the managing of those schools – in particular TQM – a point made by six CEOs of America's largest businesses (Robinson, Akers, Artzt et al., 1991). Today's organization must have embedded knowledge built in, in the form of policies, practices and values which allow the organization to tap this resource by learning through dialogue in which team members get beyond competing amongst themselves and start performing effectively as a team.

We have now reached the end of Part II which describes how and why organizations are evolving. In Part III you can read how learning to improve is supported by technology, teams and projects.

Pause for thought

1 Learning can be exhilarating. It can also be humiliating – especially when the learner's mistakes are pointed out. When you are acting as a coach or mentor, what should you do when your student makes a mistake?
(a) Be discrete? You know your student doesn't need telling, so you ignore it.
(b) Be open and supportive? Use the mistake as the focus for learning and further practice.
(c) Be advisory? Wait for your student to ask for help.
(d) Be questioning? Ask the student to review the situation and how you can help.
   What would be the consequences of your responding in each of these ways?

2 A colleague in your work group who has not shown much interest in training before, now wants to do a fine arts course in the evenings at the local college, and asks the company to pay the fees. Should you –
(a) Oppose the request because it is irrelevant to the group's work?
(b) Suggest an alternative, more relevant course of study?
(c) Ask your colleague why the work group should support the request?
(d) Support the request without question.

What would be the immediate and long-term consequences of each of the above strategies? How would you react if you were in your colleague's shoes?

3 In the knowledge-based organization, what characteristics should a leader have? List four characteristics in order of importance, either from those shown below, or from elsewhere.

knowledgeable
questioning
supportive
enthusiastic
sociable
administrative
manipulative
likeable
forceful
retiring
generous
motivated

References and further reading

Badaracco, J. L. (1991) *The Knowledge Link - How firms compete through strategic alliances.* Harvard Business School Press.

Fairtlough, G. (1994) *Creative Compartments – A design for future organisation.* Adamantine Press.

Griffiths, J. (1993) Driven towards leanness – Rolls-Royce Motors has radically transformed its working practices. *Financial Times,* 10 March.

Kolb, D. A. (1984) *Experiential Learning.* Prentice-Hall.

Lessem, R. (1993) *Business as a Learning Community. Applying global concepts to organizational learning.* McGraw-Hill.

Matthews, C. (1995) How we changed gear to ride the winds of change. *Professional Manager,* Vol 4, No 1.(January).

Quinn Mills, D. (1993) *Rebirth of the Corporation.* John Wiley

Robinson, J. D., Akers, J. F., Artzt, E. L., Poling, Galvin, R. W. and Allaire, P. A. (1991) An open letter: TQM on the campus. *Harvard Business Review,* November/December.

Semler, R. (1993) *Maverick! The success story behind the world's most unusual workplace.* Century.

Senge, P. M. (1990) *The Fifth Discipline – The art and practice of the learning organisation.* Doubleday.

Part III: Methods and tools for managing knowledge

New occasions teach new duties: Time makes ancient good uncouth;
They must upward still, and onward, who would keep abreast of Truth.
From 'The Present Crisis', by US poet, diplomat and
Minister to Britain, James Russel Lowell (1819–1891).

If you can accept the overall strategy for managing knowledge put forward in Parts I and II, you may now be ready to read Part III, which focuses in from the big picture onto some of the methods and tools needed to implement it. Teams, networks and projects occupy centre-stage in this part of the book. None of these are new, but when examined through the inform-and-entrust lens, it is clear they need to be used in new ways.

Chapters 5 and 6 deal with the computers and software which can lend power to any knowledge-intensive system. The chapters are written for users, and potential users – not for programmers. Some readers may choose to skip over parts of Chapter 6 which deal with quantitative techniques, without risk of loosing the overall message of the book.

Chapters 7 and 8 examine how the self-managing team can raise the quality standards, amplify the creativity and increase the output of knowledge workers.

Chapters 9 and 10 describe the new ways knowledge workers can use forecasting and planning techniques in today's turbulent business environment. Again, some readers may safely choose to skip the mathematics in these chapters.

5 The new technology – computers and communications

Why read this chapter?

Wait! Don't skip this chapter – it is for managers, not computer nerds and techies. It is about how to exploit computers, not how to operate them. Information technology is the most powerful labour- and time-saver ever developed, and the management of knowledge depends heavily on it. Today, most knowledge workers use computers in their jobs, and often use electronic networks to gather material and ship their output to their customers. But in addition to speeding up and automating existing procedures, the technology is making possible completely new ways of working.

The silicon chip and the telephone network are as basic to the information age as was steel and the railway network to the industrial age. Just as steel made possible the steam engine, the silicon chip also makes possible entirely new ways of working. It was easy to see that a steam engine could replace a water wheel, but knowledge work and its raw material, information, are different. In digital form information can exist in several places at the same time, and processing and shipping can be instantaneous. It is not at all easy to see the big opportunities which these new capabilities bring, partly because knowledge work is intangible, and partly because we are blinded by old paradigm, command-and-control assumptions.

How do computers fit in with the new inform-and-entrust approach? What types of computing system do we specifically need to support knowledge management? We will examine the potential of some new developments, but mostly, we will stick to general principles and longer-term trends. That way we will be equipped to take full advantage of future new developments as they emerge. The emphasis will be on supporting knowledge work.

Automating and informating

During the industrial age we discovered it was possible to improve productivity by providing workers with increasingly sophisticated machinery. In the fields, the scythe gave way to the threshing machine, then the combine harvester. And in the factories the centre lathe gave way to the capstan, then the bar-fed automatic. At the dawning of the information age it was therefore natural for us to see the computer as a more sophisticated adding machine or typewriter, which could increase productivity and reduce the number of workers needed for office jobs. And computers can indeed be used just to automate jobs – to replace people with machines and thus save on direct labour. That is what happened in the 1960s when computers were first used by companies for payroll processing. A whole class of clerical worker – the comptometer operator – was wiped out in the space of a few years. But when computers are used, new types of information become easily accessible, and this opens up entirely new possibilities, beyond just automating the job.

For instance in retail stores, when computers replaced mechanical cash registers, the main payoff came from automating some of the tasks of the check-out operator, such as looking up the list price of different items. But new possibilities also emerged: the data on items purchased entered for the primary purpose of calculating what to charge the customer, could then be used for secondary purposes such as sales analysis, stock control and reordering, which are management tasks. Of course this information was stored on the till roll in the days of mechanical cash registers, but in such an inaccessible form that it was seldom referred to. Shoshana Zuboff (1988) recognized this ability of computers to make information which was entered for one purpose, easily available for several other, secondary purposes. She identified it as a powerful new function, beyond the automating of work, for which she coined the term 'informating' the work.

Let us compare the results of automating and informating in the command-and-control regime and in the more liberal inform-and-entrust environment.

Command-and-control: computers to control

When computer-based management information systems were first introduced to support management decision-making, they were designed around the mainframe computer, but this solution which

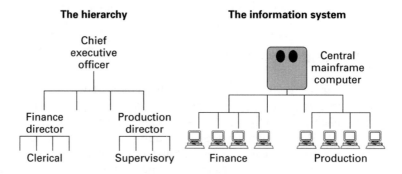

Figure 5.1 *Central mainframe computing*

was the norm in the 1960s and 1970s is less common now. With its single database, guarded by the high priests of data processing, it was ideally suited to the command-and-control approach – information could be strictly controlled and access only allowed on a 'need to know' basis, in line with a person's function and status. It closely mirrored the organizational hierarchy and did little to improve communication through levels and between departments, Figure 5.1.

The management information system based upon a central mainframe accessed through remote terminals in different departments is being modified and replaced by distributed systems based on networks of personal computers, often linked to a mainframe server, which can hold shared data and software. The new networks allow processing and storage to be carried out locally within specific departments, and should also allow the results to be passed on to other departments through the network. The human resources manager now has an HRM system, the production manager a production and inventory control system, the finance manager an accounting system, and so on, Figure 5.2. And when the people in the finance department need to know the value of stocks held in order to prepare the balance sheet, they should be able to access the inventory records of the production department through the network. This of course is a big improvement, because managers are able to get on with their own functions without being dependent on other departments, but it has disadvantages as well.

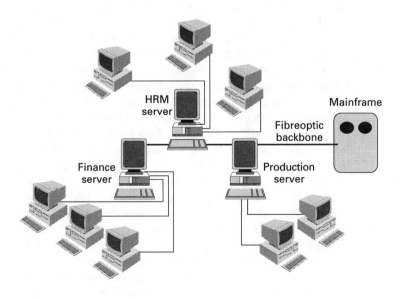

Figure 5.2 *Distributed client-server computing*

Apart from some technical problems which are bound to yield eventually to advances in technology, this approach has the major disadvantage of reinforcing traditional ways of working. All it does is automate existing work methods and consolidate existing departmental procedures and boundaries. It completely overlooks what Michael Hammer and James Champy (1993) describe as the disruptive power of information technology, 'its ability to break the rules that limit how we conduct our work' – its ability to support business processes which cut across traditional departments and thereby bring massive improvements in competitive advantage.

Big systems can screw up in a big way

We will return to the theme of business processes later in the chapter, but first let us take as an example a type of computer system which has been around for decades, with its roots in the old industrial era, namely MRP systems – materials requirement planning systems. MRP systems were one of the first applications for mainframe computing in business, after payroll and accounting systems. They were designed to control stocks of parts and rates of production in factories making mass-produced products such as washing machines, cars and television sets. Typically there are many different manufacturing processes which feed parts to sub-assembly tracks, which in turn feed into final assembly tracks. The whole system has to march to the same drumbeat, or chaos results – a shortage of a single component in one of the processes can bring the whole manufacturing system to a halt. Equally, if some process in the system runs too fast, surplus work-in-process soon begins to build up. Before computers were available to control the whole system, the final assembly tracks determined the throughput, and all the sub-assembly lines and processes supplying parts had to keep up. Needless to say, most of these used buffer stocks at each stage to make sure they never ran short, and as a consequence, the whole system required huge amounts of work-in-process (WIP – partly finished products at any stage between raw materials and finished product), which made the system extremely inflexible. Storage space required for WIP nearly doubled the factory size, and typically the value tied up in WIP would be equivalent to about two months worth of production, or nearly 20 per cent of annual revenue. So what did the command-and-control merchants of the time dream up to control this immensely complex manufacturing system? You guessed it: an immensely complex computer program for planning in detail a weekly schedule of exactly how much material should be ordered, how many parts should be made, how many sub-assemblies should be put together, and how many final assemblies should be produced. To implement the plan, the system would then print out purchase orders for suppliers and works orders and schedules for the various stages of production in the factory.

Just to give you some idea of the complexity of MRP systems, let me tell you how they handle batch sizes and lead times. The batch size is the quantity to be delivered, or produced in one lot, and the lead time is the time which will elapse between the order being placed and the batch being delivered. MRP systems assume that parts and materials will be ordered and made in their so-called economic batch sizes. This is the batch size which in theory produces the best compromise between two types of cost: the ordering or set-up cost which falls with batch size, and the storage cost which rises with batch size, Figure 5.3. This economic batch size varies for each order: large, expensive things are ordered in small batch sizes, whereas small, cheap things are ordered and stored in large batches. And each order has its own lead time, dependent on the amount and complexity of work to be done to fulfil the order, which should be worked out from work study data and machine capacity figures.

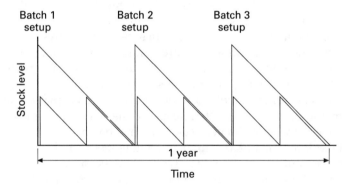

With 3 batches there are only 3 set-ups, but stock levels are high.
With 6 batches there are only 6 set-ups, but stock levels are lower.

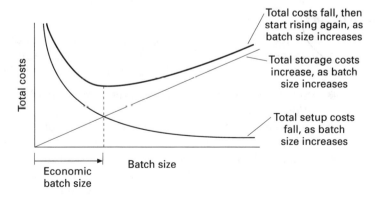

Figure 5.3 *The economic batch size*

In principle the concept is simple and logical, but the sheer volume of data which must be kept up-to-date creates an unbelievably massive task. How many separate parts go into a single TV model in a manufacturer's range? It must be hundreds. Now bear in mind that some parts may be common to a range of sub-assemblies and some sub-assemblies may be common to a range of finished products, and you can see that great complexity can arise out of the detail. In fact companies can only manage to do an MRP run once a week, which must usually be done overnight because processing the data ties up the mainframe computer for so long – literally for hours. To install the hardware and software for such a system often cost between half and one million pounds, and required a heavy overhead in the form of a white collar army of programmers, purchasers, stock controllers and expediters to make it work on the shop-floor.

In theory we can describe this as the automating of production planning and control, with the information being extracted from the job and given to managers, to leave repetitive manual tasks for the workers, who are not paid to think or plan their work beyond meeting the schedule. In practice this is planning and analysis overkill. In line with the command-and-control philosophy the intention is to plan everything to the last detail so that any bunch of idiots can execute it just by following instructions. This meaningless work produces alienated and uninvolved workers. And to make matters worse, much of the basic data is often suspect. The lead-times are full of fudge factors and guestimates. The economic batch size calculations do not take into account the high intangible costs of the inflexibility they cause and the low quality standards they can tolerate. And without special precautions, the computer stock records quickly get out of line with physical reality.

So how did this mess occur, what alternatives are there, and what did manufacturers do to improve the situation?

How did it occur?

It occurred because of our implicit assumptions about the roles of management and workers, and how to use technology. These assumptions, which are now being challenged, are as follows:

- Managers plan and control; workers are not paid to think, just to follow instructions.
- Managers can handle any job and any level of complexity, given sufficient technology.
- Productivity can best be improved by eliminating the last few direct labour jobs; not much can be done to reduce the indirect programmers, planners, accountants and controllers.
- It is better to spend money on technology than on education and training.
- Work is best organized to fit within traditional departments, rather than to support fundamental business processes.

The knowledge-based alternative: just-in-time systems

The alternatives are to use methods which do not rely on intensive use of computers – such as Japanese JIT (just-in-time) methods, or use them intensively but in such a way as to help workers do their job rather than to control them.

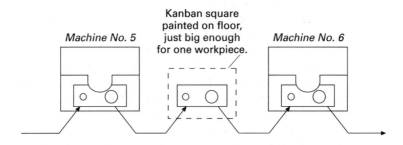

Machine No. 5 waits until the kanban square is empty, before working on the next workpiece.
Work is 'pulled' through the manufacturing system. There is never more than one workpiece between machines.

Figure 5.4   *Just-in-time (JIT) production*

JIT production requires minimal centralized control, and can be achieved without the use of computers, Figure 5.4. The JIT system operates with the absolute minimum of work-in-process, in which each work station stops work as soon as it has produced a part, and waits until the next work station downstream starts work on that part before it too starts working again. The system needs only a simple signal called a 'kanban' – in Japanese the word means visible record – to signal from one work station back to its upstream feeder work station to recommence working. A kanban can be a simple card sent back, or a square painted on the floor only big enough to store one item of work-in-process between two work stations, or some other very simple device. JIT is sometimes described as a 'pull' system, in which work is pulled through the factory – in contrast to the batch system in which each process pushes work forward to build a buffer stock in front of the next process.

The JIT system will not tolerate machine breakdowns, or manufacturing quality problems. If any work station breaks down, all the other stations before and after in the line also grind to a halt. Also, if any work station makes a defective part, all stations downstream will have to wait until the station makes a replacement part. Clearly the JIT system requires a committed and responsible work-force, who use their heads to prevent problems arising. The implicit assumptions which support the JIT system are as follows:

- Workers are better placed to anticipate problems and think about how to improve the system than the managers who know less about the details than the workers do.
- Managers should coach workers, encourage learning, and support them with resources.
- The level of complexity in business today is now so high it is more than can be handled by managers alone, even with the most advanced technology.
- Decision-making and problem-solving must therefore be spread across all workers.
- The best way to improve productivity is to eliminate where possible, indirect work such as programming, planning, accounting and controlling, because they add no value to the product.
- Success depends on ability and commitment of the whole workforce, not just management; it is often better to spend money on education and training before anything else.
- Work should be organized around fundamental business processes rather than to fit within traditional departments.

Before we leave this whistle-stop visit to the subject of JIT, it is worth mentioning that one of its main advantages is to cut down the time it takes for work to pass through the whole manufacturing system from raw material to finished product. In the old batch production system, each item of work-in-process had to queue along with the other items in its batch to be processed at each stage of production, Figure 5.5. In the JIT system, an item can go straight from one process to the next, all of which are now free of the log-jams of batches waiting to be processed. The actual value-adding time per item at each stage remains unchanged, but by cutting out the queuing, the lead-time from raw material to finished product is typically reduced from months to hours. The JIT manufacturing system is much more flexible – it can quickly be adjusted to meet changes in demand – and it will not tolerate poor quality.

The principles of JIT which were developed for manufacturing can also be applied very effectively to the intangible world of pure knowledge work. There is a very important difference however: an item of manufactured work-in-process can only exist at one place at a time, and so must pass through processing stages in sequence. But when knowledge work can be converted into digital form, it can exist in many different places at the same time and it may then be possible for several processing stages to be carried out at the same time instead of one after the other in sequence. This can reduce even further the throughput time from raw material (information) to finished product (service delivery), to produce improvements which will delight customers – at least for a while until the new level of performance becomes the industry standard. It is an example of effective, appropriate use of technology to support people and business processes.

Batch production

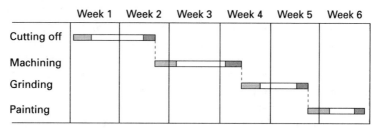

Each item must wait for all other items in the batch to be processed before being moved to the next process.
Throughput time: 6 weeks.

Key: Batch waiting to be processed
Batch being processed
Batch waiting to be taken to next process

Just-in-time production

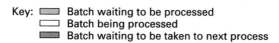

Each item is transferred to the next process as soon as it is ready.
Throughput time: 2 days

Figure 5.5 *Batch versus JIT production*

The response?

MRP consultants invariably found that their A-class clients – those who claimed to be perfectly satisfied with their new systems – formed much less than 10 per cent of all clients. And so what did manufacturers do to improve the situation? They stuck to their guns and tried even harder to make command-and-control work. They threw more money and technology at the problem: they bought MRP 2 (manufacturing resource planning) software, similar to MRP but even more complex, with capabilities expanded to control all production resources – money, people, machines, as well as materials. And they strived for even greater levels of automation and control – the factory of the future, in which paperwork and direct workers are eliminated wherever possible. In the car industry General Motors spent forty billion dollars by 1987, trying to make it work and ended up with a 20 per cent loss in market share and going from being the lowest-cost to the highest-cost producer amongst the American Big Three. Contrast the General Motors approach with that at Semco, Ricardo Semler's

Brazilian engineering company. A different industry, admittedly, but still with complex production planning problems. There they stopped using their expensive MRP system for anything other than playing simulation games to help them understand their system better, and re-organized production around small, self-managed teams of highly committed and involved workers, who ordered their own materials and planned their own work.

What old-paradigm assumptions led General Motors and others into the trap? It is easy to be wise after the event, but we are beginning to see now what they should have done. What new-paradigm assumptions would have served them better?

Inform-and-entrust: computers to add value

This is a new but rapidly developing field with few practical examples, though there are some which we will look at shortly. But first, let us start by reviewing the assumptions of the new paradigm which lead to this knowledge-based approach.

First, the purpose of business is no longer mainly just to make a profit, as business schools used to teach. We are all individuals who have a stake in the activities of business, as employees, customers, members of the community and shareholders (directly or through pension schemes) all at the same time. The profit motive on its own is too crude and simplistic and we are no longer willing to accept it. We don't want maximum dividends from our share holdings if it means our environment is polluted, we are exploited as employees, and ripped off as customers. What we want is a better deal in all our roles: better quality of life, better quality, better value. The purpose of business must therefore be to attend to all its stake holders and to add value – that is, add quality without adding cost – to the products and services offered. And the only way this can be done is through learning and improved knowledge.

Another new-paradigm assumption is that economies can be achieved by combining tasks, not by dividing them up into specialized parts, as advocated by Adam Smith during the industrial age. It worked then for pin-making, but it does not work now for knowledge work, and the principle of division of labour has routinely been taken too far in most manufacturing work as well. We should thank Adam Smith for his principle of the Division of Labour: it helped us advance in the past, but a counterbalance is now overdue – nobody has made a pin manually this century. The economies of division of labour were twofold: savings when a worker did not have to change over from one task to another, and gains when workers worked faster with special tools on simple operations. These savings were achieved for simple repetitive physical tasks performed by workers with no expectations or education. But if we take into account the alienation caused by such mind-numbing work, there have probably been no net savings made this way for many years. In the 1970s when Volvo in Sweden were busy organizing their car assembly around highly motivated work groups with combined tasks and multiple skills, British Leyland were still hell-bent on forcing their alienated workers onto assembly tracks to perform divided tasks requiring little skill – and effectively bankrupted themselves in the attempt. Meanwhile at Volvo, any direct, measurable losses incurred by lower efficiency – as narrowly defined – were more than compensated for by indirect savings from better quality and more consistent production from a committed and involved work-force.

A new principle: the combination of knowledge

Of course there may always be some types of work where the division of labour principle is appropriate, but in our knowledge-based economy there will be fewer repetitive tasks requiring limited knowledge, as more of them are automated. What we need is another principle – the Combination of Knowledge, perhaps? – which is seen to apply in even greater measure than division of labour, especially where knowledge work is concerned. The economies of this principle are also twofold: the direct economies of combining tasks, which are well-known to industrial engineers, and the indirect, unmeasurable and unpredictable, but nevertheless enormous benefits of having highly motivated, committed workers who are continually improving their own performance. The collision of ideas occurring in a tight-knit multi-skilled team produces a kind of fusion, fuelling creativity and generating new knowledge. These economies apply in particularly full measure when the tasks of planning and doing are combined, thus allowing Kolb's learning cycle to operate, Figure 5.6.

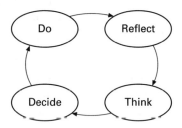

Figure 5.6 *The Kolb learning cycle*

Before we leave the issue of division versus combination, let me reinforce the rationale with an appeal to reason, and a parable. First, if you are asked to do a part of a job which by itself is empty of any meaning or purpose, you probably won't feel much personal commitment to its achievement, and there will be no scope for you to learn and improve your performance. If we want people's commitment we must therefore give them meaningful work. Meaning resides in the way things are put together, and is lost when things are divided up. Take a diamond gemstone and a rabbit dropping. Keep dividing them up and what are you left with? Eventually the same thing in both cases – a bunch of protons, neutrons and electrons. And the same effect occurs with information, too. Take a digital recording of Vivaldi's 'Four Seasons', and a copy of Microsoft's Excel spreadsheet software, and divide them up. Again, in both cases you are left with the same thing, a few unintelligible binary digits – a short string of 0s and 1s. Meaning is progressively destroyed as work is divided up.

Now the parable. A couple of years ago I was working with some colleagues in Budapest at a time when private enterprise was looking westward and to the future, but state workers were still bound by values and beliefs rooted in their recent communist-controlled past. I queued at a post-office to buy stamps for postcards, and on being served, was asked to pass the postcards to the attendant, who proceeded to lick the stamps and apply them to my cards, before placing them in a mail-bag. Unemployment was high as Hungary made the uncomfortable conversion from a planned to a free market economy, and the attendant was stretching out her work by adding serial tasks to expand her role – an understandable reaction from anyone who is paid for their time, not for their knowledge or performance. I would have been happier to queue less and take on the tasks of stamping and posting the cards – tasks I would have done concurrently rather than serially, applying the stamps and posting them as I walked out of the post office.

Later, from a tram on the way to Margaret Island in the Danube, I watched a workman sand papering the cover of some tramway equipment in the street. Obviously he too was paid for his time, not for results, as he was sanding on auto pilot, watching the world go by and paying no attention to what he was doing. And on Margaret Island, there was a group of workers sweeping leaves. When they got the leaves in a pile, they would scoop them up and put them in a large sack, but it was a gusty day and often they would almost have the leaves in a pile when a gust of wind would scatter the leaves again. This did not concern them in the least: they were not paid to keep the paths clear of leaves, or to think. They were paid to sweep and so it was natural for them to welcome the extra work. Things will change as the free market economy develops.

To summarize then, command-and-control leads to division of labour and complex systems of meaningless tasks, both of which are good for managers in the upper half of the organization. Division of labour allows managers to secure their positions in the hierarchy by legitimizing the principle of divide and rule. And complex systems require complex planning, analysis and control – management tasks which make lots of work for middle managers.

By contrast, inform-and-entrust encourages everyone to combine knowledge and tasks to produce simple systems of meaningful work which is managed by the workers themselves, supported by simple-to-operate technology, and thereby removing the need for an expensive top-heavy overhead structure of indirect planners, analysers and middle managers. It brings the combined brain power of the whole work-force to bear upon the problem of how to compete with the best in the world, by designing and operating highly effective and efficient business processes.

Business processes

A process is a collection of one or more operations for converting inputs into outputs, Figure 5.7. An oil refinery converts crude oil into petroleum products. A CD player converts digital information into musical sound. And a business process converts raw materials and information into finished products and services. So what?

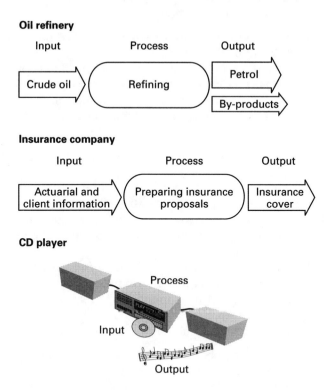

Figure 5.7 *Examples of processes*

So Hammer and Champy (1993) argue convincingly that we have lost sight of this simple fact, and much of what goes on between the inputs and the outputs of most businesses is irrelevant to the conversion process. This state of affairs has arisen from out-dated (old paradigm) assumptions about how things should be done, and poor knowledge of what is now technically possible. Michael Hammer is a consultant and professor at MIT, and James Champy is CEO of CSC Index, the leading authority in the implementation of business process re-engineering. In their book they use real companies and actual examples to show how the principles of re-engineering can yield massive improvements in performance. Through zero-based design – engineering the process from scratch with absolutely no preconceived assumptions – they aim for, and show it is possible to get nearer tenfold than 10 per cent improvement in the performance of many businesses.

Typically a business consists of a few basic business processes with inputs and outputs such as:

- manufacturing: procurement to shipping,
- sales: prospect to order,
- order fulfilment: order to payment, and
- service: inquiry to resolution;

and by thinking of these as processes we can focus on what is essential to convert the inputs into outputs.

Hammer and Champy describe the new world of work as it should be today, and list the changes that occur when a company re-engineers its business processes. Take a look at their list and judge for yourself how far it fits with the new-paradigm thinking needed to manage knowledge effectively:

- Work units change – from functional departments to process teams.
- Jobs change – from simple tasks to multi-dimensional work.
- People's roles change – from controlled to empowered.
- Job preparation changes – from training to education.
- Focus of performance measures and compensation shifts – from activity to results.
- Advancement criteria change – from performance to ability.
- Values change – from protective to productive.
- Managers change – from supervisors to coaches.
- Organizational structures change – from hierarchical to flat.
- Executives change – from scorekeepers to leaders.

Before reading their book I fell into the trap of thinking that business process re-engineering was little more than a modern combination of method study, organization and methods, and systems analysis and design. The big difference is that all of these old techniques were applied within existing functional departments and the existing hierarchy, whereas re-engineering takes none of these for granted, and uses the latest information technology to invent radically new solutions. Clearly therefore, it can only be invoked from the top of the organization, and initially will almost certainly need external help from consultants, which is how Hammer and Champy earn their crust. They make the point that processes that have been re-engineered once will someday have to be re-engineered all over again – but by that time the company should have learned how to make re-engineering a way of life and should be able to cope without the aid of external consultants.

Hammer and Champy identify modern information technology as an essential enabler in re-engineering, and show how most managers do not appreciate the new possibilities that have opened up recently. Read their book: in Peter Drucker's words 'Re-engineering is new, and it has to be done'.

Meantime, let us turn to three developments in information technology which are currently generating interest because they may enable new ways of engineering some business processes, and which promise to support the knowledge management approach. They are work group computing, object-oriented systems and multimedia communications. We will avoid technicalities as far as possible, and instead concentrate on their strategic implications.

Work group computing

According to the organization chart (Figure 2.1), information is supposed to be processed through the organization hierarchy. The lines on the chart show the few officially sanctioned channels for flows of command and control information. There are other informal channels too, but communications such as memos and reports still usually follow official channels, and when they don't, they are marked 'cc' or 'For information'. When the first business information systems were being set up, it was natural for the designers to follow the pattern of the formal organization chart, and create hierarchical databases and systems based upon the central storage and processing of information. In fact it was the only technically feasible option at the time, but it fitted well with the command-and-control approach to management.

Today however, the logic of inform-and-entrust requires a different overall architecture for our business information systems – one which supports the new non-hierarchical organization based upon small self-managed teams, and which recognizes the great importance of free and open, formal and informal communications. Was it just by luck that computers and communications developed sufficiently for this to be implemented? The personal computers which popped up like mushrooms throughout the organization during the early 1980s were later joined together in small, local networks to serve individual departments. These were arranged according to the client/server model, in which several client PCs are served by a more powerful server PC with more storage, containing shared data and software. And later still, the servers were connected up to the corporate mainframe which co-ordinated communications between the departmental client/server networks, to form a network of networks, Figure 5.8. However, the physical network cabling and computer hardware is still usually arranged according to the departments and levels of the organization chart. Thus the whole organization may, to some extent, be hard-wired to the old paradigm, and business process re-engineering often means having to re-wire the corporation. Fortunately however, this need not be done all in one go, as used to be the case with the old centralized systems. With the more recent distributed systems, some progress can be made by modifying, replacing or combining existing local networks.

Stage 1: Payroll processing on the mainframe

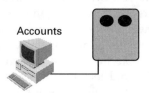

Stage 2: Other departments start using the mainframe

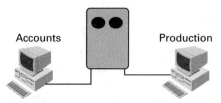

Stage 3: The personal computer arrives

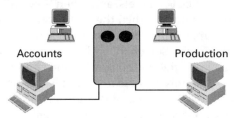

Stage 4: The personal computer prevails

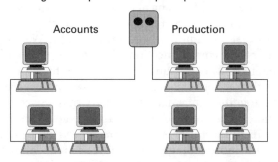

Figure 5.8   *Evolution of computer systems in business*

So what is work group computing, and how does it differ from office automation which has been around for a while now? Hardware and software product offerings are evolving rapidly, and in such circumstances the meaning of the jargon takes time to settle down. However, work group computing has come to be associated with the recent interest in re-engineering, self-managing small teams, and empowerment. There are shell products such as Lotus Notes, and Microsoft Windows for Work groups which provide a basic environment in which members of a team can share files distributed across the local network, and communicate with each other through electronic mail. These shells can also be supplied with specialized groupware modules for scheduling group activities, automating work flow, searching remote databases, processing document images and work group conferencing – as well as any of the usual word processing, spreadsheet and other applications packages.

In practice, implementations of work group computing tend to polarize into systems which automate work flow, and systems which support ad hoc co-operation and communication – that is, either automating or informating the process, Figure 5.9.

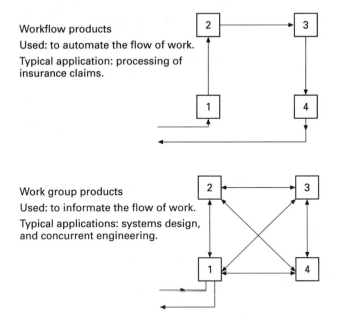

Workflow products
Used: to automate the flow of work.
Typical application: processing of insurance claims.

Work group products
Used: to informate the flow of work.
Typical applications: systems design, and concurrent engineering.

Figure 5.9 *Work group computing*

Work group computing can bring big improvements in three ways: by doing things concurrently when they were done consecutively before, combining them when they were done separately before, and automating routine tasks when they were done manually before. Groupware benefits knowledge work just like JIT and automation benefit manufacturing – by simplifying, combining and automating. For instance, insurance companies often used to handle claims in batches, passing them serially through many small divided-up component tasks of the whole business process of dealing with claims, Figure 5.10. As with batch production in manufacturing, this resulted in throughput times measured in weeks, even though the actual processing of a single claim usually took less than an hour. Compare this with the typical result of re-engineering the process, in which claims mail is scanned into a document image processing computer system so it can be processed in several places at once, then passed on one claim at a time instead of in batches, Figure 5.11. When claims are

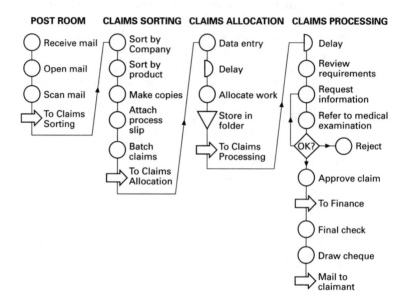

Figure 5.10   *A typical flow diagram for claims processing in an insurance company*

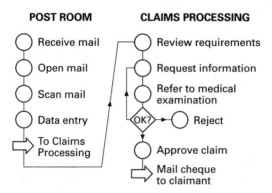

Figure 5.11   *A typical simplified flow diagram for claims processing in an insurance company, after the process has been re-engineered*

handled concurrently instead of consecutively by members of a multi-skilled claims team, customers are delighted at having their claims settled the next day instead of the next month, and productivity also goes up dramatically: tenfold increases are common, and hundred-fold not unknown.

Another good example of technology supporting new forms of work group is the move by progressive manufacturers to replace the traditional 'over-the-wall' method of product development, with the new, concurrent engineering approach. Traditionally, companies keep their design and development offices separate from the manufacturing facilities. It fits with the command-and-control paradigm to separate the planning of design from the doing of manufacture. The knowledge work is done separately from the physical work, and when the design is completed and drawn up by the design office, it is thrown 'over the wall' to the factory to be made. Unfortunately however, the designers never know as much about the details of the process machinery as the operators do, and it is common for designs to arrive in the factory which are difficult, expensive and sometimes impossible to make. Now if it costs, say, £20 to change the detail of a design while it is being designed, it is likely to cost £200 to make the same change once the design is finished, and may cost £2000 once manufacture has commenced. Although these costs are difficult to measure and impossible to anticipate in detail, avoiding them nevertheless produces a direct payoff for abandoning the traditional approach in favour of concurrent engineering, in which production staff are involved in the design process. Responsibility for the business process of new product development – concept to prototype – is given to a multi-skilled team, who handle the stages concurrently instead of consecutively. This was impractical in the days of pen and ink drawings, when only the designer had a complete and up-to-date view of the design during its development. But with computer-aided design and networks it is possible for the current state to be displayed any time in several places all at once. With the right hardware and communications links, all members of the team can share the same view of the design as it develops, and can contribute to its development, regardless of whether they are in the design office or on the factory floor. Ideas collide, and in addition to the direct savings from fewer late design modifications, guess what else happens? That's right, the time from concept to prototype is dramatically reduced, and design productivity enormously improved.

Object-oriented systems

The corporate world has recently started showing renewed interest in object-oriented (OO) languages and programming procedures. These have been around for many years, but until recently, they have never been more than a specialist, fringe interest in the world of corporate computing. But now that situation seems about to change, as the OO approach promises a better fit with new-paradigm thinking. Many writers are claiming that 1995 will be 'The Year of the Object', but at the time of writing it is too early to say how big an impact OO systems will have on the development of business information systems. It is worth raising the topic so you are aware of these developments, but our conversation will be brief: you can be better informed and more up to date by keeping an eye on journal articles and the computer press.

So why are businesses showing interest in a completely new way of programming – even when warned of the heavy up-front costs and long lead-times for learning and benefiting from the new programming methods? The answer is that, once installed, OO systems are much quicker and cheaper to develop and maintain – in other words, OO systems are more flexible and much easier to keep fine-tuned to shifting business needs in today's changing environment. It is claimed that OO systems can be developed between twice and ten times as fast as conventional systems. A rigid, monolithic and hideously expensive information system written in conventional code can lock an organization into a particular mode of operating at least until the system pay-back period has expired. This might be several years for a complex MRP system for instance – which could be a problem if you discovered the advantages of JIT during that period.

OO programming is not new. It has been used by academics for many years, in specialized areas such as the development of artificial intelligence – the intelligent knowledge-based systems or expert systems, touched upon briefly in Chapter 3. However, although not new, it is radically different from the procedural programming which until recently has exclusively been used for business systems. Most conventional languages such as Cobol and Basic, are used to construct programs in the form of an algorithm, or list of instructions which will achieve some desired result when executed in the correct sequence. Conventional programs consist of lines of code to be executed in order, and program instructions are held separately from data files, but OO systems contain 'objects' which are part procedures and part data. These software objects are used to represent real-world objects, such as products, customers, and sales orders, and they are written so they can interact with each other just as their real-world counterparts do. Objects can therefore be used to model the way a business works, and to build a system to manage the business.

Two new facilities make OO systems attractive: software re-use, and inheritance. Fast and flexible systems development is possible with OO programming because once the basic software objects for the business have been written, new systems can be created with very little extra coding. In fact a library of standard objects can be built to support re-use, and progressively reduce the need to write large amounts of new code. Programmer productivity is enhanced further by the ability of objects to be linked in parent-child relationships, so that the child object inherits characteristics from the parent object. New types of object can thus be defined in terms of existing ones. For instance using inheritance, a system for a financial institution might require objects for Savings Account, and Current Account, which could both inherit characteristics from a more general object called Account, which defines characteristics common to both. Software re-use and inheritance together have great potential for dramatic improvements in program quality and programmer productivity. These improvements, together with the modular nature of objects, allow information systems written using OO methods to evolve with the business, rather than locking the business into a particular way of working until the system is replaced with a more up-to-date system sometime in the future. Information systems serve the organization and therefore must reflect its structure. As organizations become more flexible and fluid, pressure will grow for more flexible and adaptable information systems – and OO methods are one key to unlock the information systems bind.

This sounds like the best thing since sliced bread. So what are the problems? The main ones are lack of standards, and the uncertain lead-times and investment required. There is therefore significant risk of backing the wrong horse. And standards may be very important in the future, if objects start to be accessed across networks between organizations, or if written and sold for use in systems adhering to one particular standard. There are many different developers of OO programming tools, and two main pressure groups trying to dominate the market. On the one hand there is an alliance called the Object Management Group, and on the other there is Taligent, a company set up by IBM and Apple, two of the biggest computer companies. OMG and Taligent are on divergent paths and it may be years before one or other prevails. And to complicate matters further, in the meantime conventional programmers may come up with procedural ways of delivering similar benefits.

A survey at the 1993 UK Object World conference revealed that the main reasons delegates saw for moving to object-oriented development methods were: flexibility, reduced time to market, ability to handle complex applications and programmer productivity. One of the most important overall reasons cited for adopting object development was the ability to fine-tune software to meet changing business needs. However, some delegates saw signs that the traditional approaches to software development will catch up with object technology in the near future. Time will tell.

Object-oriented information system for a team-of-teams organization: National & Provincial Building Society

In 1991 David O'Brien agreed to take over as chief executive at N&P, the 2500 strong Bradford-based building society. Then N&P was a bureaucratic hierarchy with eight levels of management and 35 clerical grades organized within traditional functions and departments. O'Brien was hired to transform N&P into a non-hierarchical team-of-teams organization with every team responsible for managing a different business process. By 1994 the new structure was in place, with a single Direction Management Process Team of senior managers, 16 Implementation Management Process Teams, and Customer Engagement Teams in each of the 500 branches up and down the country (Irving, 1994).

These changes are not just cosmetic: N&P has the chance to become one of the few truly knowledge-based, inform-and-entrust organizations in the world. O'Brien's view was that the work should all be done by computers, and people in the organization should be freed to use their knowledge and think up creative solutions to customers' problems. This dramatic culture-change from the days when people were hired to get work done, is underpinned by a new language:

- Teams engage in team play, not teamwork. Work is done by computers.
- Team players have roles – not jobs; and they have leaders – not bosses.
- Teams are not accountable, but they do carry lots of responsibility.
- Teams are not monitored, but they do measure their own results.
- Teams don't have meetings, but they do have events which are action oriented.

Excellent communications between the Direction Management Process Team and all other players at N&P have been ensured through a unique Understanding Process which measures the number of issues requiring clarification at team-understanding events. And N&P has chosen an innovative IT strategy by moving its core business systems to object technology. In May 1994 *Computing* magazine reported that the £12 million contract was awarded to Unisys to supply 320 Unix server machines and about 2000 client PCs, along with Unisys' Navigator software, and consultancy services. During 1995 Navigator will be installed throughout N&P's network – including all its 500 branches – ready to go live by the end of the year. O'Brien believes it to be the most suitable technology for his organization. He says: 'Most organizations are looking at objects from their existing hierarchical company design, that's why objects haven't got off the ground commercially. You have to redesign your business to take advantage of them.'

Recent events underline the considerable personal risk undertaken by architects of such radical change. Although O'Brien was widely credited with turning round the society, on 28

September 1994 he was ousted from his position as chief executive in a boardroom coup. The chairman of N&P, Lord Shuttleworth, said that O'Brien's management style and methods were not the reason for his exit; however he was reported as having created an unsettling work environment.

It is too early to say how far N&P's new chief executive, Alistair Lyons, will continue with the initiatives started while O'Brien was in charge, especially as at the time of writing, N&P have just accepted a takeover bid of £1.3 billion from Abbey National. This is 1.75 times the value of net assets – a premium of half a billion pounds. What do Abbey National think they are buying? Just a future stream of earnings from N&P? Or the embedded knowledge at N&P which could boost Abbey National's earnings too, perhaps?

Multimedia communications

The third IT development promising new ways of working and therefore generating interest in the corporate world, is multimedia. This is the technology that allows files to contain not only text and graphics, but also sound and video clips. It is supported by three separate technologies – those of the PC, the TV and the 'phone – and offers brilliantly enhanced, powerfully effective communications. The advantages are obvious in publishing, broadcasting, marketing, entertainment, training and education, as well as in business communications. No wonder there is so much interest in the information superhighway, and such a scramble to grab a piece of the action.

Multimedia is still very much in its infancy, and applications are limited by technical constraints. The PC was not originally designed to handle sound and video sequences, and multimedia applications often therefore push at the limits of hardware and network capacity. When the personal computer first appeared in the early 1980s, it came with just 64 kilobytes of memory which was big enough to store 64,000 keystrokes, or about twenty pages of text. By the mid 1990s, a fairly ordinary multimedia PC would have perhaps eight megabytes of memory, big enough to hold the equivalent of around 15 paperback novels. However, digitally recorded sound is very memory-hungry, and that same eight megabytes would only hold about one minute of a Beethoven sonata. And video sequences are even worse: eight megabytes would only hold a few seconds of TV quality, full screen colour video.

The problems arise because the 'phone, the TV and the PC were all developed by separate industries. The computer can only handle the 1s and 0s of digital signals, and was originally designed just to display alphanumeric keyboard characters. The 'phone was designed for spoken words, and the TV for quality sound and video, but the TV and 'phone don't use digital signals. Now we are demanding that the PC handle the lot, and this means that sound and video must first be coded as incredibly long strings of 1s and 0s, which produces some very large files. One picture is worth a thousand words – so the saying goes – but in computer memory, one picture can occupy the space of a hundred thousand words. However the PC can now just about cope with big multimedia files, and future technical advances will surely improve the situation.

Multimedia CD-ROMs

Apart from games, perhaps the best known examples of multimedia are the CD-ROM encyclopaedias such as Microsoft's Encarta, and the Software Toolworks product, based on the American Grolier Encyclopaedia. To use them you need a modern PC with CD-ROM drive to read the disk, speakers to deliver the sounds, and circuit cards to drive these devices. Then, with the Grolier product if you want to find out about J. F. Kennedy you can search the data in a variety of ways. One way is to search for the word Kennedy and in a few seconds you will be presented with a list of over a hundred articles. You can narrow the search by adding other words to your search criteria, such as President, and Cuba. This reduces the list to six articles. By selecting the first title in the list you are presented with a 13 page article on John F. Kennedy, and the options to see a photograph of the man, or hear an audio clip of one of his speeches, or play a thirty second colour video sequence to see and hear him delivering his inaugural address: 'Ask not what your country can do for you, ask what you can do for your country ...' In the mid 1990s multimedia is something new, and to see and hear Kennedy saying these words in the Capitol is a far richer experience than to read fine print from some dusty tome – unless you have an exceptionally vivid imagination.

Because multimedia is still new, we are easily pleased. There are few competing products in the marketplace, and a few years from now we will look at these first implementations in amusement rather than awe. Economic and technical limitations restrict the length of the audio clips to about 45 seconds, and the video displays are grainy, jerky sequences in a window only 45 millimetres high by 65 wide. But despite these temporary shortcomings, we can see that multimedia is a technology with a great future.

Multimedia support for training and learning

Computers are becoming easier and more fun – and they encourage you, the learner to take control of your own learning by allowing you to concentrate on the parts most relevant to your needs. It used to be easier to learn from a book than from a computer screen, but the ability to create multimedia objects (of the type described earlier) and link them one to another has changed all that. When you open a typical multimedia file, it may look initially just like any other file, displaying text and graphics. But it contains 'jumps'. A jump is a small part of the text or graphics which may perhaps appear as an icon, or button, or highlighted region, as in a hypertext document. If you click on a jump with the mouse, you see or hear something. This may be just some more text defining jargon or explaining something, as in hypertext documents – or it may be an audio clip, or a colour video sequence with sound, as in CD-ROM encyclopaedias.

Multimedia authoring is a new discipline and the principles are still being refined. However, a carefully crafted multimedia document engages the ears as well as the eyes, and draws you into an interactive voyage of discovery. The top-level text should not go into detail which you may not need, so when you read it through you can decide for yourself if you want to drill down to the lower levels where the details and the examples are stored. These lower levels can be separate objects 'linked' to the top-level text, perhaps not even stored locally, and only accessible through the network. The Microsoft Windows operating system provides an environment in which objects can be linked and embedded in this way. Also there are special multimedia authoring packages which are kind of enhanced word processors – wordsoundvideostructurers perhaps – to allow writers and trainers who may have little programming knowledge, to be multimedia authors.

It is early days, but there is little doubt in my mind that multimedia will become a major force in publishing, with the potential to transform education and training. Imagine trainees interacting with computers as intensely as our sons and daughters do when playing Sonic the Hedgehog or Donkey Kong. Imagine students in control of their own learning and freed from the lecture room. The educational sector produces only information and knowledge products, and should therefore be one of the main exploiters of information technology. The sector is labour intensive and a costly burden on tax payers, yet still depends heavily on ineffective lectures. When Learning Process Re-engineering eventually arrives in our schools and universities, our educational system will be transformed. But before that, our private sector educators and trainers will pave the way.

In this chapter we have reviewed the state of development of information technology, and focused on some developments with potential to support knowledge work in an inform-and-entrust environment. In the next chapter, we will take a critical look at some of the decision support software which is currently available. Most of the techniques have been available for some time, and so were developed during the command-and-control era. We will question whether it is still appropriate to use them, or whether they should be modified or scrapped altogether.

Pause for thought

Before you respond to the following suggestions, beware of taking the easy way out by just saying it can't be done. Remember computers are building a reputation for doing things better and much cheaper both at the same time.

1. Which aspects of your products and services are really valuable to your customers, and what would amaze and delight your customers if it were feasible to offer it to them? Could computers help make it feasible?

2. Could information technology make it possible for you to offer a new or improved service at the customer's location, at a time convenient to your customer, rather than at your time, in your place?

3. How might your existing competitors gain an edge on you by using information technology? How might it be possible for new competitors from some remote corner of the globe to take market share from you, using computers and communications technology?

4. Could the new technology enable you to offer your products –
   faster,
   cheaper,
   with more features,
   at higher quality,
   designed to suit the particular needs of an individual customer?

5. Is it possible that the new technology could be used to relieve people of repetitive work and unleash their critical and creative skills? Under the right circumstances, could this then bring greater profits and other benefits at the same time as reducing costs?

References and further reading

Hammer, M. and Champy, J. (1993) *Re-engineering the Corporation. A manifesto for business revolution*. Nicholas Brealey.

Irving, J. P. (1994) Linkage between innovations in service delivery and organisational change: a strategic management perspective. MBA dissertation, Oxford Brookes University.

Zuboff, S. (1988) *In the Age of the Smart Machine*. Heinemann.

6 Computer solutions – can you trust them?

Why read this chapter?

A whole range of software lies waiting to help you in your computer at work, and it is all only a mouse-click or a key-press away. There are software products to boost the quantity of your knowledge work by automating it, and there are products to improve its quality by informating it. Most general purpose software such as word processors and spreadsheets can help you produce greater quantity and better quality, but you often end up with no net productivity gains because you spend the time saved by automation on striving for better quality. Knowledge workers identify very strongly with their work: they know they personally are judged on the quality of their work – a strong incentive to strive for higher standards.

The menu options or Windows icons on our screens are so numerous that no one ever gets around to exploring them fully. You probably know very well how your word processor and spreadsheet works, but what about the special applications which you use only occasionally? You need to know exactly what processing goes on between data input and information output – otherwise you won't trust the results or may be misled by the results.

In this chapter, you will be able to consider some of the benefits and dangers of turning to your computer for help in your day-to-day decision-making. Four types of decision-making model commonly available in computer-based decision support packages are described: decision analysis, linear programming, queuing and simulation models. The purpose is to provide a broad understanding of these specialized techniques, not to develop your mathematical skills.

The reflective, responsible manager

The human brain is a lazy organ. It devotes much of its time to finding ways of avoiding having to think. It has to do this, because despite its enormous processing power, it would otherwise be overwhelmed by data input. During your waking hours your eyes channel a constant flood of visual data to your brain. At the same time your ears and your other three senses are adding to the deluge. But you can only think about one thing at a time, as you will be aware if you have ever tried to answer the phone in the middle of your favourite TV programme. So how does your brain cope with all the visual and audible data streaming in? The answer is it ignores most of it – your brain has learnt how to manage by exception: it knows what it can safely ignore, and what needs attention. When very young we learn to relegate monitoring of our environment to a subconscious level, to focus only on the new or unusual, and ignore the rest. Our subconscious brain handles routine monitoring, thus freeing our conscious brain to wrestle with the unusual. In fact this relegating of tasks to a subconscious level is a very important aspect of how we learn, because it allows us to do regular, mundane tasks without having to devote conscious effort to thinking about them. How else on a Sunday morning on the way back from the newsagent would it be possible for you to walk, chew gum and read the newspaper, all at the same time?

Typing is an example of a task in which subconscious processing goes on. Can you type? If so, you can concentrate on the message and at the same time effortlessly transcribe characters onto the screen at the rate of three or four key strikes per second: it is almost as if your fingers know where the keys are. You perform the mundane task of striking the right keys with no conscious effort, yet if asked to say where the letter 'k' is on the keyboard, you have to consciously stop and think.

Our subconscious helps us cope with information overload. When dealing with complex situations, we depend on our reflexes, intuition, instincts and training. Part of learning a new skill involves training ourselves to respond automatically, without conscious thought. When you first started learning to drive a car, you had to devote conscious effort to staying the right distance from the kerb, but now you can effortlessly steer down the High Street, change gear – and jump on the brakes in an emergency – all without any conscious thought. Most driving you do on auto pilot, which leaves you free to think about your shopping.

So are there any parallels between learning to type or drive, and learning to manage at work? There are some similarities and some important differences. Both situations are characterized by information overload: there is more to think about than we can cope with at a conscious level – too much processing and decision-making for us to handle in the time available. But in contrast to driving or typing, when managing, the results of our actions are often difficult to discern, impossible to measure and may turn up elsewhere, perhaps much later. This makes it difficult for us to learn appropriate reactions, and to practise them until they become instinctive. If we wish to develop our ability as managers, we must accept that however much we learn there will always be boundless room for improvement. A learning approach – experimenting and reflecting – and years of experience are needed to build 'profound knowledge', William Edwards Deming's term for the deep understanding we need of our operations and management systems (1986).

So how do managers cope with information overload? Some get trapped into fire fighting mode, others break out by prioritising and delegating, and some may turn to the computer for help.

Decision support systems

Amongst the menu items and icons on your screen, there will probably be some decision support packages, specially written to support the decision-making process. These capture some of the mathematical analysing and modelling techniques commonly taught on business courses. If the program is a well-designed tool, it will make accessible to you the embedded knowledge of a mathematician, without your having to understand or use the mathematics directly yourself. It is probably true to say that most tools for manual skills contain the embedded knowledge of experts, the details of which we don't bother or need to understand. You don't need to know about car engines to be a good driver, or about electrical circuits to play a compact disc. With these devices we learn empirically, seeing immediately the results of our actions. But if we use a computer package to help us make a management decision, we may never know how good the decision was, because there are so many uncontrolled variables, and the results may only be observable elsewhere and much later. So in knowledge work and decision-making, if we use a decision support package it is important we understand fully how the package works. It is not enough to say 'I don't understand how it works, but others have used this tool safely and successfully, so it must be OK.' When we use passenger jets or motor way bridges we can rely on reputation, and observation of others' experience. But the packaged products of knowledge workers can only be depended on when used appropriately.

Management science, business statistics and quantitative methods

Most educational courses in business administration and management include a 'quants' module. It covers topics which fall into two broad categories: mathematical models for dealing with particular problems which crop up in management, and general tools for statistical analysis which are widely used in many disciplines. Quants is seldom the most popular subject to say the least, perhaps because managers often neglect their mathematical skills while developing their people skills. Perhaps also because successful practising managers are seldom seen demonstrating their mathematical prowess, whereas they are constantly seen communicating, motivating, inspiring and leading their people. But how do they decide in which direction to lead? Some exceptionally gifted managers seem to be born with the right instincts, and succeed by relying on gut feel, but the rest of us can improve our performance by using proven methods and sound principles. As suggested earlier, quants can help us in two ways: mathematical models for aiding decision-making in particular circumstances, and general statistical techniques to help us make sense of business problems. I don't believe any manager, however gifted, can reach her or his full potential without a grounding in basic statistics.

Statistical techniques allow us to assess more accurately the importance of different factors affecting decisions generally – like for instance the riskiness of different alternatives, or the significance of results from incomplete data. These factors are particularly important in project work, and we will return to the subject in later chapters, though for a fuller treatment you will need to refer to specialist books on statistics for managers, such as Curwin and Slater, *Quantitative methods for business decisions* (1994) or Morris, *Quantitative Approaches in Business Studies* (1993).

Mathematical models, however, are each designed to help only with a particular type of decision in circumstances where narrowly defined conditions apply. The idea is that you should be able to construct a model of the real-world system you are managing, or customize an off-the-shelf one, then experiment with it to see how it behaves. It is cheaper and quicker to experiment with a model than with the real-world system, as any aircraft designer can tell you. With a good model it should be possible not only to answer particular questions, but also for you to subject your model to different conditions and thus develop a feel for how your real-world system might behave in a variety of different future circumstances. A cash-flow forecast developed on a computer spreadsheet is an example of a model. You can play 'what-if' games to see how sensitive your model is to changes in interest rates for instance. By changing the interest rate used, you can immediately see the results cascade down to the bottom line for each month of the coming year.

The usefulness of a model depends very much on how faithfully it represents the real world: simple models based on simple assumptions tend to be unrepresentative, and have poor predictive ability.

Let us cast a critical eye on some well-known mathematical models for decision-making, in the context of the self-managed team environment which we expect to be common in future.

Decision analysis

'Has he luck?' Napoleon habitually asked this question to assess a man's probable practical value in war time. In peace time today managers also need luck, though they should not depend on it, for there is always risk in decision-making. To be a good manager you must make good decisions quickly, before you have all the facts, because the future won't wait. That is why decision-making is difficult: some of your decisions are bound to turn out badly – it is the nature of the game. So the best you can hope for is to improve your batting average. But how? Decision analysis can help ensure you consider all the options, and then help you adopt an appropriate strategy for choosing from amongst the options. We will argue the pros and cons of the method shortly, but first let's see how it works.

The decision analysis method requires us to reduce what is often a continuous spectrum of choice down to a few discrete choices. It also requires us to reduce the infinite variety of possible futures which may affect our chosen option down to a few discrete 'states of nature'. The problem can then be drawn up as a table, or as a tree structure. It is rather a rough cut approach but has the advantage of throwing the problem into sharp relief.

Here's an example. Fashion Foods is a small company supplying quality fast food outlets with deep frozen prepared meals for serving straight from microwave to table. The business is growing fast, and they need to add to their product range. However they only have the resources to develop one new product out of three main contenders. The future market conditions under which the product will be sold will be affected by levels of unemployment, interest rates and so on, but are expected to be either favourable or unfavourable. The payoffs estimated for each combination of product and market condition are as follows:

Table 6.1 Payoff (£000s)

Choices	States of nature:	
	Favourable market	*Unfavourable market*
Bayou Pie	300	−200
Pizaz Pizza	80	80
Pistoffee Ice	90	−20

Uncertainty

The two directors, Harriet and Tim have no view as to how likely it is that the market will be favourable. They do not even feel justified in assuming that favourable and unfavourable conditions are equally likely. They must therefore decide which product to develop under what mathematicians would describe as conditions of uncertainty. There are two decision criteria which they could use: Maximax and Maximin. Harriet is an optimist and always expects things to turn out well: she would feel comfortable with choosing the largest of the best payoffs of each product. This is called the Maximax criterion, because the product with the maximum of the maximums is chosen. Tim on the other hand, is a pessimist and always assumes that whatever decision is eventually made, it will turn out to be the worst choice for the conditions that actually prevail. He would therefore favour the product which yielded the 'best worst' payoff. This is called the Maximin criterion, because the product with the maximum of the minimums is chosen.

By collecting the row maximums and the row minimums in a couple of extra columns added to the table, we can easily identify which products satisfy the Maximax and Maximin criteria.

Table 6.2 Payoff (£000s)

| | States of nature: | | | |
Choices:	Favourable market	Unfavourable market	Row maximums	Row minimums
Bayou Pie	300	–200	**300**	–200
Pizaz Pizza	80	80	80	**80**
Pistoffee Ice	90	–20	90	–20

Three hundred in bold print in the Maximums column indicates that Bayou Pie satisfies the Maximax criterion, and 80 in bold print in the Minimums column indicates that Pizaz Pizza satisfies the Maximin criterion.

Risk

Before Harriet and Tim could agree, they read an article in *Fast Food Journal*, which persuades them there would be a 60 per cent chance of a favourable market for their products. With probabilities available for the states of nature, it now becomes possible for the decision to be taken under what a mathematician would describe as conditions of risk. They therefore did another analysis, taking into account this new information, and calculating the expected monetary value (EMV) associated with each product. This is a kind of weighted average which takes into account the greater probability of a favourable market. It is equal to the average payoff for a choice, if the same decision were faced and made the same way many times. Take Bayou Pie for instance; on the 60 percent of hypothetical occasions when there would be a favourable market, a gain of £300,000 would be made. However on the other 40 per cent of hypothetical occasions when there would be an unfavourable market, a loss of £200,000 would be made. The net result would be an average gain in the long term of $(0.6 \times £300,000) - (0.4 \times £200,000) = £100,000$. We can collect the EMVs for each product in another column to the right of the table, and then choose the product which yields the maximum EMV.

Table 6.3 Payoff table (£000s) showing EMVs

| | States of nature: | | |
Choices:	Favourable market	Unfavourable market	EMV
Bayou Pie	300	–200	100
Pizaz Pizza	80	80	80
Pistoffee Ice	90	–20	46
Probabilities:	0.6	0.4	

In fact Bayou Pie wins with its EMV of £100 which is greater than the other two of £80 and £46. However, it is important for Harriet and Tim to realize that if they use the EMV criterion and go ahead with Bayou Pie, they will never receive £100,000: it is a purely hypothetical average. On this single occasion they will actually receive either £300,000, or they will lose £200,000, depending on whether or not the market conditions actually turn out to be favourable. Remember, the EMV criterion is designed to improve your batting average over the long term, and in theory the averaging should work well in an organization when applied to most projects. The averaging principle will then work over many similar projects in the same way as it would do over the same project repeated many times. A word of caution however: it is quite possible for a particular project to have a small risk, say 10 per cent, of a fatally large loss along with other outcomes with good positive payoffs. In these circumstances the figures may still produce a large positive EMV for the project. But clearly it would be foolish to decide on a project because it has the best hypothetical average and in so doing take on a real 10 per cent risk of wiping out your organization.

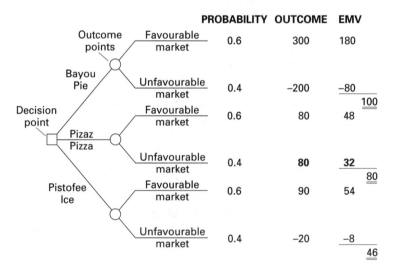

Figure 6.1 *Decision tree for the Fashion Foods decision*

Finally, note that this situation could be represented in the form of a tree structure, Figure 6.1. The tree is useful for representing multi-stage decision-making situations which could not be shown in a simple table. Single-stage decisions such as the Fashion Foods example are normally dealt with using a table. This brief discussion of decision analysis is only an introduction to the subject, which you can study in greater depth by referring to specialist books on quantitative methods, such as Render and Stair, *Quantitative Analysis for Management* (1994).

Critique

The method tends to be simplistic, which is its strength and its weakness. By reducing continuous ranges of choices and states of nature to two or three discrete cases, it becomes possible to analyse the model; however it then bears only a passing resemblance to reality. This could be rectified by having, say, three or four states of nature instead of just two, but then we run into trouble with estimating their probabilities with any degree of accuracy. It is difficult enough setting two probabilities: in times of rapid change the past is a poor guide to the future, and estimates of probabilities can be highly subjective – often little better than guesses. This also applies to the accuracy of the payoff estimates, which will depend very much on the experience of the estimator.

There is another problem, too. Books on quantitative methods often concentrate on the mathematics and in so doing, seem to suggest that managers make decisions in a linear, irreversible series of stages. It is often suggested that managers should:

1. define the problem,
2. draw up the payoff table,
3. assign the probabilities,
4. estimate the payoffs,
5. calculate the EMVs,
6. make the decision, and
7. execute it.

In fact managers seldom work in this way; they tend to keep going back to adjust their estimates and recalculate. They look for ways of reducing the down side, include contingency plans and seek escape routes to use if things go wrong. In other words they don't just accept the problem as originally defined: they seek constantly to redefine it. It is therefore quite unrealistic to view decision analysis as a way of automating the decision-making process. It should be seen as a method of viewing the problem in a new light, and from a different angle. It can provide another way for managers to interact with the available data. The discipline of preparing estimates of payoffs and risks attached to different choices is in itself a valuable exercise which will add to a manager's depth of understanding and quality of decision. The final course of action may not depend just on the EMV and may bear little resemblance to any of the choices available in the problem as originally defined for the decision analysis exercise.

Linear programming

With misgivings I have taught this subject to hundreds of students because the syllabus required it, but I have never met a manager who has actually used it in their job. Like the tool on the Swiss Army penknife for getting stones out of horses' hooves, the problems it was designed for seldom seem to exist. The arguments for continuing to teach it seem somewhat tenuous; for instance that it is an exercise in conceptualizing, or re-framing problems in mathematical terms. That is indeed useful, but unfortunately, linear programming implies many wrong messages about organizations today and how managers should manage them. As you read this section, see if you agree.

Courses in management science and operations research often start with linear programming, as it is one of the simpler modelling techniques. It requires a problem to be described in terms of a set of simple equations which will plot as straight lines – hence the name. One equation must define the objective to be optimized, and the rest impose constraints on the variables. The product mix problem is often used as an example to illustrate the technique.

The product mix problem

For instance, suppose you want to maximize profits from a small business with four workers making chairs and desks. How many chairs and desks should you make, if every chair makes a profit of £15, and every desk makes a profit of £45? You cannot make an infinite number of chairs and desks because of the constraints imposed by your workers: they have limited time available, and different skills. One worker can only fabricate the parts for chairs and desks, and another can only assemble them. The third worker is the only skilled upholsterer for chairs, and the fourth is the only laminator for the surface of desks. The times required per chair and desk in each skill area are as follows:

Table 6.4

Worker	Worker time required for chairs (mins/chair)	desks (mins/desk)	Worker time available (mins)
Fabricator	16	40	960
Assembler	12	48	960
Upholsterer	20	–	960
Laminator	–	64	960

Expressing the problem as a mathematical model

If we use the variables x_1 and x_2 to represent the numbers of chairs and desks made, then the profit Z can be found from the equation:

$$Z = 15x_1 + 45x_2$$

This is a straight line equation, and is the objective to be optimized – that is, maximized in this case. It is therefore called the objective function. The constraint equations can be derived easily from the table above. They are:

$$16x_1 + 40x_2 = 960 \quad \text{(Fabricator constraint equation)}$$
$$12x_1 + 48x_2 = 960 \quad \text{(Assembler constraint equation)}$$
$$20x_1 \qquad = 960 \quad \text{(Upholsterer constraint equation)}$$
$$64x_2 = 960 \quad \text{(Laminator constraint equation)}$$

Defining feasible solutions

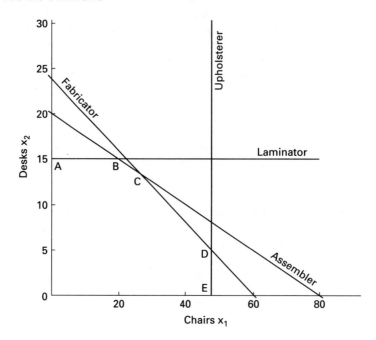

Figure 6.2 *Making chairs and desks: charting the constraints*

These formulae will also plot as straight lines, as you can see in Figure 6.2. The horizontal axis measures the number of chairs that might be made, and the vertical axis the number of desks. Thus any point on the graph indicates a potential production plan – the co-ordinates of the point being the number of chairs and desks in the product mix. The constraint lines do not all cross at a single point on the graph. If they did, the co-ordinates of the point would be the values of x_1 and x_2 which satisfy all four of the constraint equations – the only feasible product mix. However, there is no such point on the graph through which all four lines pass, and so there is no single unique solution for the four simultaneous constraint equations. The chances of it happening will always be remote, but this does not matter, because strictly speaking we should not think of the lines as defining exactly what the values of x_1 and x_2 should be. Instead we should think of the lines as limits defining the upper boundary of a range of values which it is feasible for x_1 and x_2 to have. Take for instance the Fabricator constraint equation. Each chair takes 16 minutes to fabricate, and each desk takes 40 minutes, so if you plan to make 2 chairs and 2 desks, how much of the fabricator's time will it take? Two times 16 for the chairs and 2 times 40 for the desks makes 112 minutes total, which is less than the 960 minutes available, so the plan is feasible. You can easily see this on the graph because the co-ordinates of the product mix are $x_1 = 2$, and $x_2 = 2$, which indicates a point near the origin, below and to the left of the Fabricator line and so within the feasible area. But if you plan to make 20 chairs and 20 desks, it will require 1120 minutes, which is more time than the 960 minutes available and so this more ambitious plan is not feasible. On the graph, the point $x_1 = 20$, $x_2 = 20$ plots further away from the origin, and in fact lies above and to the right of the Fabricator line, outside the feasible range, indicating that this proposed product mix is not feasible. Each of the other constraint lines also define an area which is feasible, so for a product mix to be entirely feasible – that is, within the capacity of all the workers to produce in the time available – it must have co-ordinates which lie below and to the left of all the constraint lines.

The point must also lie above and to the right of both axes, because it is not feasible to make a negative number of chairs or desks. So, the axes and the constraint lines together define a feasibility polygon OABCDE. Stick a pin into the graph, inside the polygon, and read off where the pin is on the two axes. These co-ordinates represent a feasible product mix. The polygon contains many points for many feasible product mixes. Our objective however, is to find a feasible product mix which will also maximize profit.

Deriving an optimum from amongst the many feasible mixes

To find the optimum we must now turn to the objective function, the straight line equation which defines profit:

$$Z = 15x_1 + 45x_2$$

We need to show this line on the graph as well, so we can see exactly how it can help. Like the constraint equations it slopes down to the right, but there is a complication. It has an unknown constant Z, which means we cannot find the points where it cuts the axes. We can only plot it by giving Z a value, the profit, so let's do that. In fact let's take two values of Z and plot the line twice, so we can see what happens to the line as the profit increases, Figure 6.3.

You can see from the graph that the profit increases as the line moves further away from the origin, which if you think about it seems right. The more chairs and desks you can make, the more profit you will make. At the origin a product mix of no chairs and no desks will make no profit, whereas far above and to the right of the origin, an infinite number of chairs and desks would make an infinite profit. The

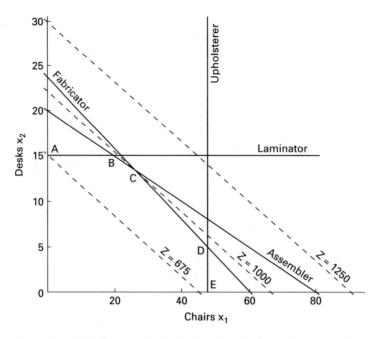

Figure 6.3 *Making chairs and desks: locating the optimum feasible product mix*

line marked Z = 675 joins up all points which produce a profit of £675. It is similar to a 100 metre contour line on a map which joins up all points which are 100 metres above sea level, or an isobar line on a weather map which joins up all points of equal pressure – in fact Z-lines are sometimes called iso-profit lines. The £675 iso-profit line cuts through the middle of the feasibility polygon, and so there are many points which are both on the line, and inside the polygon. Any one of them will produce a profit of £675 and will also be feasible.

Now look at the £1250 iso-profit line. This Z-line falls entirely outside the feasibility polygon; it joins up many points, none of which are feasible, but all of which in theory would produce a profit of £1250. You probably realize the maximum feasible profit lies somewhere between the Z = 675 line and the Z = 1250 line, and will be parallel to both. But where? And what product mix will produce this maximum profit? One simple practical way to find out is to use a clear plastic ruler. Lay the ruler across the graph with its lower edge on the Z = 675 line. Now carefully move the ruler away from the origin, keeping it parallel to the Z-lines. As you do this, you will see that less and less of the ruler edge cuts across the feasibility polygon. Eventually as you keep moving the ruler further away from the origin, you will reach a position where the ruler edge only touches the polygon at one point – in fact at the corner labelled C. At this point, you have found the Z-line with the largest possible Z-value while still touching the feasibility polygon. The optimum product mix therefore lies at point C on the graph.

You can read off the co-ordinates of this point from the graph to get the optimum product mix, and use the formula for Z to calculate the maximum profit. The optimum solution is to make 26⅔ chairs, and 13⅓ desks, which will give a profit of £1000.

Developments of the method

The graphical method is very useful for explaining how the technique works, but has a major disadvantage. It can only handle very simple problems, such as product mix problems for companies which only have two products, one for each axis of the graph. Know of any such companies? Me neither, but it doesn't matter, because the Simplex technique is an equivalent algebraic technique which does not depend on graphs, and which can therefore handle any number of products.

It is useful that we can express the linear programming model in algebraic form, because then it can be computerized and developed further. Once the model is set up, you can play 'what-if' games to see how sensitive the model is to small changes in the variables. For instance in the chair and desk example, you might consider paying your fabricator overtime to get him to work for more than the present 960 hours maximum. This will move the Fabricator constraint line further away from the origin, changing the position of point C and increasing the total profit. But by how much? Enough to pay for the overtime? The computer makes it easy to answer questions such as these.

Another limitation of the basic method is that it is only suitable for solving the product mix problem, and the similar ingredient mix problem in which the objective is to minimize, say, the total cost of a food product made up of several ingredients. Each ingredient has a different cost, and offers a different balance of one or more components such as vitamins, fat, fibre and salt. The food must provide these components within acceptable limits, which can be represented by constraint equations. And to minimize cost, the iso-cost line must be moved as close to the origin as possible, while still touching the feasibility polygon. However, the limitation of the basic method to product- and ingredient-mix problems has also been pushed back by the mathematicians, and there are adaptations of linear programming which can be used for solving the transportation problem and the assignment problem.

The transportation problem is one where there are a number of factories, each of which can supply a number of warehouses. All routes from every factory to every warehouse can be shown as a matrix of cells with the factories listed down the rows, and the warehouses across the columns, Figure 6.4.

Each factory has a total availability, each warehouse has a total requirement, and each route has a different unit cost of transportation, shown as a small figure in each cell. The problem to solve is how to meet the requirements from the availabilities at minimum total cost.

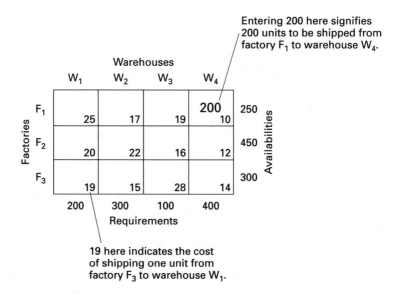

Figure 6.4 *The transportation problem: which factories should supply which warehouses to minimize total shipping costs?*

Take a look at the example in the figure and see if you can calculate the minimum cost transportation schedule. One way which will get you close is to allocate to the lowest cost cells first, but surprisingly, this way cannot be relied on to yield the lowest total cost. If you try it out, you may begin to see why.

The technique can also be used to maximize profits through supplying products to markets, in which case the small figures in each cell will represent the unit profit associated with each allocation, and the aim is to maximize the total profits from all the allocations.

The other adaptation, the assignment problem, is a special case of the transportation problem in which each supply point has just one unit available, and each demand point requires just one unit. The technique can be used to allocate tasks to workers, jobs to machines, or any other situation where not more than one resource may be assigned to one use, and not more than one use may be assigned to one resource, Figure 6.5.

The small figures in the cells may again represent the costs or times to be minimized, or profits to be maximized, of each possible assignment. It has obvious applications in the field of production planning. Assuming they are costs in this example, see if you can find the lowest cost schedule of assignments. Once again, merely allocating to the lowest cost cells first may get you close to the optimum, but will not guarantee it.

There are routines with names such as the Hungarian method, the North West Corner rule, and Vogel's method for homing in on the optimum answers in linear programming, but computers have

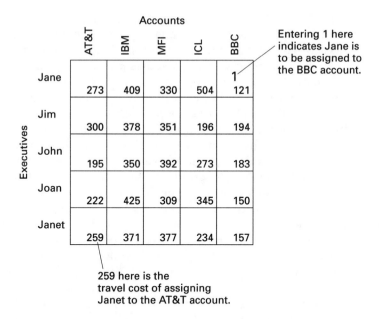

Figure 6.5   *The assignment problem: which executive should be assigned to which account, in order to minimize total costs*

removed the need for anyone but programmers and mathematicians to learn the details of these techniques.

Critique

Linear programming is a powerful and valid mathematical approach. However it only has limited applications in business, and there is the risk it might be applied inappropriately. It is appropriate for linear programming to be incorporated in computer programs for automating some of the routine short-term planning and scheduling which goes on in many organizations. For instance, some highly automated factories have a central computer which optimizes the flow of work-in-progress through all the individual machines. The routing of jobs through the factory depends on at least four things: the priority rules for jobs, the availability of machines, the mix of jobs on hand, and the cost of each route. If a machine breaks down, or an urgent job arrives unexpectedly, the central computer must immediately reschedule all the jobs. If the times and costs of each job on each machine are known, it would be entirely appropriate to use linear programming in the computer routine for dynamically rescheduling in this way.

However, it is not usually appropriate for linear programming to be used by a manager to optimize a big, longer-term decision – and in any case, managers should be looking for creative ways of overcoming constraints rather than planning to live with them. The reasons why it is not appropriate to use linear programming for the strategic decisions usually quoted as examples in business texts, are as follows.

First, linear programming assumes linearity – or in other words, it assumes that simple, proportional relationships exist between the important variables. For example the objective function formula for profit assumes that every extra product sold will contribute to profits by the same amount. It assumes that if profits increased by £5000 when sales increased by 100 units, then sales of a further 100 units will also bring a further £5000 profit. However, higher sales can often only be secured through greater effort – and cost. Eventually, the cost of extra sales may be so heavy that no profit at all is made. In fact it is only safe to assume linearity for small changes in any of the variables concerned.

Second, linear programming assumes certainty – in other words that we know exactly what the costs and availabilities of our resources will be, and what the profits per unit will turn out to be during the next period. This may have been true in times past when the business environment was reasonably stable, but in the current business climate it is difficult to think of anything we can be certain about in the longer term. Bear in mind also that linear programming models can be very sensitive to errors in the values used. When two lines intersect at an acute angle, a small change in the position of one of the lines will cause a large shift in the point of intersection at which the optimum solution may lie.

To conclude then, linear programming should be left to mathematicians and computer programmers, and should only be applied, if at all, to short-term problems in business. It encourages constrained thinking, which is the kiss of death to knowledge work. In knowledge-based industries the potential of knowledge is boundless: new knowledge can always push back old constraints. For most managers, linear programming therefore has an insignificant role to play in the new world order, in which chaos theory – the theory described by James Gleick (1988), of non-linear systems, complexity and unpredictability – invalidates the old belief that linear approximations can be used to describe non-linear relationships.

Queuing theory

Queues – called waiting lines in the USA – are everywhere. In the developed world, we all spend the equivalent of weeks every year just standing in line, queuing. You get up in the morning and wait for your son to get out of the bathroom. On the way to work, you queue at ticket barriers, or traffic lights. And at work, you queue at the photocopier, at the drinks machine and in the canteen. You wait for your letters to be typed and for your phone calls to be connected – and your 'in tray' documents wait for your attention. When you travel on business, your jet circles the airport waiting its turn to land. But of greatest concern to you as a manager, your customers wait in line for you and your organization to fulfil their orders and meet their needs. If they wait too long, you know some of them will go to be served elsewhere next time if they can.

Nobody likes being kept waiting, and queues always detract from quality of service to some extent. As managers we operate in an age of unprecedented competition in which quality of service and customer care are immensely important. We should therefore do all we can to reduce queuing and eliminate it wherever possible. And to do this, we need to study in more detail how queues behave. You might think there isn't much to study, as queues are just the result of demand exceeding capacity, and all you need to do is increase capacity. It is true you are faced with a trade-off: the cost of customer dissatisfaction and lost sales will fall as the cost of providing capacity rises, Figure 6.6. But as we shall see, queues are not quite as simple as they seem, as long queues can still form even when demand is less than capacity.

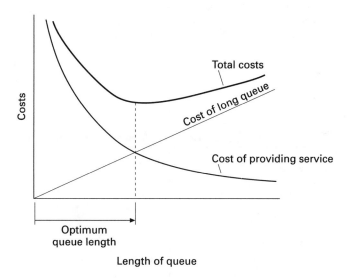

Figure 6.6   *The queuing trade-off: the costs of customer dissatisfaction versus the costs of providing extra servers*

How can a queue form if the average arrival rate is slower than the average service rate? If the arrival rate is constant and less than the service rate which is also constant, there can never be any possibility of queues developing. For instance, if a customer arrives every minute, exactly on the minute, and is served in just fifty seconds, there will be no queue and the server will be idle, waiting for the next customer to arrive for ten seconds each minute. However, queues do form when there are variations in the arrival and service rates. For example, a queue can form when a few arrivals occur in quick succession, even though the average arrival rate is less than the average service rate. This short-term problem can be made worse if some of these arrivals take rather longer than normal to serve. Remember, the arrival rate is only faster than the service rate on average, and in the short-term there can be variations in both the arrival rate and the service rate. It is these variations which allow queues to develop. Then, if the average service rate is only a little faster than the average arrival rate, it may take some time to reduce the queue length. And during this time, it is likely that two or three more arrivals may occur in quick succession. Thus, the queue length will fluctuate about some constant average greater than zero.

A good point to start is with the work of A. K. Erlang, a Danish telephone engineer who researched the problem of telephone calls queuing to be connected. He published his research findings in 1917, and when the discipline of Operations Research was born in the 1950s, his work was extended to business problems more generally.

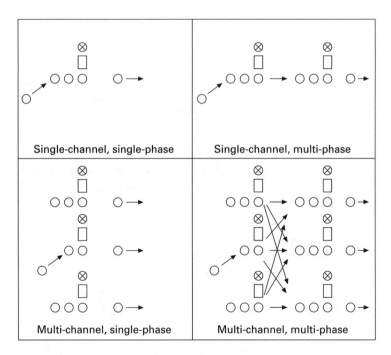

Examples:
SCSP: box office at a small theatre.
SCMP: flight boarding (show boarding pass, then go through security check).
MCSP: banks, post offices.
MCMP: Argos stores (queue to place order, then queue to collect goods).

Figure 6.7 *Queuing systems*

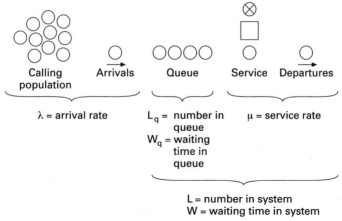

NB: All variables are averages

Figure 6.8   *Components of a queuing system*

The queuing theory formulae

Erlang's work has been encapsulated in a set of formulae. These predict the average queue length, and average waiting time, given the average arrival rate and average service rate for a queuing system. This sounds like great news – computers store and use formulae, so we can just type in the arrival rate and the service rate and get the answers we need – right? Well usually no, unfortunately. Let us see why.

Queuing systems are analysed as a single queue leading into a single service facility (single-channel) or into several service facilities in parallel (multi-channel). Also, they can be of the type where the service is provided at a single stage (single-phase) or at several stages in series (multi-phase), Figure 6.7. There are three main components to any queuing system: the calling population and the arrivals it generates, the service facilities and the departures that exit the system, and of course the queue itself.

Erlang's formulae for single channel, single phase systems are shown below, using the following symbols:
If

λ = the mean arrival rate

μ = the mean service rate

L_q = the mean number of people in the queue

L = the mean number of people in the system

W_q = the mean waiting time in the queue

W = the mean waiting time in the system

Then:

$\lambda/\mu = \rho$, a ratio known as the utilization factor, or traffic intensity

$$L_q = \frac{\lambda^2}{\mu(\mu-\lambda)}$$

$$L = \frac{\lambda}{(\mu - \lambda)}$$

$$W_q = \frac{\lambda}{\mu (\mu - \lambda)}$$

$$W = \frac{1}{(\mu - \lambda)}$$

Also, the probability of no one in the system, $P_0 = 1 - \rho$ and if the probability of the number in the system, n, being greater than k, is $P_{n>k}$, then $P_{n>k} = \rho^{k+1}$.

Here's an example of how they might be used. Suppose you own and run a corner newsagent shop, and between 8 and 9 am, customers arrive on average at the rate of two per minute. If you can serve four customers per minute, taking money for newspapers and cigarettes, then:

$\lambda = 2$ customers arriving per minute on average, and
$\mu = 4$ customers served per minute on average.

So, according to the formulae:

$L = 2/(4{-}2) = 1$ person in the system (i.e. the shop) on average.
$W = 1/(4{-}2) = 0.5$ minutes, or 30 seconds time per customer in the system, on average.
$L_q = 4/4(4{-}2) = 0.5$ customers in the queue on average, and
$W_q = 2/4(4{-}2) = 0.25$ minutes, or 15 seconds time per customer in the queue, on average.

These results are consistent, and show that an average customer spends 30 seconds in the shop :15 seconds waiting in line, and 15 seconds getting served. And there is more information we can get from the formulae:

$\rho = 2/4 = 0.5$ which is the utilization factor. It predicts that between the hours of 8 and 9 am you will be busy serving only 50 per cent of your time on average. Also:
$P_0 = 1 - 0.5 = 0.5$ which is the probability of there being no customers in the shop, which again is consistent, predicting that 50 per cent of the time there will be no customers in your shop.

And finally, if you want to find the probability of more than, say, two people being in the shop at any one time, the calculation is:

$P_{n>2} = 0.5^3 = 0.125$ meaning that there will only be 3 or more customers in your shop 12.5 per cent of the time.

The remarkable elegance and simplicity of Erlang's formulae belies the complexity of their proof, which requires familiarity with probability theory and differential calculus – mathematical skills which most managers are hardly noted for having! However, this would not matter if there were many well-known cases of managers having successfully used the formulae to solve problems at work. We drive over motorway bridges and fly in aeroplanes without first checking the stress calculations, not because we trust the designers and their mathematics, but because many other people have successfully gone before us. There are one or two celebrated cases where queuing theory has yielded accurate predictions, but by and large such cases are thin on the ground, and Erlang's formulae are not widely used by managers. However they still regularly appear in the quants syllabuses of business courses.

Perhaps the biggest difficulty with the queuing theory formulae is that they only give accurate results when a set of restrictive preconditions apply. Erlang had to define the conditions, or the problem would never have been simple enough to model as a set of equations. The assumptions are as follows:

● FIFO: first-in, first-out. No queue-jumping. Arrivals are served in the order in which they arrive.
● No balking: all arrivals join the queue, however long it is. No one shops elsewhere, or comes back later.
● No reneging: all arrivals stay in the queue, however slow it moves. No one gets fed up and leaves before being served.
● The average arrival rate is known and does not change over time. No rush-hours.
● Arrivals must conform to a Poisson frequency distribution. This has a bell-shape similar to the normal distribution for a low average arrival rate, but is skewed to the right if the average arrival rate is higher.
● Arrivals are independent: no one joins because an earlier arrival has joined. No family, or group arrivals.
● Arrivals come from an infinite, or very large calling population which is not depleted by members leaving it to join the queue.
● The average service rate is known and does not change over time.
● Services must conform to a negative exponential frequency distribution. This decay curve falls off rapidly, showing there are many short service times, and very few longer service times.
● Service times are independent of one another. No speeding up if customers are waiting.
● The average service rate is faster than the average arrival rate.

Critique

Can you think of any circumstances in which all these conditions apply? Toll booths on a motorway might come close: no chance of balking or reneging there. But can you think of any other examples?

And here's an even more pertinent question: what use is it anyway to know the average queue length and the average waiting time in the queue? You won't win much sympathy from a customer who has just waited half an hour to get served by telling him the average waiting time in the queue is only five minutes. This is the age of competition and choice – remember? Balking and reneging are the norm, and each customer is an individual who is easily affronted by being batched up and averaged, along with 20 other customers. You are the manager, and I am sure you are more interested in the exceptional cases, at the margin where customers choose to stay or leave – perhaps never to return. But unfortunately Erlang's formulae can tell us nothing about maximum and minimum waiting times, or actual variations in queue length. They deal only with averages and probabilities.

There are some approximate rules of thumb which emerge from Erlang's formulae. For instance if you chart queue length against the utilization factor ρ, you will see that queues only begin to be a problem for utilizations of over 80 per cent. Below $\rho = 0.8$, average queue lengths are zero or in the low single figures, but above $\rho = 0.8$ the average shoots up rapidly, reaching infinity at $\rho = 1$, Figure 6.9. Around the 80 per cent mark, the curve is changing rapidly, so quite a small increase in service rate or reduction in arrivals, can dramatically reduce queues. One practical example of this is that the morning traffic queues in my area disappear during the school half-term, when the small proportion of cars normally delivering kids to school in the morning is not present.

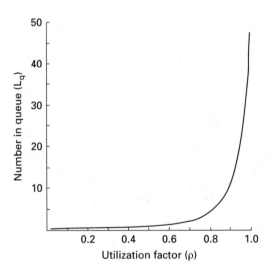

Figure 6.9   *How queues grow when the utilization factor increases*

Another point which emerges from Erlang's work is that the predicted averages are halved if all variability is removed from either the arrival rate, or the service rate. For instance, queue lengths will be halved if you can somehow arrange for the figure for service time to be a constant instead of an average – perhaps by replacing a human server with an automatic facility. So long as the service rate is greater than the arrival rate, any queues that form are entirely due to the two sources of variability. Remove one of the two sources and you remove half the queue. Remove both sources and you remove the queue entirely.

However if you want to know about maximum queue length, maximum waiting times, and how often these are likely to occur, we must turn to some other method of analysis. And fortunately there is a powerful, flexible alternative to the queuing formulae, which can provide these answers. Also, it can allow managers and business students to develop a deeper understanding of how queues behave, and relieve managers from ever again being faced with having to substitute values into formulae which they understand very little, and trust even less. The alternative is simulation.

Simulation

This is a dynamic modelling technique. We came across models before, in linear programming, but this time we also create a set of realistic inputs to our model, so we can study how it behaves. Simulation in business is equivalent to studying a model aircraft in a wind tunnel. Aircraft designers know that the stresses and strains in a wing spar vary linearly across its depth, and so they use the appropriate formulae in the design of the wing. But no designer or mathematician has been able to come up with formulae to describe the optimum profile for an aerofoil section. Wing design therefore relies heavily on trial and error – the testing of models in wind tunnels and computers.

Simulation can be used to study business problems where there is an unpredictable, random element to the way in which tasks occur. For instance, it is impossible for a hospital to know when the next cardiac arrest will occur, and a maintenance team cannot know when the next breakdown will happen. The technique is therefore particularly useful in areas such as maintenance planning, stock control and queuing, in which a realistic stream of arrivals, breakdowns or customers can be generated by a technique known as the Monte Carlo method.

The Monte Carlo method

John von Neumann was one of the most celebrated mathematicians of recent times. He was born in Hungary in 1903 and was 27 when he first came to the USA to lecture at Princeton University. Within a year he was made a Professor of Mathematics, a post he held until his death in 1957. He was a pioneer in the field of computer science, and is perhaps best known for having first proposed the stored program technique in the design of the modern digital computer.

> In 1937 von Neumann adopted American citizenship, and during World War II he became involved in the Manhattan project to develop the first atomic bomb. He encountered some extremely complex problems while studying radioactivity at the secret Los Alamos scientific laboratories on top of a remote mesa in New Mexico. There were no computers, and radioactivity was too complex to analyse by conventional means, so he developed a simulation method to study the sporadic emission of neutrons. Because of the randomness of the emissions, which was akin to the randomness of a roulette wheel, he called it the Monte Carlo method.

The Monte Carlo simulation technique

This method produces a realistic stream of input values suitable for feeding into a mathematical model to see how it behaves. The method takes random numbers from a table or generated by computer, and uses them to produce values which individually are random, but collectively form a particular pattern. In fact the figures can easily be made to fit any desired frequency distribution, while remaining random within that constraint. As an example, let's start with the simplest of real systems – one which is so familiar that we know how it behaves, one which we could test directly at no cost anytime, and so would not normally bother to model – the flip of a coin.

Imagine you are sitting in a pub with me one evening, and I suggest we play a game of chance based on spinning a coin. The rules of the game are simple: we spin a coin and if it lands heads up, I pay you £2, but if it lands tails up, you pay me 50p. However, before each spin you must pay me a 70p entry fee. If you have £4 with you, would you play?

For this simple example you could reason that half the spins will be heads and half tails, so two average spins should result in one head and one tail. The head would win you £2 and the tail would lose you 50p, which comes to £1.50 over the two spins. The average for a single spin is therefore half as much, making 75p. So, even after paying a 70p entry fee you will be left with winnings of 5p per spin on average.

However, for more complex problems, you could arrive at much the same conclusion with the more structured approach of decision analysis which we covered earlier in the chapter. You would calculate the expected value to you of each spin – the average outcome in the long term. This is calculated as the value of each possible outcome multiplied by its probability:

Table 6.5

Spin	Probability	Value (p)	Probability × Value (p)
H	0.5	200	100
T	0.5	−50	−25
Totals	1.0	150	75

Thus the expected, or average value of a spin is 75p. But the entry fee is 70p for each spin, and this must be deducted from the average, leaving a net expected value of each spin to you of 5p. So the expected monetary value (EMV) of your winnings for 1000 spins is 1000 times 5p, which comes to £50. But remember, the EMV is only a hypothetical average. In reality your actual winnings are unlikely to be exactly £50, though they will be close to it. According to decision analysis, this is an excellent opportunity for you, and you should go for it. In the long term you are sure to win, but there is a risk: remember you only have £4 in your pocket. If you have a run of bad luck early in the game, you might lose your £4 and be unable to continue playing because you couldn't pay the entry fee.

To keep our simulation as simple as possible, let us use a set of ten single-digit random numbers. The first number is 1, the second is 2, and so on, through to 9 which is the ninth, and 0 which is the tenth. By definition, random numbers are all equally likely to occur, so each number has a 10 per cent chance of occurring. In other words each number has a probability of 0.1 and if we plotted the numbers from a random number table as a probability histogram, they would appear as a perfectly uniform distribution, Figure 6.10. Now to simulate the spinning of a head or a tail, we need to produce from the random numbers a probability of 0.5. This we can do by putting together any five numbers each with a probability of 0.1. For instance any number from 1 to 5 inclusive could be taken to indicate a head, and any number from 6 to 0 inclusive to indicate a tail, Figure 6.11. So, as half the numbers indicate a head and half indicate a tail, we can simulate ten spins by simply reading off the numbers from a random number table, and recording the outcomes, as follows:

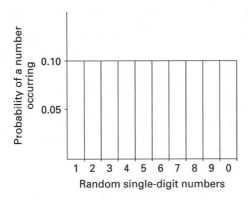

Figure 6.10 *Random numbers are all equally likely to occur*

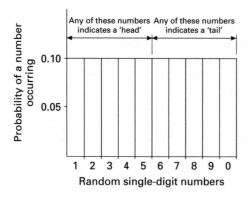

Figure 6.11   *Using random numbers to simulate the spin of a coin*

Table 6.6

Spin no.	RN	H/T	Fee	Win/lose	Value	Cumulative value
1	6	T	−70	−50	−120	−120
2	2	H	−70	+200	+130	+10
3	1	H	−70	+200	+130	+140
4	7	T	−70	−50	−120	+20
5	9	T	−70	−50	−120	−100
6	0	T	−70	−50	−120	−220
7	8	T	−70	−50	−120	−340
8	5	H	−70	+200	+130	−210
9	8	T	−70	−50	−120	−330
10	6	T	−70	−50	−120	−450

Look at the figures in the first row of the table. For spin number 1, the random number 6 is drawn. This lies in the range 6 to 0, and so indicates a tail, T. The next two figures, the fee and the winnings or losses are added together to give the value of this first spin. And in the last column, the cumulative or running total of value is recorded. As you can see, for this particular simulation, the cumulative value ends up at -450p or £4.50 in the red.

But what good is this? If we were to run the simulation again, we would get a different result, possibly showing a positive balance at the end this time. True, this simulation is too short, and on its own does not tell us much. However, set it up on a computer spreadsheet for 100 throws – then run it 100 times and count how many times you get a negative cumulative balance of greater than £4. This is really useful information to help you decide whether to play the game with me. By studying the various runs, you will get a much better feel for what to expect in the game. This is the true advantage of simulation: by playing with the model, you can understand much better the behaviour of your real-world systems. As you watch the simulation play through on your computer screen, you can see probability at work and feel its effect: it becomes a real influence you have to contend with – not just an abstract concept. Simulation adds depth to your knowledge – helps you make the decision instead of making it for you in the form of a single, optimum solution based on averages.

I'm sure you can think of situations in business where an investment project may be threatened if it takes longer than expected to come good, and where it would be useful to anticipate future difficulties. Of course most business problems are more complex than the flip of a coin, but simulation can often still help. As an example, let us return to Erlang's queuing problem.

Simulating a queuing problem

The American Direct Bank is planning to locate a drive-in banking facility, close to a group of superstores which will be opening soon near an exit from the M40 motorway. The bank wants its customers to get served without ever having to queue for long. Of course queues can develop because of variations in service time, even when the average service rate is faster than the average arrival rate. So, from surveys of their drive-in services in the USA the bank has produced a table of service times and their probabilities, which shows how service times will vary at the proposed drive-in facility. (Table 6.7)

Table 6.7

Service times (minutes)	Probability
1	0.1
2	0.25
3	0.3
4	0.2
5	0.15

The bank has also collected survey data to show how UK customer arrival times will vary because these variations too will make queuing problems more likely. (Table 6.8)

Table 6.8

Inter-arrival times (minutes)	Probability
1	0.1
2	0.15
3	0.35
4	0.15
5	0.15
6	0.1

These probability tables are all we need to run a queuing simulation to help us decide how many service channels should be provided. The simulation will show how queues develop, and make it easy to calculate what the average and maximum queue lengths and waiting times will be. Here's how.

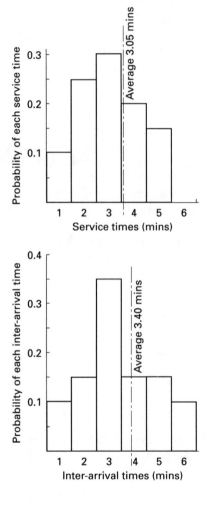

Figure 6.12 *Probability histograms of service times and inter-arrival times*

First, let's chart the variations in service times and arrival times as probability histograms, Figure 6.12. We don't need to worry whether these distributions conform to the negative exponential and Poisson shapes, because unlike the Erlang formulae, simulation can handle any shape. By eye however, you can probably see that on average the arrival rate is slower than the service rate, and so a single channel service will probably be sufficient, so let's start on that assumption.

There are three stages in running a queuing simulation, which are:

● preparing look-up tables to generate service times and inter-arrival times, then
● running the simulation to produce a table of results, and
● analysing the results.

Look-up tables

The procedure for generating a realistic stream of service times and inter-arrival times is the same for both, so let's start with the service times. Then we can just repeat the procedure for inter-arrival times. The service times need to be random and variable, while at the same time conforming to the pattern shown in the probability distribution. We need to convert random numbers into service times. Our look-up table must therefore have random numbers listed against service times, so when given a random number, we can look up the service time it indicates. First, as in the coin spinning example, we need to divide up the random number range in proportion to the probabilities for each inter-arrival time. But this time we need to divide up the range more finely, so we use two-digit random numbers starting at 01 and ending with the 100th number which will be 00.

Refer back for a moment to the original table of service times, Table 6.7. On the first row you can see the probability of a service time of one minute is 0.1, which means there is a 10 per cent chance of taking one minute to serve a customer. So in our simulation we must arrange for 10 per cent of services to take one minute. We do this by allocating 10 per cent of the random number range – ten of the 100 numbers – to the inter-arrival time of 0.1. So let's use the first ten numbers, from 01 to 10 to indicate an inter-arrival time of one minute.

Moving down Table 6.7, on the second row the probability of a service time of two minutes is given as 0.25 or 25 per cent. So we need to allocate the next 25 random numbers to a service time of two minutes ... and so on. When we get to the last row of the table, the last remaining random numbers will be allocated and every random number will be associated with a particular service time. Then, to generate a realistic stream of service times, all we need to do is generate a string of random numbers and look up the associated service times.

In practice there is an easy way of making these allocations. There are two steps, adding a couple of extra columns to the original probability table. First as an intermediate step, we add a cumulative probability column, which starts at the top for a time of one minute with a cumulative probability of 0.1 on its own. Then for two minutes in the second row of the table it rises by 0.25 to 0.35. In the third row it rises by a further 0.3 to 0.65, and so on, to the last row which has a cumulative probability of all the individual probabilities, which must always come to 1.0. This is now shown in Table 6.9.

Table 6.9

Service times (minutes)	Probability	Cumulative probability
1	0.1	0.10
2	0.25	0.35
3	0.3	0.65
4	0.2	0.85
5	0.15	1.00

In the cumulative column, the figures after the decimal point indicate the end of each section of random numbers to be associated with each service time. Thus the first section starts with the first available number, 01, and ends at 10. Then the second section starts at the next available number, 11, and ends at 35. The next starts at 36 and ends at 65 ... and so on. This is shown in Table 6.10.

Table 6.10

Service times (minutes)	Probability	Cumulative probability	Random number range
1	0.1	0.10	01–10
2	0.25	0.35	11–35
3	0.3	0.65	36–65
4	0.2	0.85	66–85
5	0.15	1.00	86–00

By plotting the random numbers as a probability distribution, we can show how the whole range of random numbers has been divided up in proportion to the individual service times, Figure 6.13. From this you can see that there will only be a 10 per cent chance of picking a random number in the range 01–10, which would indicate a service time of one minute. However, there is a much bigger 35 per cent chance of picking a random number in the larger range 36–65, which would indicate a service time of three minutes. The look-up table is very easy to operate: if you draw a random number 72 for instance,

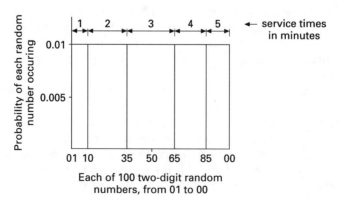

Figure 6.13   Probability distribution of one hundred random numbers divided up in proportion to the probabilities of five service times

this lies in the range 66–85 and so indicates a service time of four minutes.

Before we can run the simulation, we must repeat this procedure to produce a look-up table for inter-arrival times. However I hope you can see by now that the procedure is perfectly straightforward and with a little practice becomes very easy. The result is a look-up table for inter-arrival times as shown in Table 6.11.

Table 6.11

Inter-arrival times (minutes)	Probability	Cumulative probability	Random number ranges
1	0.1	0.1	01–10
2	0.15	0.25	11–25
3	0.35	0.60	26–60
4	0.15	0.75	61–75
5	0.15	0.90	76–90
6	0.1	1.00	91–00

Now all we need to run the simulation is a table of random numbers if we are doing it manually with pencil and paper. Alternatively, if we construct the look-up tables on a PC spreadsheet program such as Microsoft Excel, there is an in-built function which can produce the random numbers automatically. To get the most out of simulation, you really do need to use a PC. But more of that later.

Running the simulation

There are three parts to the simulation, which is best constructed as one big table. The left-hand part of the table generates arriving customers, the right-hand part shows them being served, and the middle portion monitors queue length and waiting time. Table 6.12 shows what a short run of ten customers might look like:

Table 6.12 The American Direct Bank. Simulation of the first ten customers to arrive

1	2	3	4	5	6	7	8	9	10
Cust. No.	RN 1	Inter arr. time	Arr. clock	No. in queue	Enter service clock	Time in queue	RN 2	Service Time	Depart clock
1	54	3	3	0	3	0	23	2	5
2	50	3	6	0	6	0	99	5	11
3	66	4	10	1	11	1	54	3	14
4	12	2	12	1	14	2	60	3	17
5	74	4	16	1	17	1	19	2	19
6	39	3	19	0	19	0	94	5	24
7	85	5	24	0	24	0	51	3	27
8	32	3	27	0	27	0	05	1	28
9	55	3	30	0	30	0	80	4	34
10	91	6	36	0	36	0	02	1	37
Totals:		36		3		4		29	
Means:		3.6		0.3		0.4		2.9	
Maximums:		6		1		2		5	

The column headings from left to right are as follows:

1. **Cust. No.:** This is a running total of customers arriving.
2. **RN 1:** This is a random number series, used with the look-up table for inter-arrival times to produce simulated arrivals.
3. **Inter arr. time:** This is the inter-arrival time indicated by RN 1 in the look-up table.
4. **Arr. clock:** This is the clock time at which each customer arrives. It is a cumulative, or running total of inter-arrival times.
5. **No. in queue:** This is the number of people queuing, including the new arrival.
6. **Enter service clock:** This is the earliest time the customer can be served, and is the later of two times: the arrival time of that customer (shown in column 4, same row), and the departure time of the previous customer (shown in column 10, previous row).
7. **Time in queue:** This is the elapsed time between the customer arrival time shown in column 4, and the enter service time, shown in column 6.
8. **RN 2:** This is a second random number series, used with the other look-up table to produce simulated service times.
9. **Service time:** This is the service time indicated in the look-up table by the RN 2.
10. **Depart clock:** This is the time that the customer leaves the system after being served. It is the service time from column 9 added to the enter service clock time from column 6.

At the foot of the table there are some totals, some means which are just the totals divided by the ten customers who arrived during the simulation, and some maximums. These are useful for the final stage, the analysis of results.

Analysing the results

A simulation run of just ten customers is nowhere near large enough to provide useful results. You should really run sufficient customers to give an average inter-arrival time close to the expected inter-arrival time, and an average service time close to the expected service time. You can calculate these expected times from the original survey data by multiplying the times by their probabilities and adding them up. For instance, the expected inter-arrival time is:

$$1 \times 0.1 + 2 \times 0.15 + 3 \times 0.35 + 4 \times 0.15 + 5 \times 0.15 + 6 \times 0.1 = 3.4 \text{ minutes.}$$

This means that on average, 3 minutes and 24 seconds elapses between the arrival of one customer and the next.

The expected service time is calculated in the same way, and comes to 3.05 minutes, which means that on average it takes 3 minutes and 3 seconds to serve a customer. So customers are being served faster than they are arriving, and if the customers arrived and were served in exactly these times, the bank cashier would be idle between customers for 21 seconds. It is useful to calculate the expected arrival and service times before you do the simulation, especially if it is not obvious from the distributions which is the largest. The easiest way is to add yet another column to the original probability data, to hold the product of the probability and the time in each row. Then the expected value is found by summing these values at the foot of the column.

Of course all queuing situations can be simulated, even where the service rate is slower than the arrival rate. Erlang's formulae could not cope with that – they would give meaningless negative answers for queue length and waiting time – but simulation just shows the queue length continually growing. You could even calculate the average queue length and waiting time – but they would not be much use, and would more or less double every time you doubled the length of the simulation run.

The full power of simulation is only available through implementing it on your PC, because it is only a little more difficult to run a simulation for 100 customers than it is for ten. Also, once set up, you can run the whole simulation including calculation of the means and maximums at the foot of the table, in a couple of seconds. You can therefore run the simulation 20 or 30 times in the space of a minute, by pressing a key which forces the spreadsheet to recalculate. When it recalculates, it produces new sets of random numbers each time, and as the figures cascade down through the table, you get a different answer on the bottom line each time. Most of the runs will be quite similar, but occasionally the variations in arrival and service times can interact to produce a result further from the average. By watching the values on the bottom line, and also columns 5 and 7 in the body of the table for queue length and waiting time, you can develop a much better understanding of how queuing systems behave. You can gain the equivalent of maybe several years experience in the space of a few minutes.

Critique

Simulation is a powerful and versatile technique for developing a better feel for the behaviour of a system. However it does require some simple statistical knowledge and a confidence with using numbers, which not all managers may have.

Like all powerful tools, simulation has the potential for harm as well as good, and even for a numerate manager there is the danger of expecting too much of the model – of believing it to be an almost perfect representation of reality, and devoting too much time to refining and studying it. It should be thought of as just one way of re-framing the problem, one which will have imperfections, but nevertheless has the capacity to add depth to our knowledge of the problem in question.

The technique is open to anyone with some basic statistical ability, and a familiarity with spreadsheets such as Excel. There are also special simulation languages which are ideal for simulating production scheduling and inventory problems, for instance. You might find it worth while to learn one of these if you need to build lots of simulation models.

Pause for thought

The computer was built for the knowledge worker. It can amplify your skills and boost your productivity. But it is such a complex tool that you and I and everyone else must inevitably have gaps in our knowledge of it. So would you like to be honest with yourself and own up to those areas where your knowledge is a bit thin? What are your computer training needs? Until you identify them you cannot do anything about them.

1   Are you familiar with the Windows environment? If not, run the tutorials which are available in the Help menus of Program Manager, or your word processor or spreadsheet. Do you know:

- how to use Help, and navigate around inside the facility to find the solutions to your problems?
- how to use File Manager to list the filenames on a disk, or to create directories on a disk for holding different categories of files? Are you confident at copying files between directories or between disks?
- how to have more than one application running at the same time, how to switch quickly between them and how to use the Clipboard to carry data across from one application to another?
- where the user manuals are, or who to ask for help with these or other problems which all of us have, but feel too embarrassed to admit to?

2   Think of a situation recently in which you had to choose between different investment options. Can you draw up a decision table or tree to analyse it better? It is one thing to solve decision analysis problems at the end of the chapter in a statistics book, but quite another to frame real problems in this format for yourself before solving them.

3   Do queues feature in any of your problems at work? The chances are that they do in some form or other – either customers or work waiting for your attention, or machines waiting for maintenance. What data would you need to collect before you could do a Monte Carlo simulation, to help you understand the situation better?

References and further reading

Deming, W. E. (1986) *Out of the Crisis*. MIT Center for Advanced Engineering Study.

Curwin, J. and Slater (1994) *Quantitative Methods for Business Decisions*. Chapman and Hall.

Morris, C. (1993) *Quantitative Approaches in Business Studies* (3rd edn). Pitman.

Render, B. and Stair, R. M. (1994) *Quantitative Analysis for Management* (4th edn). Allyn and Bacon.

Gleick, J. (1988) *Chaos. Making a new science*. Heinemann.

7 Team knowledge as a business resource

Why read this chapter?

The team is the basic organizational unit in knowledge-based organizations. The purpose of the team is to create, develop and exploit the knowledge resource and bring forth its fruits. Within a team-of-teams organization, process teams drive the semi-permanent revenue-generating processes of the organization, and temporary project teams are formed to meet new opportunities as they arise by bringing together an appropriate mix of skills and experience. In this chapter we will look at team communications, team building and the team-roles played out by members.

The team as business unit

Small teams are becoming the basic unit of many organizations now, functioning like cells clustered together to form a living organism. They can be thought of as little businesses, co-operating and competing with other little businesses in the same field. The small team provides the right environment for knowledge to take root and flourish. Large size, force and power are no longer decisive. In the information age knowledge, creativity and the good idea can outwit brute force and will increasingly prevail. But where do good ideas come from, and how can we recognize them when we encounter them?

We have all read stories of tycoons who started with nothing and had to hawk their ideas round to a succession of bank managers before they found someone to back them. And you must have felt the same frustration when your boss turned down that good idea of yours which needed more investment than you could authorize. But unlike the budding tycoon, you work in an organization and in the traditional hierarchy your idea often only gets one chance, so it has always been (and still is) important to present ideas well. In a command-and-control regime there is no one else to turn to if your boss rejects your idea. You must present it as easy to implement, with a large, early and apparently certain net payoff, even if it means massaging the facts somewhat. Despite our obsession with quality and customer care, a payoff of some kind will always be important for proposals to be approved. But in the new team environment, ideas can be developed and debated, and may never be vetoed. However, even in the new environment, not all ideas can be implemented. Your proposal will be one of many you and your team colleagues are considering, and you will only have time jointly to carry forward the most attractive ideas. And massaging the facts is pointless in the team context where truth, openness and trust are valued qualities – you would only be fooling yourselves.

A project starts as an idea in someone's mind. It must then be thought through and developed into an executable proposal, along with costs, projected cash flows and paybacks, which we will look at in more detail in Chapter 10. Then it must be carried forward to a successful conclusion, despite all the unanticipated problems and setbacks which are bound to occur. And at each stage, ideas and creative solutions are required.

New ideas

Let us examine the process of capturing a good idea and converting it into a new source of revenue. The idea must first occur to someone before it can be developed into a project proposal or business plan, and be approved and implemented. The original germ of the idea arrives somehow in the creative right-hand side of the brain of one person. We don't fully understand how ideas arrive: they come in a flash – hence the light bulb turning on over the cartoon character's head. Consider your own experience: one moment there is just a confusion of thoughts and memories chasing each other around inside your head, and the next moment there is an interesting comparison or contrast which suggests a new possibility. Confusion and profusion lead to fusion – the joining together of random thoughts in Brownian motion. For new ideas to form, there must be a concentration of many random thoughts in the melting pot (an open mind), and the opportunity for something to crystallize (time for reflection). Proven group methods for idea generation such as brainstorming demonstrate the need for these conditions.

We all have opportunities to reflect – moments when our mind is quiet, often away from work painting the spare room at the weekend, or reading a book such as this, or jogging in the morning – and often that is when our best ideas begin to take shape. But we don't all concentrate on the same things, and the people who are most likely to have a new idea about a process at work are the people who are closest to the process – the staff performing it. Suggestion schemes have been around for many years, which shows we have always known that operators can use their heads as well as their hands, but paying operators a special bonus for using their heads reinforces the belief that operators are paid their wages only for using their hands. Until the advent of quality circles, there was no systematic attempt to tap into this rich source of value. The quality circle was the forerunner of today's multi-skilled self-managed small team, and it marked the beginnings of the new, knowledge management paradigm. Quality circles and quality improvement groups are not specially rewarded for using their heads – they are expected to, and so they are only paid extra for out-of-hours work. If a bonus is paid, it will be shared by the team, not taken by an individual. Teams are trusted with access to information, they are encouraged to learn skills of data collection and analysis, problem-solving and decision-making. They are assumed to be mature and responsible adults and they are provided with time, place and opportunity for discussion. Add a little recognition and applause for success, and you have the makings of a turned-on team.

Even in quality circles, the seed of a new idea must begin to germinate in the mind of just one person, but the co-operative team environment is fertile ground: true teams value new ideas and give them proper consideration, whoever introduces them. But the old paradigm scarcely recognized that anyone other than managers could use their heads, and many new process improvement ideas must have withered and died because they formed where they were most likely to form – on the wrong side of the management-worker divide. And even amongst old-paradigm managers, the competitive cult of the individual prevented co-operative, constructive debate, and thus destroyed any chance of new, partly formed ideas being given a fair hearing. So a manager would work in private until the new idea could be developed and presented as a great opportunity to make or save money.

Project proposals and business plans

To improve its chances of acceptance, your new idea should be written down. You will need to develop it into a proposal with a payoff. This is work for the logical, left-hand side of the brain.

Project proposals and the business plans of budding tycoons are so similar it is scarcely worth distinguishing between them. They both start with an idea for making or saving money, or for providing a better service. The project proposal is less extensive in scope than a full business plan, as it is set in the context of an existing business, or part of a business. It does not normally need to start from scratch and cover every aspect of business, from raising funds, finding personnel and premises, through design and production to marketing, sales and invoicing – as is the case with the business plan. But apart from scope they are the same, so let's just talk in terms of projects. Projects have recognizable phases, from idea through preliminary research, data collection and analysis, to proposal, execution and final review. Right now, though, we are concerned with the proposal which must be prepared and written up for circulating and presenting to a small audience. The proposal is a critical stage in the life of the project, with two functions. It acts as a lens to bring the idea into focus, and it acts as a communication to sell the idea.

An idea in your head can seem very attractive, but it remains fluid and can assume different shapes and proportions depending on the angle you view it from. But when you start setting it on paper, some difficult decisions have to be made. The discipline of writing forces you to firm up on exactly what you are proposing, and in particular, how you expect it to work out in the future. While writing the proposal, you may be aware of a kind of internal debate going on inside your head, between the creative right and the analytical left side of your brain. Sometimes you will get as far as writing something down, and it is not until you read it back to yourself that you see the flaws. So the writing of the report in itself helps bring your ideas into focus, even though it is not the main motive for the writing, which of course is to sell your idea to others. And at that stage a new debate begins, within your team now, in which your idea will be further tempered, tested, improved upon – and perhaps progressed a step closer to implementation. The idea is no longer entirely yours now: it belongs to the team. You have traded it for an enhanced standing and reputation amongst your team colleagues.

Team processes

Ideas are the seeds of the knowledge harvest, but of course there is more to farming than sowing and reaping. Tilling, weeding, watering, winnowing, storing and taking to market – all spring to mind as useful analogies for essential team processes which must be performed for the knowledge resource to be exploited. Of course we cannot take the analogy too far because, as we saw in earlier chapters, there are big differences between knowledge work and physical work such as farming. However it is appropriate to draw some comparisons. For instance, just as farmers will not last long if all they do is sow seed, neither will knowledge teams get far if all they do is sit around having ideas. So what other processes must teams perform? The processes of the team are powered by individuals in the team fulfilling particular roles.

Team roles

Meredith Belbin (1993) has studied team roles for over twenty years. In his books he records the conclusions he and his colleagues at Henley Management College arrived at, during a series of experimental studies which lasted nearly a decade. The purpose of the studies was to try and understand how individual managers behave in the context of a working group, and to design tests that could be used in recruiting and selecting managers to work in groups. You may question the motive for the work, which assumed it would be possible for a remote manager external to the group to determine its make-up and thus influence its performance. However the results are still relevant: Belbin's conclusions can help groups understand their own internal processes, which is useful in their own self-management.

He has defined nine team-roles that team members can perform. There is an implication that members are inherently predisposed to particular team roles. Whereas this may be true for a particular environment, such as within traditional hierarchies, a change in team environment – or objectives – can make it possible for members to change their predominant team-role contributions. Indeed it may be essential for them to do so, as Prime Minister Winston Churchill, who was an excellent war-time prime minister, found to his cost when the war ended. Different environments and objectives call for different leaders, as anyone who has been on an outward bound course will know. If Winston Churchill and his cabinet had ever faced a trek through the Welsh mountains, he would probably have fallen in behind the leadership of a cabinet colleague more familiar with that situation.

Belbin's nine team-roles, and their contributions

Plant: This is the creative, imaginative role, contributing unorthodox solutions for difficult problems. The name is intended to suggest the planting of idea seeds in the group, rather than suggesting the person is a spy planted in the group by senior management.

Resource Investigator: This role calls for an enthusiastic extrovert who is a good communicator. It is filled by someone who can use the phone and other networks to explore opportunities and develop contacts.

Co-ordinator: Teams need a confident, mature person to chair meetings, clarify goals, promote decision-making and delegate tasks.

Shaper: Teams also need someone to keep the pressure on, to set challenges and overcome obstacles. This role requires someone with dynamism, drive and courage.

Monitor evaluator: A discerning person with sober judgement who can take a strategic view of all options is needed for this role.

Teamworker: A mild, co-operative, perceptive and diplomatic person is required for this role. Someone who listens, builds, averts friction and calms the waters.

Implementer: This role is performed by a conservative person who can turn ideas into practical actions. It requires discipline, reliability and efficiency.

Completer: Teams must deliver on time, and therefore need an anxious, painstaking, conscientious person to fill this role, who will search out errors and omissions.

Specialist: This role provides knowledge and skills in rare supply, fulfilled by a dedicated, self-starting single-minded person.

These team-roles add to our understanding of useful team behaviour by categorizing it into clusters with appropriate names which most of us can recognize. We have all seen co-odinators in action or worked with teamworkers. Categorizing in this way is a classical research method which was widely applied by Victorian botanists and palaeontologists in the study of our physical world. The method was appropriate then for describing the immutable species and types in their disciplines – as it is now for describing the possible range of behaviour that humans may exhibit as members of teams. However whereas ranunculi and ammonites remain immutable, human behaviour can change. We call it learning. Belbin does acknowledge this, but a more appropriate terminology would distinguish more clearly between the behaviour and the person – for instance Shaping as a process, rather than Shaper as a role. Belbin believes each individual has a natural tendency towards particular roles within a team, and that each individual should play to his or her strengths. That may have been appropriate in rigid hierarchical organizations, but specialization and division of labour such as this is less appropriate in the multi-skilled self-managing teams of today's new flexible organizations. Teams last just for the duration of the project – they form, dissolve and reform as new needs arise. In this environment, individuals need to be versatile, and they should improve on their weaknesses as well as developing their strengths. And for knowledge to flourish, there are two team roles which all team members must be reasonably good at, and seek to improve – those of teamworking and communicating.

Team building

What is the difference between a team and a work group? What characteristics does a team have, beyond what a work group has? The word 'team' is borrowed from the world of sport, and is used in the business context because of its many positive connotations. Teams have fun, and their members are there voluntarily. They have esprit de corps, bound together by a common purpose and sharing common values. They are self-motivated to improve their performance and have a strong desire to win. Team members feel personally responsible for fulfilling particular functions, and the worst fear is the fear of letting the side down. This is in stark contrast to the work groups of some command-and-control organizations where members are press-ganged into performing rigidly defined tasks which they neither understand fully nor care much about. It would be more appropriate to describe groups such as these as flocks unthinkingly following their leader, or squads drilled to follow procedures and respond predictably.

Seen in this light, it is easy to see how the need for flexibility and responsiveness in today's business climate has led to the team being welcomed as a versatile and effective organizational building block. But how can teams be created? Once again we can draw upon experience from the sporting world.

Getting the right people together

In a local sports club, the responsibility for picking the team rests with the player-captain, who invites other players onto the team for the next match or for the season. Then the team trains together to improve their group performance. This is the most democratic model, with members remaining on the team voluntarily only so long as they find the experience satisfying. The team represents the club as a whole, which is financed and run by its membership to meet a variety of social needs as well as winning matches.

In larger sports clubs, finance, ownership and operating at a profit become much more important, and this has a bearing on how the match teams are picked. The success of the match team can have a big influence on takings at the gate, and so large clubs tend to be run more like businesses, with match teams being selected by a manager or a selection committee. Neither the manager nor the committee model appears to be entirely satisfactory, according to press reports on football and cricket team selection in the UK.

In commercial organizations, both the local club and the large club approaches are used. The large club model, with a manager or committee deciding the composition of teams has been the norm in the past, though there are exceptions. For instance Tom Peters (1992) describes what happens at big American consultancies such as EDS and McKinsey, where nearly all the work is done through projects, and the organizations are just big collections of project teams that are continually forming, changing, dissolving and re-forming. At these companies, a consultant can put together a project team by inviting candidates with the required qualities and experience to join up. Of course candidates or their existing project leaders could reject the invitation, but the whole system operates on a quid pro quo basis, and people who refuse invitations may later have their own invitations refused when they too are trying to put together a team. Consultancies sell knowledge, and they are at the forefront in developing knowledge management structures. The evidence seems to suggest that invited, voluntary membership of teams is the most appropriate model for organizing to exploit the knowledge resource.

However, operating with voluntary invited membership of teams presents problems even to EDS and McKinsey. They employ tens of thousands of consultants around the world and in practice this makes it extremely difficult to find the best available candidates for a particular client project. The key resource of a consultancy is the knowledge of its consultants, and the problem is how to bring this knowledge to bear on client problems. The best candidates are those with the most relevant knowledge, but no one knows what everyone knows in a big consultancy. So a consultant trying to put together a team for a particular project must first do some research, to find out if any colleagues have been involved in similar work. And the key to this initial research is networks: human networks based on address books, friendships and business relationships; and electronic networks starting with the company information system and databases, but maybe eventually reaching out beyond the boundaries of the company through global telecommunications to wherever the desired knowledge may be held. After a few years building up their contacts, many managers claim they almost always know someone with the right knowledge – or failing that, they know someone who knows someone. However, EDS and McKinsey do not leave to chance this important stage in the life of the project. They have special databases and directories for holding and locating project reports, and have support staff whose purpose is to maintain the databases, help consultants with their problems, and insist that consultants provide the latest updates. This is knowledge management par excellence, and if you want more details you can find them in Peters' *Liberation Management* (1992), a large part of which is devoted to networks and knowledge management structures in different companies.

Getting the group to perform as a team

When a group of individuals is brought together for the first time, all they may have in common is perhaps an allegiance to a larger organization, and a statement of group purpose. Initially the group is just a collection of individuals, and does not become a team until the group members have got to know each other through communicating, training, working and playing together. There must be an emotional payoff for each individual to remain voluntarily as a team member, based on mutual respect, fun and the great feeling of belonging to, and contributing to a winning partnership.

A group must pass through various stages on the road to becoming a team. Most of the pioneering research work into group dynamics was done in the 1950s and 1960s, and one of the better known descriptions of the stages in team building is that of Bruce Tuckman (1965):

- **Forming:** getting together and settling membership.
- **Storming:** the individual struggles for team control, and roles within the team.
- **Norming:** making clear agreements and goals.
- **Performing:** actually doing the work.

This is one perspective of the stages in team building, as seen by a leader or external observer. Another view is offered by Will Schutz, who describes the stages as felt by an insider – a member of the initial group:

- **Inclusion:** am I a part of this group?
- **Control:** what will be my role and status?
- **Affection:** will I get the emotional satisfaction I want from this group?

This view is particularly helpful because it relates what we see happening in groups to what we know about the psychology of motivation, and what we know to be true from our own experience of groups. It gets closer to recognizing that being a member of a team is both demanding and rewarding: we all strike our own psychological contract and on balance membership must be worth the sacrifices. In fact being part of a team can be extremely satisfying, but no one can command a group of people to work as a team. Like throwing a party, all the leader can do is plan the environment, provide the right atmosphere, and hope things will start to swing. If it doesn't work for you, you will withdraw emotionally: you may be one of the group, but by not joining in you will not be on the team.

Team formation and performance depend entirely upon communication: without it a group cannot even start any of Tuckman's four stages. Also, it seems that team performance is closely related to quantity and quality of communication amongst the team members – and not just task-related communications. Exceptional team performance can only be achieved when the barriers are down and members are communicating well. Openness depends on trust which depends on openness – a loop which can spiral upward as a virtuous circle to exceptional performance, or downward in a vicious spin to disintegration. Fairtlough (1994) starts his book on the theme of openness, and Senge (1990) also devotes a chapter to the subject. On many occasions he quotes Bill O'Brien, the inspiring CEO of Hanover Insurance whose policies led to Hanover becoming one of America's most successful insurance companies. Here's one quote:

> The impulse toward openness, as O'Brien says, 'is the spirit of love.' Love is, of course, a difficult word to use in the context of business and management. But O'Brien does not mean romantic

love. In fact, the type of love that underlies openness, what the Greeks called agape, has little to do with emotions. It has everything to do with intentions – commitment to serve one another, and willingness to be vulnerable in the context of that service. The best definition of the love that underlies openness is the full and unconditional commitment to another's 'completion,' to another being all that she or he can and wants to be.

Communication at this level can only be initiated and sustained by regular face-to-face meetings in a variety of social as well as business contexts, so that members can get to know each other as whole human beings. Only then can the highest levels of trust and commitment be achieved. But of course most of the work towards task completion goes on outside of meetings, sometimes by members in widely dispersed geographical locations. Then of course, members must keep in touch through phone, fax and computer, not as substitutes for face-to-face meetings but as additional forms of communication which can sometimes allow the time between face-to-face meetings to be extended. The phone is mostly used to allow people to communicate at the same time while at different places, though with answering machines it is possible to communicate at different times as well as different places. Multimedia computer conferencing can offer a richer form of same time, different place communication, in which people can see and hear each other while sharing a common view of their knowledge work on screen. The computer also enables different time, different place communication through e-mail and bulletin boards.

KPMG Peat Marwick use groupware to win business

In his Sunday newspaper column, Tom Peters (1995) described how the consulting group KPMG successfully uses groupware to create value through pooled knowledge. When they responded to an invitation to bid for conducting a major technology overhaul for an insurance company, KPMG beat EDS, IBM and Coopers & Lybrand to win the business. Nothing unusual so far, so why the fuss? Two (perhaps three) reasons.

First, the request for the bid was received at 3 pm on Friday, yet the thick proposal complete with graphics and diagrams was finished and delivered to the client less than a normal business day later at noon on Monday. This would not have been possible without a very efficient way of bringing organizational knowledge to bear on the problem. This was achieved with the support of KPMG's new Knowledge Manager system.

Second, the proposal was prepared over the weekend by four partners in four different cities, using FirstClass groupware. We are not supplied the details but we can imagine the hectic scene when the bid invitation arrived on Friday afternoon. Someone would have to decide what skills were required on the team, then locate partners who had these skills and were free to take on the work. The team would initially get together in network cyberspace, to agree an overall approach and decide how to share out the work. Then they would each individually work on their own sections of the report, perhaps accessing remote databases to download blocks of text, facts, graphs and flow diagrams, which would then be assembled and customized for the report. Sections would be pasted into the draft report, a common view of which all four partners would share as it gradually took shape. And finally, there must have been a joint discussion of the overall impression created by the report, and some final polishing before printing and delivering it to the client.

And third? The third reason is that although Tom Peters believes fervently in electronic networking and customer responsiveness, he does not believe it possible over a single weekend to produce a report capable of breaking new ground and leading the insurance industry in a whole new direction. His view is that you should 'Groupware yourself to the hilt. I'm all for it. But use the technology to do something with pizzazz, not just to be a lightning-fast drone.' He believes professionals should not respond to stupid requests from clients: professionals should not take business that does not help them grow or turn them on.

The desire to maximize profits is seldom the main motivating force for the true knowledge worker.

Communication across the four combinations of time and place are therefore:

- **Same time, same place:** for instance face-to-face meetings.
- **Same time, different place:** the best known example is phone conversations.
- **Different time, same place:** where the night shift takes over from the day shift, for instance.
- **Different time, different place:** computer conferencing, bulletin boards, voice mail, e-mail, fax, etc.

Robert Johansen, David Sibbert and their team (1991) refer to these as the 4-square map of groupware options – or teamware options, as perhaps it should more rightly be called. Their book interprets groupware as more than computer hardware and software, to include any tangible or intangible tools for assisting the work of teams. I commend it to you if you are in any way involved in team building. As a team themselves the authors are acutely aware of the importance of good communication, and their well-written book is an excellent object lesson, the contents dealing with electronic and other tools for teams, and turning groups into teams.

Team self-management

What exactly do we mean by self-management? The 'self' part is clear enough, and for a definition of the word 'management' we could turn to the Management Charter Initiative, or the Institute of Management, or one of many recent books on the subject. But to throw into sharp relief the differences between 'management' and 'self-management', I shall use a definition of management developed in a book written at the end of the old industrial era. The authors Ernest Dale (an academic) and L. C. Michelon (an industrialist) wrote *Modern Management Methods* in 1966 and it remained in print for over twenty years, into the beginning of the information age. They define management in terms of nine functions.

The management functions

- Planning
- Organizing
- Co-ordinating
- Staffing
- Direction
- Control
- Innovation
- Representation
- Communication

In fact these functions are derived from an earlier book of one of the authors, published in 1953 at a time when there were probably less than 100 computers in the whole of Europe and the information age had not yet begun. As you read the quotes that follow, judge for yourself how things have changed since then.

> **Planning.** The basic management function is planning, which begins with setting objectives and includes specifying the steps needed to reach them. ... Naturally the fundamental objective of any business is to make a profit and to increase it. ... The manager far down the line may believe that his objectives come down from above and that he cannot change them. And this is true when objectives are formally stated to him by higher management, in his job description or other directives.

The authors revealed their contemporary attitudes to gender, hierarchy, the single-minded pursuit of profit, and the roles of managers and managed. It is a snapshot of the crude, one-way dictatorial approach to planning adopted by managers in the industrial era. But since then, passing fashions such as joint consultation and management by objectives introduced for a while some dialogue between manager and managed into the planning process. But now in the knowledge-based organization it is apparent that plans developed by teams for themselves, are superior to those of a remote manager developing plans mostly in isolation, which the group has no choice but to follow. Not only are the plans of better quality because more knowledge has been brought to bear, but they will be implemented better because the teams own them and are committed to their successful implementation.

> **Organization.** Organization includes dividing the work into missions that can be handled by one person. ... The principal functions that must be carried out if the plans are to become reality must be described and arrangements must be made to prevent the duties of two positions from overlapping and to ensure that various units are not working at cross-purposes. ... The manager should also take pains to understand what is known as the 'informal organization' ... and learn how to encourage the good results it produces and discourage the bad ones.

Once again the attitudes of the era are revealed. A static business environment was assumed, in which it was possible to divide up the planned work into permanent duties which could be defined in fixed job descriptions. It was also assumed that the manager knew everything about every job. How else could the manager ensure there was no overlap of duties – or uncovered gaps between duties? And furthermore it was assumed that individuals in the group did not communicate much and were quite likely to work at cross-purposes unless the manager took special care to avoid it. However the authors did acknowledge the possibility of an informal organization, but seemed distrustful of it. If group members were allowed to communicate amongst themselves they could co-operate – but might they also conspire?

A static business environment, omniscient managers, exploitation and mistrust were the norms. It sounds like a Charles Dickens novel now, but how many managers still try to organize like this today? The division of labour supports the old, hierarchical method of organizing, but 'divide and rule' now appears to be a very expensive way of avoiding the need to trust people. We now know that teams are quite capable of organizing themselves, though not without some overlap of duties. Indeed overlap is valued because it creates opportunities for communication, co-operation and improvement.

> **Staffing** ... to fill the positions with the most qualified people available ... [and] supplement the abilities of his people by training ... [and] observe their performance and to judge where they are deficient.

In those days it was the prerogative of senior management to move people around like chess pieces. It seemed to be the only way of managing those lower down the hierarchy, who at best were regarded as less able, and at worst untrustworthy. By contrast, those at the top were considered to be the able and trustworthy executors of shareholders' wishes. Employees were a resource to be exploited, so of course managers should pass judgement on them and decide what training they needed.

Since those days, we have seen personnel management gradually evolving into human resource management or HRM, though in 1995 the debate still continued on precisely how it differs from personnel management. One champion of the cause is David Guest (1987) who defined HRM in terms of four goals – integration, flexibility, quality and commitment – and drew up a table contrasting the new HRM approach with that of personnel management, Table 7.1. Although Guest has his critics, it is clear that a number of big UK companies are indeed moving in this direction. There seems to be agreement that old-style managers cannot know as much about the jobs their people do as the people themselves know through doing the work. Similarly, old-style managers were seldom fully aware of training needs and deficiencies because they were mistrusted by their people, who therefore found ways of concealing their deficiencies. Now, the HRM view is that team members who trust each other know their own abilities and training needs, and can monitor their own performance far better than any remote manager could ever do.

Table 7.1 Stereotypes of personnel management and human resource management. Source: Guest (1987)

	Personal management	*Human resource management*
Time and planning	● Short-term ● Reactive ● Ad hoc ● Marginal	● Long-term ● Proactive ● Strategic ● Integrated
Psychological contract	● Compliance	● Commitment
Control systems	● External controls	● Self control
Employee relations	● Pluralist ● Collective ● Low trust	● Unitarist ● Individual ● High trust
Preferred structures and systems	● Bureaucratic/mechanistic ● Centralized ● Formal defined roles	● Organic ● Devolved ● Flexible roles
Roles	● Specialist/professional	● Largely integrated into line management
Evaluation criteria	● Cost minimization	● Maximum utilization/ (human asset accounting)

The HRM role then, is to support empowerment through coaching, and to offer training which team members themselves see as worthwhile and relevant to their needs. Thus the HRM approach is well-matched to the needs of the knowledge-based organization. HRM forms a large sub-set of the inform-and-entrust, or knowledge management approach. Understandably however, it focuses on the human element, mostly neglecting the massive impact of information technology on communication, and the leverage this can bring when applying knowledge to processes and products.

> **Direction** ... that is, telling people what to do and seeing that they do it to the best of their ability. Since the manager must work through other people, he may stand or fall by his ability to get them to produce the needed results.

There is no place for this function in the knowledge-intensive organization. When openness prevails, telling people what to do is at best pointless and redundant. When people are kept fully informed, they do not need telling what to do beyond what is in the terms of their engagement. They will realize for themselves and just do it, obeying the 'law of the situation' as discussed in Chapter 3. There is of course a need to keep the whole organization on track, but this unifying, strategic responsibility of the directors is an entirely different function, in no way related to direction as defined by Dale and Michelon. The directors' role should be to maintain and improve the culture, the mission and the shared values of the organization – which gives a very different meaning to direction, far from telling people what to do and seeing they do it.

> **Control** ... means checking on progress to determine whether plans are being fulfilled. If performance is falling short of what is necessary to fulfil the goals, the manager must take steps to correct the difficulties.

Planning and control go together: to control means to follow a plan. We have already seen that teams should make their own plans, and so logically the team should also be responsible for controlling and holding to those plans. So the only change needed to this quoted definition is substitution of the word 'team' in place of the word 'manager' – it is the team which must take steps to correct any difficulties they may encounter.

> **Innovation** ... No country and no company can expect to stay on top, or near the top, if it continues doing things in the same old way simply because that way has brought success in the past. And innovation is not a job for the research department alone. Innovations must be developed by every manager who wants to be worthy of the name.

Of course we all agree with the general sentiments here. In 1966 when Dale and Michelon wrote their book, innovation was just beginning to be recognized as important. Now of course, it is so important it cannot be left to a few remote managers. Innovation is the basis for progress, improvement and competitive advantage. It is a core theme of knowledge management – the responsibility of the team, not of some uninvolved manager remote from the action.

> **Representation** ... the manager must represent his company to the outside world. ... to more groups than ever before. These groups include the financial community, the general public, the local community, labour unions, industry associations, and innumerable governmental bodies.

What did Dale and Michelon mean by representation? It is not entirely clear, but from the context they appeared to mean stating a position, making a case or putting a point of view. In other words, more to do with talking than listening.

Until recently most government departments insisted that all letters sent out had to be signed by the department head. The rule was absolute and even applied when the head had very little knowledge of what the letter was all about because the work it referred to had been entirely handled by a subordinate. The head acted as gatekeeper, policing the flow of information into and out of the department, and in these circumstances, representation was entirely the responsibility of the head. Perhaps even today there are some last outposts where this practice still survives, but not for much longer. The concept of organization as fortress, with a single gatekeeper controlling the outflow of all information, is a major handicap. In the information age, free flow of information is vital to success. This can only be achieved through many channels, not through a single gateway policed by the manager.

Representation could have another meaning, namely the function performed by a representative who is fully empowered to speak, listen and act on behalf of the team. This richer meaning is much more helpful. Representation in this sense is compatible with the knowledge-based approach, and a legitimate function of the self-managing team. Of course not every team member will be able to represent the team in every respect, and the team may still need to appoint gatekeepers to protect those few categories of information which must remain confidential, such as personal details of employees, and new product details. Even in these areas however, there is a tendency to over-estimate the risks and undervalue the benefits of openness. For instance, there is no point in refusing to give the home phone number of an employee if it is freely available in the public phone directory.

Here's another example: suppose a car-maker discovers for sure that their rival is developing a particular type of car, and even finds out some of the details of the design. The discovery is unlikely to do them much good because coming from behind and arriving in second place with a copy is hardly a recipe for success. Success comes from the total effect of choosing, combining and implementing a particular set of design details. In other words, success depends on bringing the total knowledge of the organization to bear on the problem, not just on a product specification. And as we saw in Chapter 3, it is this embedded organizational knowledge which makes the difference – and unlike the migratory knowledge in a product specification, it is impossible to copy overnight.

The risks of increased openness are therefore greatly exaggerated, whereas the costs of reduced openness tend to be invisible and are thus under-estimated. They include the costs of poor response, mistakes and misunderstandings which occur because of poor communications along the supply chain when secrecy, mistrust and win-lose negotiations are the order of the day.

> **Communication** ... is shown encircling all the management functions, since none of them can be performed without it. The organization structure is designed to set up 'channels of communication' through which information is passed downward and upward. ... organization is sometimes described as a 'system of communication' ... control systems are actually systems of communication.

The authors very clearly reveal their mechanistic, command-and-control mindset in this introduction. It implies the organization is a machine in which people with their own needs and abilities are irrelevant distractions which must be held in check. People are not actually mentioned in this introduction: it suggests the organization is about as human as a digital telephone network. In this context, channels of communication were assumed to be mere conveyor belts which added no value to the processes of the organization. This is a false assumption.

Although communication was regarded as important then, it is so much more important in the knowledge-based organization that what is needed is scarcely in the same league. Dale and Michelon only referred to communication as the medium through which the other management functions were implemented, without actually adding value in its own right. It consisted of sending messages – instructions sent down the hierarchy, and later, reports sent back up. But on-going, two-way communication – an open dialogue – is much more than a conveyor belt to carry information between people: it is an essential part of knowledge processing. It is instrumental to learning and central to the knowledge creation process. Many ideas must be brought together to achieve the critical mass for creative fusion to occur. This can only occur through free and open dialogue. Communication adds value.

Communication adds value

Because this important concept is so consistently denied by the command-and-control approach, let us examine it more closely from the knowledge perspective, by using a metaphor proposed by Gareth Morgan (1986) – that of organization as brain. A computer works entirely by switching internal circuits on and off and we believe the human brain works in much the same way. Circuits are switched on and off by brain cells (neurons) firing, to make connections at the synapses between adjacent brain cells. Similarly in learning organizations, we may think of the organization as a brain, in which organizational learning and thinking occurs when the people in the organization – the 'brain cells' – connect by talking.

How brains connect

Neurologists believe the human brain stores simple memories in individual brain cells, and complex thoughts as circuits along which tiny electric currents flow when we recall them. These circuits are defined by the particular neurons and the particular synapses between them that connect up to form the circuit. When a synapse fires for the first time, it becomes more likely to fire again, and thus a new experience in some way burns a new circuit through the brain. When a memory is recalled, the circuit is activated and the current flows again, burning the circuit more deeply. Thus when the current flows, not only is the original experience played back, the record is also established more securely in memory. This theory provides an explanation for rote learning, and the fact that our memories fade unless we regularly recall them. According to this theory, thinking and communicating within the brain are very closely associated – in fact almost one and the same thing.

There is some physical evidence to support the theory. For instance, the nerve cells which simply communicate messages along the spinal column are very similar in structure to the brain cells in the cerebral cortex which are responsible for memory, thinking and reasoning. And at the top of the spinal column where it thickens to join the brain, lie the cranial nerves responsible for involuntary control of heart-beat and breathing, and reflex actions such as vomiting, coughing and sneezing. Thus there appears to be no clear distinction between the nerve cells in the brain used primarily for thinking and those in the spinal column used for communicating with the rest of the body. And furthermore, it is even believed that the intelligence of the human brain is more dependent upon the number of association fibres connecting different regions of the brain, than upon the total number of cells in the brain.

It seems that communication is necessary for two distinct functions – creativity and co-ordination – which correspond to the separate phases in Kolb's learning cycle – those of thinking and doing. These can be separated to some extent for physical tasks and industrial work, but are much less distinguishable for knowledge-based work. The intelligence of the learning organization is the product of an on-going and wide-ranging debate, akin to the tiny currents that flow between different regions of the brain. By contrast, the slowness of bureaucratic organizations is caused by the inhibited dialogue at the top, and the simple nature of the task-oriented communications passing through the hierarchy, akin to the effector-receptor signals passing along the spinal column. Learning in teams and organizations occurs through dialogue, not dictation, but of course this takes time and the bigger the team, the more time it takes up, as you may know from your own experience of sitting on big committees. Beyond a certain point, bigger teams, like bigger brains, do not result in greater intelligence. Very big teams are more difficult to co-ordinate and spend more time on conveying basic information, which leaves less time available for creative dialogue.

This poses a major problem. How can we bring sufficient brains to bear on really big knowledge-based projects without creating such a large co-ordination overhead that it reduces progress to a snail's pace? That is the subject of the next chapter.

How Aughinish Alumina Ltd are achieving the impossible by running their entire plant using leaderless, self-managing work teams

According to traditional received wisdom, Aughinish Alumina Ltd (AAL) is a strategic impossibility. AAL is a continuous-process plant on an island in the Shannon estuary in Ireland, importing expensive bauxite from Guinea and using standard rate electric power to refine it into alumina. They are selling in over-supplied world markets in competition with low-cost producers in Australia, Brazil and Jamaica, who sit on top of bauxite mines and use cheap electric power and cheaper labour. In 1992, their owners Alcan (Canada) had over-capacity and were selling alumina cheaper than it was being produced by AAL, with little prospect of the market improving. So how come the plant isn't derelict and quietly rusting away in the mists and rain that sweep in from the North Atlantic?

On the face of it, AAL was not much different from many other plants around the world which have been shut down by their owners because they were no longer profitable. In 1992 it was a traditional command-and-control hierarchy, in which the five levels from managing director to front line workforce had recently been brought down from eight levels in 1988. Also, there was a worsening climate of indstrial relations. Negotiations to secure more craft and operator flexibility had been going on for three years and there were 43 unresolved grievances lodged by the trade unions against the company.

But AAL had three things in their favour. First, the plant which only came on-stream in 1983 cost US $1 billion, can scarcely have reached payback and was still fairly new. Second, if the plant had shut, local employment prospects for most of the 570 workers and managers were very poor indeed. And last but by no means least, the company had always invested heavily in developing the workforce by offering them many opportunities for training.

Here is an example where starting to manage the knowledge resource actually made a difference. Less than two years later in 1994, using only leaderless teams, 25 per cent fewer people ran the plant to produce 20 per cent more alumina, and AAL were on course to achieve by 1995 their survival target of a US $25 per tonne cost reduction on 1992 prices.

Pat Sweeney, Human Resources Co-ordinator at AAL, and John Taylor (1994), Development Consultant from Sheffield College, Yorkshire, describe how – to the delight of Alcan (Canada) – this remarkable success story was achieved.

In late 1992, corporate messages to AAL left them in no doubt as to the vulnerability of the plant, and a strategy team with Pat Sweeney as a member was formed with the aim of reducing costs so that AAL could sell alumina for at least the cost of its production, even at the most depressed time in the economic cycle. The objective was a 20 per cent reduction in controllable costs through:

- **technology gains:** stretching plant productivity and efficiency, and,
- **people gains:** harnessing the discretionary (knowledge) capability of the workforce.

How?

By informing and entrusting – how else? The 'technology gains' come mostly by the continual improvement efforts of front line workers, not by top management command. And the 'people gains' come by enabling people to see the situation for themselves and putting them in charge of their own destiny. Informing – or more accurately, communicating – lies at the centre of the transformation: the 'organization as machine' became the 'organization as brain', and this could only have happened through everyone doing a lot of communicating.

In August 1993 the strategy team produced a video and three booklets, outlining a five-year survival plan. There was one booklet on the new values, teams and working practices, and what it would be like in future to work at AAL, a second booklet giving details and advice on the AAL voluntary severance programme, and a third one on AAL's enterprise support scheme to help people start their own businesses or re-train. The human resource facilitators were involved in many group and invividual meetings, providing the chance for much discussion and critical debate, and eventually 155 people left AAL under the severance terms.

By November 1993 the new values and vision based on openness, trust and self-management had been hammered out in discussion with the workforce, and a team-based organization structure was in place at AAL. The new structure – if that is the right word to describe it – consists, Semco-style (see Chapter 2), of three groupings: front-line process teams, team facilitators, and the senior management team. There is a high level of communicative competence and capacity for critical debate throughout the plant, and time and place are made available for this to continue. Individual and organizational learning is the driver for change, and gradually trust has been building, as process teams try out their new empowerment and discover its reality. Within less than a year, universal scepticism has been replaced by virtually total acceptance of the effectiveness of the new organization to deliver the business outcomes.

The verdict?

Of course there have been difficulties. Everyone has had to change. Senior management find it difficult to keep their hands off and not intervene. The same is true of the people who were middle managers and are now facilitators or in process teams. They too occasionally revert to old command-and-control modes of behaviour. And the process workers don't find all aspects of self-management easy either, especially the thorny 'people issues'. Everyone is struggling to learn new roles and new modes of behaviour, but discussion and debate, driven by the new vision and values, keep the development on course. Grievances taken up by the trade unions have dropped to zero, and problems are now resolved by the teams, sometimes with facilitator support. Teams report a widely-held feeling of common sense about the new way of working. It is not empowerment they experience, so much as the removal of barriers to sensible working.

Of course AAL may yet be overwhelmed by economic events, but for the time-being at least, they are learning to get ahead of the economic fundamentals weighing in against them. And given a further breathing space, they have a good chance of staying ahead.

Pause for thought

1

Do you recall being a member of a team which really worked well? What was it that made it a good experience for you? Could you re-create those conditions again, if necessary?

2   Are you a member of a team now? What are your answers to the questions which Will Schutz suggests we ask of ourselves, on inclusion, control and affection?

3   What role do you most naturally fall into, when you are a member of a group? Are there any of Meredith Belbin's roles which you feel you should work on to develop and add to your repertoire?

4   Under what circumstances do you have your best ideas? Is it possible for you to re-create those circumstances when you need to generate some new ideas?

5   Which of Johansen and Sibbet's four-square combinations of time and place communication do you regularly use? Jot down examples of each. Is there a combination which you do not use as much as perhaps you should? What is blocking you? How could you overcome any obstacles?

References and further reading

Belbin, M. (1993) *Team Roles at Work.* Butterworth-Heinemann.

Dale, E. and Michelon, L. C. (1966) *Modern Management Methods.* Penguin.

Fairtlough, G. (1994) *Creative Compartments – A design for future organisation.* Adamantine Press Ltd.

Guest, D. E. (1987) Human resource management and industrial relations. *Journal of Management Studies,* Vol. 24, No 5.

Johansen, R, Sibbert, D, Benson, S, Martin, A, Mittman, R. and Saffo, P. (1991) *Leading Business Teams. How teams can use technology and group process tools to enhance performance.* Addison Wesley.

Morgan, G. (1986) *Images of Organization.* Sage.

Peters, T. (1992) *Liberation Management – Necessary disorganization for the nanosecond nineties.* Macmillan.

Peters, T. (1995) An indecent proposal. *Independent on Sunday.* 15 January

Schutz, W. (1989) *FIRO: A three dimensional theory of interpersonal behaviour.* WSA.

Senge, P. M. (1990) *The Fifth Discipline. The art and practice of the learning organisation.* Century Business.

Sweeney, P. and Taylor, J. (1994) A case study of transition in a continuous process company towards empowerment using self managed work teams. Paper at HRM conference, Nottingham Business School. 14/15 Dec.

Tuckman, D. W. (1965) Developmental sequences in small groups. *Psychological Bulletin,* 63.

8 The project as a team responsibility

Why read this chapter?

Project teams assemble temporarily to develop new ideas for product or process improvement. The project allows the shifting workload of the new organization to be co-ordinated and shared out in manageable, human-size parcels. It adds structure to the amorphous, invisible world of knowledge, so the work can be scheduled to meet new objectives by particular due-dates. The PERT method for doing this was developed in the industrial era, and when applied appropriately, it has proved to be an effective tool for scheduling the intangible processes of knowledge workers.

In this chapter we will examine the project as a method of reaching for new knowledge and new goals. We will discuss project management software for scheduling projects, and describe how it may be used most effectively by teams for knowledge work, in contrast to how it is customarily used for industrial work.

Organizing for learning and creativity

The success of a team in creating value depends on the quality of the communications links between all the members of the team. The bigger the team, the more difficult this is to ensure. In a team of two, there is only one possible communication link – and that is often difficult enough, as you will know if you are married. In teams of three there are three links, along the sides of the triangle they form, and with a team of four there are six links, Figure 8.1. On a football team of 11 there are 55 links between different pairs of players, and in a rugby football team of 15 players there are over a hundred different links between pairs of players. That is too many for all the links to be fully developed, and may explain why most sporting teams are smaller than this. It is interesting to note that the smallest operational unit in most armed forces, the squad, although not a true team also consists of between five and eleven members.

Excellent communications links are not easy to maintain. The conclusion we should draw is that to perform well in a competitive business environment, self-co-ordinating, self-managed teams should be kept within the size that has proved humanly practical in other competitive environments – on the playing field and battle field. This is particularly true for knowledge work, where too much time spent co-ordinating leaves too little time for creative, productive dialogue.

Number in the team	Diagram	Number of links
2		1
3	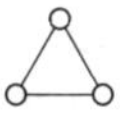	3
4	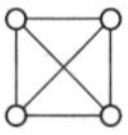	6
5	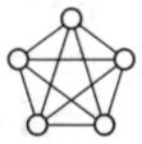	10
6	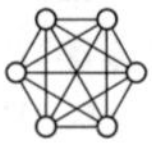	15
n		$\dfrac{n(n-1)}{2}$

Figure 8.1 *The number of links between pairs in a team*

Balancing the needs for co-ordination and creativity

A good example of almost pure knowledge work is the software engineering project, in which programmers build, in the words of Fred Brooks (1982), 'from pure thought-stuff'. Programming is a particularly fruitful example of a knowledge process from which we may learn and perhaps derive some general principles of knowledge management. There are two reasons why: first because the output of the process is in the form of computer code which can be tested to see how well it performs, and second because there are few uncontrolled variables which may influence its performance. In most other examples of knowledge work it may never be possible to gauge the effectiveness of the knowledge process because the output cannot be tested, or in cases where it can be, there are other influences which affect the outcome. For instance we can never test corporate strategy. Suppose a CEO develops and implements a particular corporate strategy, and subsequently the organization prospers or declines. In a changing competitive environment, who can say by how much the fortunes of the organization are determined by the CEO's corporate strategy, and how much by changes in the economic cycle? We cannot even know whether an alternative strategy would have been better. In other instances there may be a test of success, but seldom is the result of the test dependent only on the output of the knowledge worker.

Take for example a prosecution lawyer. The outcome of the trial is a test with a clear result, but is not just dependent on the strength of the prosecution case, but also on other factors such as the ability of the defence lawyer for instance.

Programmers, in common with CEOs and lawyers, require knowledge and understanding, along with analytical and creative skills. But unlike other forms of knowledge work, programs are immediately testable. When a programmer writes a software routine it either runs and performs as required, or it doesn't. Also, if another programmer writes a similar routine to meet the same requirements, most likely it would consist of different lines of code which we can examine. And when compared objectively, one routine will be superior because it runs faster, takes less memory, or meets the requirements better in some other way. Thus programming is unique as a knowledge process in that the quantity and quality of output are easier to measure. This makes it a particularly appropriate field of study for anyone interested in how to manage knowledge and the productivity of knowledge workers. Some research has been done into the productivity of programmers, but very little has been written on the relevance of the results to other types of knowledge work. Compared to the volume of literature on the productivity of industrial workers, remarkably little has been written on the productivity of knowledge workers apart from programmers. However there are two studies which have been influential amongst software professionals, which should be of interest to other knowledge workers.

The productivity of knowledge workers

The first study supports the generally held view amongst software project managers that the performance ratio between best and worst programmers is often greater than 20:1! The study was reported by Sackman, Erikson and Grant in 1968 and showed ratios ranging between 25:1 and 28:1 for the hours spent by worst and best programmers on coding and debugging a particular routine. Also there were substantial differences in the product. The worst programs took five times more memory, and took five times longer to run than the best programs.

How far are these results generally relevant to knowledge work? It seems likely they will be to some extent, so there must be potential for improving the productivity and quality of other knowledge workers, as well as programmers. Through further research it should be possible to find methods of improving the worst performances to a point where they are less far below the best performances.

The gasoline syndrome

The second study led to another generally held belief. The book by Fred Brooks, *The Mythical Man-month*, is a classic first published in

1972. In it, he argues that adding programmers to a software team that has fallen behind schedule, will actually make matters worse:

> ... when schedule slippage is recognized, the natural (and traditional) response is to add manpower. Like dousing a fire with gasoline, this makes matters worse, much worse. More fire requires more gasoline, and thus begins a regenerative cycle which ends in disaster.

Why should this be? If someone helps you peel the potatoes it takes half the time. And if it takes four people two days to paint a fence, eight people will complete the work in a day. But software engineering cannot be compared to familiar work such as this which, because we can see it, determines our preconceptions. Unlike peeling spuds or painting fences, software engineering is a creative, team process which cannot be split into a number of identical tasks to be completed independently without much need for co-ordination and communication. On the contrary, co-ordination is a major problem, and communication between team members is crucial to the dialogue which enables the whole-team creative process. Now considering the disproportionate effect that expanding the team has on the number of communications links between pairs of members, we can begin to see that Brooks's gasoline analogy is a good one. If you double the team, the pair links increase more than four-fold. The extra members eventually bring some extra capacity, but in addition to a once-only, up-front delay while the new members form, storm and norm, they also bring a disproportionate and continuing communication load. First, when the new members arrive, progress is halted while existing team members give time to bring them up to speed. Then, when the enlarged team starts work, progress is permanently burdened with an increased communication overhead. By the time the new members begin performing, the already tight schedule has slipped by more than can be compensated for by the net capacity increase of the new members – all because no allowance for communication is made in the estimates.

Brooks concludes that big software projects are disproportionately more difficult than small projects. For a given team, a software system consisting of 100,000 lines of program code takes much more than ten times the effort for a 10,000 line system – and this is a catch-22 for really big, complex software projects. A team of ten people will achieve high productivity, because the communications overhead is reasonably small, but the size of the task may mean it will still take several years to complete! This is far too long, because the hardware for which the software is being written will be obsolete by then, and nobody will be interested. But increasing the team size much beyond about ten, actually causes the time spent on communicating to rise much faster than the time saved on programming – thus actually making the situation worse.

So what can be done to get really big projects finished in a reasonable period of time? Brooks concludes that teams should still not be bigger than ten people with one person acting as 'surgeon', and the others providing programming, editing, administrative and secretarial support. If 200 people must be put on the job, 20 such teams should be used, and the minds of the 20 surgeons should be co-ordinated by a single system 'architect'. In other words, what we have here is a team of teams organization.

In summary then, Brooks puts the blame for the gasoline syndrome on four causes:

- the techniques for estimating knowledge work are poorly developed, and make the unreasonable assumption that all will go well,
- the techniques for estimating fallaciously confuse effort with progress, and make the unreasonable assumption that team members and months are interchangeable,
- project leaders are uncertain of their estimates, and so find it difficult to resist pressure to bring forward due-dates, and,
- schedule progress is difficult to measure and is poorly monitored.

These conclusions are not only true of software projects. They are relevant to projects in other disciplines too such as research, design, development, or any work in which value is added through the creation of new knowledge.

Planning and controlling work through projects

What is a project? The word implies a casting forward to some fixed point in the future, and so we use it to describe any planned undertaking which must deliver by an appointed time.

Much of the work done to produce industrial products and services is not organized as projects, but as routine, on-going responsibilities. Thirty years ago nearly all the work of a traditional manufacturer or a retailer was routine and continued without much change. That was OK in the industrial age which was characterized by stability – inflexible organizations operating in stable markets. In those days you would train while young for a particular type of work, and it would secure you a job for life. Any change that did come along was gradual, and could be implemented by adjusting the routines. The small extra workload caused by change could be fitted in during slack periods, or by making the customer wait a while. But for the most part, it was business as usual, planning and monitoring the flow of work through the system.

As we saw in Part I however, that scenario is being superseded. Routine work is rapidly being automated out of existence, and dealing with change is becoming the major part of most managers' jobs – and that is why the project is fast becoming the accepted way of getting work done in the information age. But continuous change, unlike continuous routines, needs to be managed in a different way. Routines are repetitive, requiring the same things to be done over and over again, and can therefore be managed by fixed methods and systems – job specifications and procedures designed to reach long-term goals, by means of a well-trodden path with clear milestones along the way. Change however, by its very nature involves doing new things, or doing the same things in new ways, and this calls for a different management approach. To start with, we may not have a clearly defined goal, or know which path to choose, or how long it will take to get there. Managing by project – defined as a planned undertaking to deliver some benefit by an appointed time – seems to be just what we need to add structure to an on-going programme of change.

Project work	*Normal work*
● Self-contained. Defined limits on time and cost.	● Open-ended. Deferrable times and costs.
● Temporary team.	● Permanent team.
● Work on several project teams.	● Work on one process team.
● Non-repetitive, new work, few precedents.	● Repetitive, familiar work, well-known procedures.
● Problems expected, new learning needed.	● Few problems, normally right first time.

Continuous change is too much for us to handle all at once. What we need are staging posts on the journey. A project therefore is a way of arriving at some desired state, or achieving some envisaged future benefit. It is the furthest outpost we can contemplate reaching in the boundless panorama of opportunities spread out in front of us. Following the Russian launch of Sputnik, the first earth satellite, the Americans set up their NASA space programme in order to regain the lead in the space race. It was a continuous programme with no clear staging posts. Then in the 1960s President Kennedy started one of the most ambitious projects ever – to put a man on the moon by the end of the decade. It was a clear goal, but initially no one knew how to achieve it, and the first problem was to map out the steps to be taken to get there.

It took eight years to achieve Kennedy's goal. Now, if we had to do it again, it would take no more than a year or two at most. Why? Because we learned how to do it in the 1960s and that knowledge gained during the Gemini and Apollo programmes is available to us now, whereas it wasn't at the beginning of the 1960s. When Kennedy first set the goal, the main obstacle was lack of knowledge. Projects always require the creation of new knowledge, or learning, because they require new things to be done for the first time. Before Neil Armstrong could make his giant leap for mankind, scientists at MIT had to devise guidance systems, materials technologists had to create new materials, and engineers had to design and build the space vehicles. In order to achieve this historic goal, existing and new knowledge had to be brought together on an unprecedented scale. It was knowledge which lifted Neil Armstrong to the moon.

Of course the Americans had previous experience of managing fairly big projects, and it was during one of them, the Polaris missile program for the US Navy during the 1950s, that they developed a powerful new method for scheduling and controlling project work. It is called Program Evaluation and Review Technique (PERT). At about the same time, another group of project engineers were facing similar problems at Dupont, the big chemicals company in America. They came up with an almost identical solution which they called Critical Path Method (CPM). Today these techniques have been captured digitally and are available to you as software packages.

Project management software

Usually these packages have the word 'project' in the title. There are dozens of products, each with their own strengths and weaknesses, but a typical and well-known example is Microsoft Project. It is a Windows product, easy to learn and ideal for any project where there are penalties for missing the due-date. It can be used to plan and control the launch of a new product, or an office relocation over the weekend to be ready for business at 9 am on Monday.

The main output of these packages is a Gantt chart. This is like a staff holiday planner with horizontal bars drawn across the dates booked by different people, but this time the bars show when each of the separate tasks of the project should be done. But don't be fooled by its apparent simplicity: by modelling the project in this way an amazing fact of real value is revealed. In big projects, most of the tasks turn out to have no effect at all on the overall duration of the project! Only a few critical tasks determine the total time needed to finish the whole project. All the rest need less time and can be done in parallel with the critical sequence of tasks.

This kind of computer support is a really powerful aid. It allows you, the project leader, to concentrate your scarce time and valuable attention on the few, critical tasks which, if they over-run will delay the whole project. All the other tasks have more time available than is strictly needed for their completion, so they can take a little longer without affecting the due-date for the project as a whole. So, for instance in a project of 100 tasks, typically only 20 of them will be critical and those are the ones you must make sure everyone knows about. Knowing which are the critical tasks is a bit like knowing which are the 20 per cent items in 80/20 (Pareto) analysis, in that it allows you to focus on the important few tasks and avoid wasting your attention where it probably won't be needed. This is a major advantage, and no project team can hope to survive for long in a competitive environment without this kind of computer support.

Computer support for task scheduling

Here's an example of how Microsoft Project could be used sometime in the future. In this scenario the new M44 east-west motorway from Harwich to Cheltenham has just been completed, and Tesda, the national supermarket chain want to open a new store in Witbury, a market town in the Cotswolds close to the motorway. Tesda have been negotiating for months with the Planning Department of Witbury Town Council, and have reached a point where they expect to win official approval at the planning committee meeting to be held next week. The committee however are expected to add some conditions to be met concerning the external appearance of the store.

Tesda's co-ordinator for the new store project has listed all the project tasks which must be completed before the store can open:

Table 8.1   Project: opening of Tesda's new Witbury store

Task name	Duration (business days)
Gain Board approval and Local Authority planning permission.	7
Finalize exterior design to meet conditions of planning permit.	5
Finalize local PR/advertising strategy, get contracts signed.	16
Local advertizing and new store opening publicity.	48
Job advertizing and recruitment of new staff.	40
Demolish old store.	5
Erection of the new store building.	30
Finalize and approve the interior design details.	10
Complete the interior decorations, and install the store fittings.	5
Finalize the computer systems design, and place contracts.	28
Delivery of the computer EPOS and EDI systems and software.	21
Install and test the computer systems.	6
Train new and existing staff on use of new computer systems.	6
Grand opening by CEO, Mayor and local dignitaries.	1
Total	228

Task relationships: one after the other, or side by side?

Naturally after the long period of negotiation, Tesda's CEO is anxious now for the store to open as soon as possible. Each day's delay puts back by a day the start of the new revenue stream from the store, and delays its break-even point. The list of tasks adds up to 228 business days, but like prison sentences, some of these times can be done concurrently. For instance, getting the advertising contracts signed, and finalizing the exterior design are independent of each other. They will be done by different people, and one need not be finished before the other begins. They can be done in parallel if necessary. On the other hand, the interior design details must be approved before the interior decorating and fitting can start. The decorating depends on the design, and so these tasks must be chained together, one after the other. The second cannot start until the first is finished. Clearly the project will not take as long as 228 days, but what's the minimum time it can be completed in? Jot down your guess now.

Let us see how project management software can help. Suppose you are the store project co-ordinator using Microsoft Project for example. These are the steps in planning the project:

1. Decide what tasks need doing. Type in the list of task names. These will initially appear as fourteen parallel tasks, all starting on the same date, Figure 8.2. If you know the duration times of the tasks, you can enter these as well, but if you don't know them yet, you can leave them out for the time being: Microsoft Project will assume a nominal one-day duration which you can easily change later.

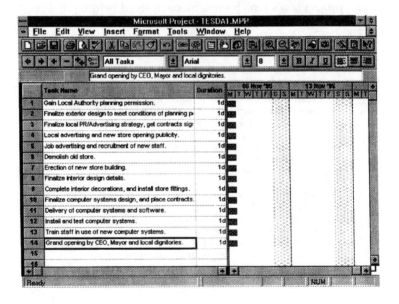

Figure 8.2 *Listing tasks with Microsoft Project*

2. Decide when to do tasks. Identify the tasks which depend on earlier tasks. Microsoft Project needs to know which are the sequential tasks that must follow on, one after the other in a particular order. Just highlight the sequence of task names, then click on the 'Link' button in the toolbar. It has a little chain link symbol on it. The Gantt chart then shows these tasks scheduled one after the other, Figure 8.3.

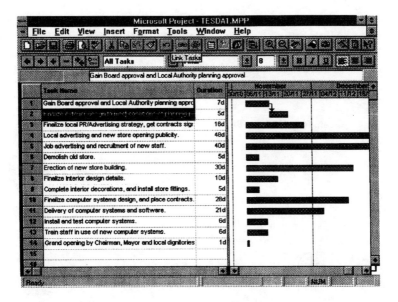

Figure 8.3 *Linking sequential tasks with Microsoft Project*

3. Decide who should do each task. Click on the (human) 'Resource' button in the toolbar. It has two little human faces on it, and it opens the Resource Assignment window, which can hold a resource list of people's names. You can add names to the resource list, and you can very easily assign a name on the resource list to one or more tasks on the Gantt chart. You do it by simply dragging and dropping the name onto the tasks you want that person to do. The person's name then appears next to the assigned tasks on the Gantt chart.

The whole process is very easy and intuitive, especially if you have used other Windows products. It just seems like common sense, but in fact behind the scenes the software is taking care of some quite complex logic – as you will know if you have ever prepared a PERT schedule manually. Before computers were so widely available, PERT 'networks' had to be drawn up using pencil, paper and eraser. The Tesda project would be shown as arrows representing the tasks, and circles representing events, or points in time between the arrows when one task finished and another began, Figure 8.4. The arrows radiate out of the starting point at the left of the paper, and converge on the finishing point at the right. In between there is a network of interconnecting sequences of tasks. One of these paths through the network is longer than all the others. It is called the critical path because it is the sequence of critical tasks which determine the shortest time in which the whole project can be completed. As you can see from the PERT network, the critical path for the Tesda project is 74 days long. How does that compare with the guess you jotted down earlier? All the other, shorter sequences of tasks have more time available than they were estimated to require, and so should not affect the total time needed to complete the whole project.

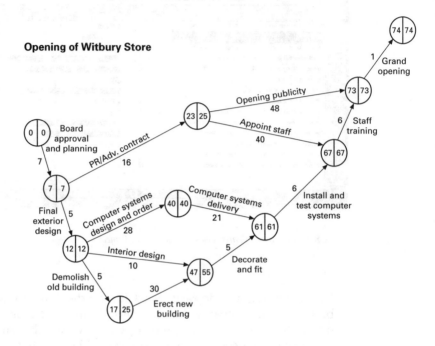

Opening of Witbury Store

Figure 8.4 *The Tesda project PERT network*

Drawing up PERT networks manually used to be a real chore, but they had to be done to capture all the task dependency relationships, and to analyse the limits between which non-critical tasks could 'float'. Because non-critical tasks have more time available than they need, they can start on time and finish early, or start late and finish on time. The digital model of the project that Microsoft Project holds can be displayed on screen either as a Gantt chart or as a PERT network if you prefer, and you can edit the underlying digital model through either of these two displays. However the network is not nearly as easy to read as the Gantt chart, and most people are only too glad to be free of working with networks.

Task types: physical tasks and knowledge tasks

This is where we raise that old chestnut again, the difference between physical tasks and knowledge tasks. It is a crucially important distinction which must be made in scheduling projects, but unfortunately it is one which seldom receives much attention. The important differences are:

- physical tasks can usually be estimated fairly accurately. They can be broken down into component parts for which we have reliable methods of timing and costing. This is not true of knowledge tasks which require learning and creativity.
- physical tasks can usually be finished quicker by putting more people to work on the task. This is not true of knowledge tasks, as we know from Brooks's study of programmer productivity, discussed earlier.

For an illustration, let's return to the Tesda project. It consists of a mix of physical and knowledge tasks. Demolishing the old building and erecting the new one are examples of physical tasks in the construction and building industry for which quantity surveyors are trained to calculate accurate times and costs. If you doubled the resources allocated to these physical tasks, you could probably halve their durations – so long as they don't start getting in each other's way. Finalizing the interior design details, however, is a knowledge task. The whole task might be the responsibility of a single interior designer. Would doubling up by adding another designer halve the time for the task? Probably not. And how much faith can we have in the estimated duration for this task? The designer probably used rules of thumb to arrive at the original estimate, and so with no hard evidence to support the estimate, might find it hard to resist pressure to reduce it, if it happened to be a critical task.

Using PERT for detailed planning and control

The problems of unreliable estimates were faced in the 1950s when the network method of scheduling was first developed. Command-and-control reigned supreme, and it was thought possible to develop plans much further then. The planners developing PERT added detailed features which subsequently proved impractical. For instance they wanted more control over the accuracy of estimates for research and development tasks in the US Navy Polaris missile project. They realized that the time needed to develop a new ceramic material for rocket nozzles for instance, depended to some extent on luck. In trying out different combinations of materials, the researchers might hit lucky and happen on a suitable mix early on in the search – or they might get through their short-list of most promising ingredients and be forced to extend the development period as they cast around for other possibilities.

Of course planning is not supposed to depend on luck, so the Polaris planners thought in terms of probability instead. They asked each task leader to give not just one estimate of project duration, but three – a most likely time, a pessimistic time and an optimistic time. These three times were then assumed to represent three points on a continuous scale of possible durations for the task in question, Figure 8.5. This probabilistic approach assumes that if the task, or a very similar one is done for the first time many times, the duration will be different each time because of uncontrolled variables, such as the order in which you try out ingredients in a research task. A weighted average of these three estimated durations is then used as the statistically 'expected' duration for each task. Then, the expected durations of critical tasks are added up to give the expected duration of the whole project.

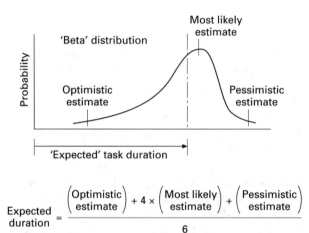

Figure 8.5 *Calculating the 'expected' task duration*

The theoretical advantage of this method is that uncontrollable variations in task durations are not just swept under the carpet and ignored, but overtly accounted for in the planning process. At one stage, the American Department of Defense insisted the method be used for their big, publicly funded projects. Unfortunately however, many of the assumptions made are just not valid in practice, and this probabilistic approach so widely taught in business schools is rarely if ever used in the management of real projects (Anthony, Dearden and Bedford, 1984). There are two main reasons why: managers have no faith in the technique, and the statistics have never been shown to work in practice.

Managers have no faith in a technique they do not fully understand, which opens the door to pessimism and provides a justification for missed targets. Managers don't like to think they are at the mercy of chance. They feel more comfortable with clearly stated, fixed goals that they can aim for.

The statistical assumptions are faulty on several counts, but one of the most serious is the 'roundabouts and swings' assumption that worse-than-expected durations on some critical tasks will be compensated for by better-than-expected durations on other critical tasks. This cannot be true either in theory or in practice. The effect of a critical task finished late is always fully added to the project duration, but the effect of a critical task finished early can seldom be fully subtracted. This is because other parallel paths which are just sub-critical become critical before the full time saving can be made. There is therefore an in-built tendency for the actual project duration to exceed the statistically expected project duration which assumes a symmetrical, normal probability distribution of possible project durations. The symmetrical distribution is wrong because it shows that early project completions are just as likely as late project completions. In fact, projects with parallel sub-critical paths will always be more likely to finish after the expected project due-date than before it.

This tendency to over-run is true of all projects, not just probabilistic networks. We all know that projects don't finish early just by chance. It rarely happens at all, and when it does, it is always the result of effort and a cause for congratulation. No wonder project managers don't trust these statistical flights of fancy. It is a classic case of taking planning too far, to a level of complexity which falls foul of chaos theory and the unpredictability of non-linear systems. Pushing analysis to these limits was seen as appropriate in the command-and-control era of the 1950s, but today the approach is to keep things as simple as possible. The inform-and-entrust approach suggests we should use the basic Gantt chart to inform and assist teams in managing their progress, not as a tool for setting and enforcing deadlines.

Project scheduling in self-managed teams

The great value of a tool such as Microsoft Project is that it allows teams to share a much better understanding of what must be done, when, and by whom, to complete the whole project. It makes it easy to plan and display the project as a Gantt chart for all to see and understand. It is a powerful tool which can be used appropriately or inappropriately. For instance in a command-and-control organization, the Gantt chart could be used at first as a command, then later as a standard against which to monitor and control. The computer would support management in developing more finely honed original plans and thus strengthen commitment to them. But in a changing environment, plans need to be flexible.

In an inform-and-entrust organization, the Gantt chart on the computer network allows all on the team to share an up-to-date view of the current plan. If a task takes longer than planned, everyone will know about the situation as it develops, and will be thinking of ways in which the lost time can be recovered. The combined brain power of the whole team will be brought instantly to bear on the problem. With Microsoft Project it is simple to change the plan: the keyboard is scarcely needed. Tasks can be expedited or postponed by dragging and dropping them into new positions. Durations can be extended or shortened by dragging an end of the task bar to a new point on the Gantt chart. Because plans are so easy to edit and reschedule, anyone can run 'what-if' exercises and generate possible alternatives for the team to consider.

The contrast between the two approaches is another example of informating versus automating. The advantages of automating the planning process are minuscule compared to the advantages of informating the team environment. Not long ago if management got their plans wrong, that was their problem. But in the self-managed team, the uncertainty inherent in all plans is acknowledged. It is felt daily as a tangible reality which must be managed by whatever means available. Flexible plans for flexible teams is a powerful combination. It brings to the workplace the efficient, ad-hoc methods we use as a matter of course at home. For instance, what do you do in the morning before going to work? You put the kettle on first, so it can be heating while you fetch the tea or coffee. If you are late, you'll probably drink it in the bathroom, and if you're very late, you'll probably find yourself hopping around putting your socks on with a piece of toast between your teeth! Similarly at work there are very few tasks which cannot be overlapped to some extent. But it seldom used to happen, partly because sequential tasks were done by different specialists who didn't communicate freely, and partly because manually drawing up a PERT network of tasks did not encourage it. Overlapping of PERT tasks was only achievable awkwardly by splitting them into sub-tasks with parallel paths. Now however, the new team-based organizations don't contain non-communicating specialists, and tasks can easily be dragged and dropped in overlapping positions while the software takes care of the PERT network. The methods and software are available to all. In the new race for competitiveness, organizations which stick to the old ways will be left dead in the water.

Pause for thought

1   Estimate how long it takes you to get from home to work in the morning – then measure how long it actually takes. Or better still if you can, estimate how long it will take you to perform a physical task at work of some sort, then measure how long it actually takes. Your estimates will probably be closer than plus or minus 50 per cent of the actual time. Now repeat the exercise for a knowledge task, such as preparing a report, or a presentation. Do you think your estimate will still be within plus or minus 50 per cent?

2   What proportion of your day is occupied by doing regular, routine work, and what proportion by doing new things that you have not done before, and involve you in learning something new? Cast your mind back and ask where the trends are heading: towards, or away from routine work?

3 Have you got access to project planning software at work? Might it strengthen your position with your organization in these uncertain times if you could demonstrate you know how to use it?

4 Look at Figure 8.1 and calculate how many different pair-links there are in a rugby football team of 15 players.

References and further reading

Anthony, R. N., Dearden, J. and Bedford, N. M. (1984) *Management Control Systems* (5th edn). Irwin. pp 398–399.

Brooks, F. P. (1982) *The Mythical Man-month. Essays on software engineering.* Addison-Wesley.

Sackman, H., Erikson, W. J. and Grant, E. E. (1968) Exploratory experimental studies comparing online and offline programming performance. *Communications of the Association for Computing Machinery*, Jan.

9 Figuring out what lies ahead: forecasting

Why read this chapter?

This chapter is about forecasting. Forecasting has long been a key weapon in the armoury of the industrial manager: for command and control there had to be a business plan. And at the heart of the plan there was always a demand forecast, a cash-flow forecast and a profit forecast. How else would it be possible to persuade investors to risk their money on the venture?

But what place has forecasting in the chaotic, unpredictable world described by Tom Peters, James Gleick and others, where organizations survive by being flexible and responsive? Do we need to forecast if we work in an organization which has shifted to the inform-and-entrust paradigm? Of course we do: forecasting is just as important in the information age, but the inform-and-entrust environment requires us to use the techniques in a more appropriate, thoughtful way, which acknowledges the possibility of alternative futures. Forecasting should promote understanding, not blind with science. The narrow, blinkered view is too risky now.

Business planning and the techniques of forecasting will always be relevant, but they should be used to open the minds of everyone to what is possible and probable, rather than to lock everyone into working towards a single, predicted future. There are some really useful ways of forecasting the important numbers in business, and these can help us develop our understanding of how the future may pan out.

The purpose of this chapter is to review the simple techniques of moving averages and trend projection, and assess their value as tools for managing knowledge within teams. Used appropriately, these techniques are even more important in today's changing business environment.

What do we know about the future?

There are two theories about the future. The traditional view is that the world is a complex system driven by cause and effect, and it is only unpredictable because we don't yet know enough about how it works. This view sustains the belief that as we add to our knowledge of the world, we will be able to see with increasing certainty, further into the future. The latest thinking, however, is influenced by chaos theory and it contradicts the traditional view. Chaos in this context means complexity, not utter formlessness and confusion, which explains the somewhat misleading name of chaos theory for the new science of complexity. It is founded on the belief that the world is much more complex than we previously thought, and is inherently unforecastable beyond the short term. It compares management and economic systems to weather systems, which operate, so the theory suggests, as a mix of interacting sub-systems, where positive feedback can create instability and unpredictability. Thus, very small initial causes can be amplified to create monstrously large changes in effects – so much so that, to repeat Edward Lorenz's well-known quotation, the flap of a butterfly's wing in Peking today may set off a hurricane in New York next month (Gleick, 1987). So managers, like sailors, must keep a weather eye out for potential disaster – be alert and prepared mentally and physically to adapt quickly if circumstances change.

One of the reasons why Shell, the giant oil company, was able to adapt so quickly to the four-fold increase in the price of crude oil in 1973, was because they alone amongst the big oil companies had foreseen the possibility. They had used a technique called scenario planning, which was developed in Shell Francaise at the end of the 1960s, and was introduced to Shell's Group Planning Division by Pierre Wack. Shell encouraged decentralized management to make strategic decisions throughout its world-wide operations, but true to the command-and-control paradigm of the time, they were co-ordinated through a sophisticated planning system. The planning system aimed to balance the flow of products from the oil wells in the Middle East to their retail outlets around the world, and in the 1960s it all depended on a particular forecast of world economic growth. Shell realized that if the world changed and the forecast was wrong, decentralized strategic decision-making would result in anarchy. The Group Planning Division therefore started moving away from producing single forecasts, which managers were expected to work to, and began instead to produce multiple scenarios. As you can imagine, the managers at first felt insecure and let down by the planners who, managers felt, were shirking their main responsibility. Gerard Fairtlough was chief executive of Shell Chemicals at the time; he was outraged. Here's what he had to say (1994):

> How could we put forward our business plans to the group's central office unless we had something firm to work with? And why did there have to be this expensive planning set-up in the centre, if it wasn't going to help me, if the planners were going to take away my security blanket?

However, it did not take him long to see the rationale:

> ... it might actually be more useful to my part of the Shell group than official forecasts of growth rates, forecasts which I knew in my heart would probably turn out to be wrong. I began to see

that this new approach was not, in fact, one of abdication, but rather one which treated Shell's managers as adults. I decided that I was grown up and I could do without my security blanket.

As a result, Shell's managers became more aware of the uncertainty they were living with, and were able to keep in mind different possibilities when deciding on new plant and levels of stock. Thus when the oil shock eventually arrived in October 1973, Shell was prepared and coped with it better than any other big oil company.

It seems therefore that in an increasingly uncertain world, we should produce more forecasts rather than less, to produce multiple forecasts for multiple scenarios in place of just one officially approved forecast. For the multi-skilled self-managed team operating in an inform-and-entrust environment, forecasting is perhaps even more important than it has ever been before. Team members who share responsibility for performance and results cannot avoid responsibility for forecasts too. In discussing and debating likely futures, teams will communicate more effectively when they have a shared understanding of the simpler techniques for analysing and synthesizing data.

For instance, we all know what a moving average is – or if not we can easily find out from a book on business statistics. But there are many different ways in which a moving average can be used, and we probably differ in our views on how valuable the technique is. Once again, as in Chapter 6, the purpose here is not to help you develop your skill in their use. For that you should turn to a good, basic book on quantitative methods in business, such as Morris (1993) or Curwin and Slater (1994). Our purpose here is to describe the relevance and value of the techniques.

Moving averages

Edward Lorenz used the butterfly effect to illustrate the inherent unpredictability of the weather. Yet we still listen to weather forecasts for the next day or two, and they are usually right. However we now know that long-range weather or business forecasting is entirely pointless, but short-term forecasts work very well most of the time. In fact they work so well that suppliers routinely use short term demand forecasts to determine the level of stock to carry. For instance Unipart uses moving averages to track the demand for each of many thousands of car parts they supply. The calculations are embedded in their stock control software, and the results are used to compute when and how much to re-order. Without this kind of forecasting Unipart would have to carry higher levels of stock and employ more stock controllers which would add significantly to their costs.

It is this 'next-period' type of short-term forecasting for which moving averages are most useful – to estimate demand for the next day, week or month. Later we will review how they are also used to help spot trends and trend reversals.

Simple moving averages for next-period forecasting

We all use the past as a guide to the future: we call it experience. But we also know that experience gets out of date – recent experience is more relevant than older experience. And it is this principle which justifies using a moving average as a forecast. But why use an average? Why not just take the most recently recorded value and use that as a forecast? This is indeed the right thing to do in some circumstances, despite being very simple and unsophisticated. Figure 9.1 shows how it might work. Here we see a series of values charted against time – a time series. The values are the sales of a product which change from month to month, to produce a fairly smooth trace, but the trend alters now and then. In the first stage, sales are constant and the forecast is almost error free. Then in the mid stage, sales rise and the forecast responds quickly, lagging only one month behind as it tracks the rising price trend. And finally when the trend dips down again, the forecast reflects this fully the following month.

Month	Sales (1000's)	Forecast (1000's)
N	10.4	
D	10.9	10.4
J	10.5	10.9
F	10.5	10.5
M	11.0	10.5
A	10.6	11.0
M	11.3	10.6
J	11.4	11.3
J	12.3	11.4
A	12.5	12.3
S	13.1	12.5
O	12.7	13.1
N	11.6	12.7
D	11.4	11.6
J		11.4

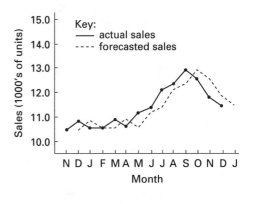

Trace of forecasted sales matches trace of actual sales, but is offset to the right by one month.

Figure 9.1 *The naive, or last-period forecast*

This is called the last-period, or naive forecasting method, and it works well for the type of data shown in the chart above. But let's see what happens with another more volatile time series, the sales of a product which fluctuate from month to month, Figure 9.2. This time the naive forecast is wrong-footed nearly every month. When the forecast goes up, the sales go down, and vice-versa. Under these circumstances it pays to look at more than just last month's sales, and take an average of the last two or more months, Figure 9.3. Then the line on the chart joining the forecasts traces a smoother path through the middle of the fluctuating monthly sales. The forecast is never completely wrong-footed, but follows the general trend. But when a new sales trend emerges, it takes a little longer to respond. A three-month moving average takes three months to reflect in full the new direction sales are taking. Even when sales start to fall, the moving average carries on rising for a while.

Month	Sales (1000's)	Forecast (1000's)
N	11.2	
D	13.3	11.2
J	11.6	13.3
F	12.7	11.6
M	12.0	12.7
A	14.1	12.0
M	12.4	14.1
J	14.7	12.4
J	13.7	14.7
A	14.6	13.7
S	14.7	14.6
O	12.7	14.7
N	13.2	12.7
D	11.8	13.2
J		11.8

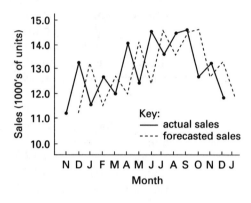

Volatile data wrong-foots the naive forecast nearly every time

Figure 9.2   *Why the naive forecasting method is wrong for volatile data*

We therefore have two conflicting requirements of our forecast. We want it to respond quickly to new trends as they emerge, but we want it to ignore transient fluctuations. But when a new sales figure deviates from the trend, how can you tell whether it is the beginning of a new trend, or just a transient fluctuation? The pattern only becomes clear later on, and there is no way of telling in advance. We want smoothing and response, but we cannot have both in full measure. If we use more months in our moving average, we get more smoothing but slow response. With fewer months we get less smoothing but fast response. Sometimes either the trend or the fluctuations predominate in our data – as in the carefully chosen examples shown in Figures 9.1 and 9.2. In the first example we needed response, and in the second, smoothing. But more often than not both types of variation occur, which calls for a bit of both, a compromise – some response and some smoothing.

The balance between response and smoothing is often a difficult choice. It is a bit like choosing between a sports car and a limousine. The sports car offers fast response but a hard ride, whereas the limo offers a smooth ride at the expense of poorer response. As time goes by however, car designers have found ways of offering both – for those who can afford it. And attempts have been made to do the same with forecasting, by using 'weighted' moving averages.

Month	Sales (1000's)	Total (T) of last 3 months sales	3 month moving average forecast (T ÷ 3)
N	11.2		
D	13.3		
J	11.6		
F	12.7	36.1	12.0
M	12.0	37.6	12.5
A	14.1	36.3	12.1
M	12.4	38.8	12.9
J	14.7	38.5	12.8
J	13.7	41.2	13.7
A	14.6	40.8	13.6
S	14.7	43.0	14.3
O	12.7	43.0	14.3
N	13.2	42.0	14.0
D	11.8	40.6	13.5
J		37.7	12.6

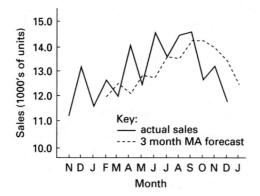

Figure 9.3   *How to do a three-month moving average forecast*

Weighted moving averages for next-period forecasting

Experience has a limited shelf-life. We should therefore take more account of the most recent month in the three-month average than of the other two months. This we can do by weighting differently the sales in each of the three months , before adding them up and dividing to find the average. A common way of producing a weighted three-month moving average is to multiply the latest sales by three, the next latest by two and the oldest by one – then dividing by six to find the average. In effect we are taking three of the latest, two of the middle, and one of the oldest figure, making six figures in all, so that is why we divide by six. Thus the latest sales have the most influence on the value of the forecast.

Another way of looking at it is that the forecast is made up by adding together three sixths of the latest sales, two sixths of the middle month's sales and one sixth of the oldest sales. You can see therefore that the latest sales have as much influence on the forecast as the other two sales figures together. Three-sixths, or half of the latest sales goes into the forecast, compared to only one-sixth of the oldest sales.

The net effect of weighting like this is to increase the response and reduce the smoothing. If you are now left with too little smoothing, you can use a four month weighted moving average, with weightings of 4, 3, 2 and 1. You would need then to divide by 4 + 3 + 2 + 1, which comes to the nice round number 10. Thus the latest price would only make up four-tenths or 40 per cent of the forecast – rather less than the three-sixths or half used before. The influence of the latest price is reduced, lowering the response and increasing the smoothing.

Striking the right balance between smoothing and response with these weighted moving averages starts to get complicated, especially if you use five or six or more prices in your average. It is not easy to judge the right weightings for a particular smoothing requirement, and it is very difficult to change the balance once you have been using a particular weighting for a while. However the good news is there is another type of weighted moving average which overcomes all these problems. It is called the exponentially weighted moving average, or more commonly, exponential smoothing.

Exponential smoothing for next-period forecasting

It is not immediately obvious, but this is in fact a weighted moving average, as we shall see in due course. It's a breeze to calculate – all you need is three values to produce the next forecast: the last forecast, the last actual sales and a constant called alpha.

The alpha constant is a figure between zero and one, which can be thought of as a proportion rather like a probability figure. You might find it helpful to think of alpha as a response factor, because if alpha is 1, the forecast comes out identical to a last-period, naive forecast – that is, 100 per cent response and no smoothing. But if alpha is set at zero, the forecast comes out as a horizontal line on the graph – a fixed value not responding in the slightest to any change in the actual sales – in other words, zero response and infinitely smoothed. Let us use for this example a response factor (alpha value) of 0.6, to give slightly more response than smoothing.

The other two values you need are the last forecast and the last actual sales. With these you can find the forecast error last month. Just subtract the forecast from the actual sales, so for instance if the forecast was 22 sales and the actual was 27, the forecast was too low by 5 sales. To get the forecast for next month, all we do is add to the last forecast a proportion of the error, to bring it up a bit, because it was too low before. How much of the error should be added? That's right, you guessed it: 0.6 or 60% of the error should be added, if you are using 0.6 as your response factor (alpha).

Month	S Sales (1000's)	E Last period error (E = S − F)	A Adjustment (A = E × α)	F Forecast (= $\frac{\text{previous}}{\text{forecast}}$ + A)
N	11.2			(10)
D	13.3	1.2	0.7	10.7
J	11.6	2.6	1.6	12.3
F	12.7	−0.7	−0.4	11.9
M	12.0	0.8	0.5	12.4
A	14.1	−0.4	−0.2	12.2
M	12.4	1.9	1.1	13.3
J	14.7	−0.9	−0.5	12.8
J	13.7	1.9	1.1	13.9
A	14.6	−0.2	−0.1	13.8
S	14.7	0.8	0.5	14.3
O	12.7	0.4	0.2	14.5
N	13.2	−1.8	−1.1	13.4
D	11.8	−0.2	−0.1	13.3
J		−1.5	−0.9	12.4

NB: A previous forecast is needed to start the forecasting calculations.
So, an arbitrary value of 10 for F (in brackets) is put in the right-hand
column of the table. Its effect is negligible after 3 or 4 months.

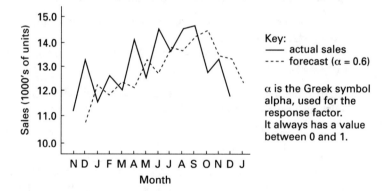

Figure 9.4   *How to do an exponential moving average forecast*

We can summarize it all in a formula:

New forecast = (last forecast) + (forecast error) × (response factor)

So using our example figures, we get:

New forecast = 22 + 5 × 0.6

= 22 + 3

= 25

You can see now how the alpha factor works as a response factor. In
this case, 60 per cent of the error has been added to the last forecast,
bringing it more than halfway to what the actual sales were last
month. But if we used a factor of 1.0, then 100 per cent of the error
would be added, to produce a forecast equal to last month's actual

sales. And using last month's sales as this month's forecast is, of course, the last-period, or naive forecasting method which you no doubt remember, gives 100 per cent response and no smoothing. So we can change our limo into a sports car, or vice-versa by changing just one figure – the alpha value. In fact we can easily fine-tune the forecasting method to suit the particular characteristics of our data, by making small adjustments to the value of alpha, until we get the balance between smoothing and response just right for our needs.

Is exponential smoothing truly a weighted average? We can see that it is by re-arranging the formula we used for the new forecast. The following formula can easily be derived from the formula we used before:

New forecast = (alpha × last sales) + (1.0 – alpha) × (last forecast)

With an alpha factor of 0.6 the new forecast can therefore be found by taking 60% of the last sales and adding 40% of the last forecast:

New forecast = (0.6 × last sales) + (0.4 × last forecast)

But the last forecast also consisted of 60% last-but-one sales and 40% last-but-one forecast. So let's substitute this into the formula:

New forecast = (0.6 × Last sales) + (0.4 × 0.6 × last-but-one sales + 0.4 × 0.4 × last-but-one forecast)

= 60% last sales + 24% last-but-one sales + 16% last-but-one forecast.

And the last-but-one forecast can also be split down into part earlier sales and part earlier forecast:

New forecast = 60% last sales + 24% last-but-one sales + 10% last-but-two sales + 6% last-but-two forecast.

At this stage in our analysis, 94% of the new forecast is derived from a weighted average of previous sales, and only 6% from an earlier forecast. And even this 6% can be shown by the same analysis to consist mostly of even earlier actual sales.

A pattern emerges as we continue this process. Each new forecast consists of a string of earlier actual sales figures, weighted less and less as they slip back into the past, plus a vanishing part of a very old forecast. Therefore, exponential smoothing truly is a weighted moving average. In theory every earlier sales figure has an effect on the new forecast, but for most practical values of alpha, the influence of very old figures rapidly disappears after five or six periods. That is why it is called exponential smoothing – because the weighting of earlier sales declines exponentially, Figure 9.5.

To sum up then, exponential smoothing is so much better than other weighted moving averages that it is the only one you should ever consider using. However, there are circumstances in which it is inadvisable to use a weighted moving average – for instance when the data is seasonal.

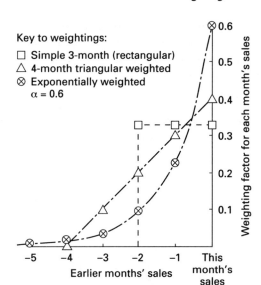

Figure 9.5 *The weightings compared for different types of moving average*

Moving averages for next-period forecasting of seasonal data

Weighted moving averages are a lousy way of forecasting seasonal sales. It's obvious why if we look at an example. Car sales in the UK are characterized by low sales in July. Potential customers put off buying until the new annual registration plates are available in August – and then they come back in force. So boom in August follows bust in July. Everyone knows this seasonal fluctuation, driven by the extra value of a car carrying the latest plates, will be repeated each year. Yet a weighted moving average will amplify the July dip in sales, to produce a low forecast for August, when sales will surely be high. It is wrong-footed in just the same way a last-period, naive forecast would be.

Simple moving averages are not much better either, except for one special type. When we discussed simple moving averages, we saw that the forecast becomes smoother as we increase the number of months in the moving average. A moving four-month average produces a smoother forecast than a three-month one. And five months is smoother than four. In other words, the greater the number of months you carry along in the moving average, the greater the smoothing effect. But this does not hold true for seasonal sales: the best smoothing is always achieved by using a twelve month moving average. Six months would be worse as you would expect, but so would eighteen months. The one and only special type of moving average you should use with seasonal data is the one which uses a complete year of data points – no more and no less. Then the average month is calculated from moving annual totals, each with a representative cross-section of seasons. Annual figures cannot be seasonal – a season is part of a year – and so by using annual figures all traces of seasonality are entirely removed. Again, a very simple example will make clear what happens.

A seed merchant sells seeds all year round, but the spring is when most people buy. Sales are 30 per cent above average in the spring quarter, and 10 per cent below average in the other three quarters. There is a consistent upward trend, and very little random variation, Figure 9.6.

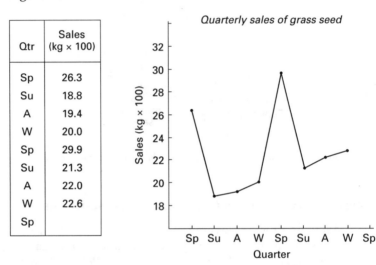

Qtr	Sales (kg × 100)
Sp	26.3
Su	18.8
A	19.4
W	20.0
Sp	29.9
Su	21.3
A	22.0
W	22.6
Sp	

Figure 9.6 *Seasonal sales for grass seed*

Now let's see what happens if we use a simple moving average of three different types: a three-quarter, a four-quarter and a five-quarter moving average, Figure 9.7. The three-quarter moving average does not always include the high spring sales. Three times a year it does, then the fourth time it doesn't. Autumn-Winter-Spring does, and so do both Winter-Spring-Summer, and Spring-Summer-Autumn. But Summer-Autumn-Winter doesn't, and so because it only sees the three low quarters, the average comes out low once a year. The three other averages all see two low and one high quarter which lifts these three averages above the fourth one. This is why, when charted, the three-quarter moving average dips down one quarter each year. And ironically the dip occurs for the quarter when the seasonal sales are high – in the spring quarter. The three-quarter average is not much good as a forecast, because it moves in the opposite direction to the actual sales for that quarter.

The four-quarter moving average always has a full, representative cross-section of the seasons: Autumn-Winter-Spring-Summer, then Winter-Spring-Summer-Autumn, and so on. Every average sees three

Qtr	Sales (kg × 100)	3-qtr MA	4-qtr MA	5-qtr MA
Sp	26.3			
Su	18.8			
A	19.4			
W	20.0	21.5		
Sp	29.9	19.4	21.1	
Su	21.3	23.1	22.0	22.9
A	22.0	23.7	22.7	21.9
W	22.6	24.4	23.3	22.5
Sp		22.0	24.0	23.2

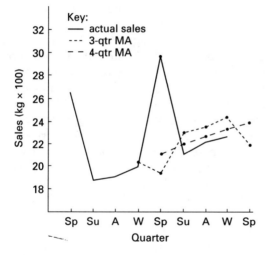

Figure 9.7 *Three-, four- and five-quarter moving averages*

low quarters and one high quarter, and so when the averages are charted, all seasonality is removed to leave just the underlying trend with no dips or peaks. This is better than having a dip where there should be a peak, but there is still room for improvement. We really want a peak in the forecast to coincide with the seasonal peak in the actual sales. We will see how this can be done soon, but first to see what happens with a five-quarter moving average, try plotting on the chart the four values in the right-hand column of the table in Figure 9.7.

You should see that the five-quarter moving average is not the answer. A year plus a quarter is used in the moving average, and by adding this extra quarter a seasonal element is added to the seasonality-free yearly sales. As the forecast rolls forward across the seasons, each of the quarters takes its turn as the extra quarter. For three forecasts in the year, the extra quarter is one of the lower quarters, but once a year it is the peak spring quarter. Thus when traced, the forecast is smooth up to and including the high spring quarter – then comes a delayed-reaction high forecast for the summer quarter. So, by increasing the number of quarters in the moving average, some seasonality has been re-introduced, to wrong-foot the forecast once again.

We must therefore return to the four-quarter moving average, from which all seasonality has been removed, and which in Figure 9.7 plots almost as a straight line. This de-seasonalized moving average is an accurate trend-adjusted forecast for the next period. But we want a forecast which follows the same seasonal pattern as the actual sales figures. The secret then is to adjust the de-seasonalized trend by superimposing on it the expected seasonal pattern. Thus the overall strategy is to analyse the historical sales figures separately for trend and for seasonality – then to combine these components again to synthesize a next-period sales figure.

The synthesis consists of two stages: find the seasonal index for the quarter in question, then multiply the smoothed forecast by this index. The forecast then behaves much more realistically. For instance, our seed merchant wants the Spring forecast to peak above the smoothed forecast, like the real sales will do, so what should be done is this. First find the average Spring sales over the last three years, then express this as a proportion of an 'average' of all quarters during the last three years, calculated as one-eighth of total sales for the two years. If the average Spring sales over the last two years were indeed 30 per cent above average, the index will come out at 1.3. Thus, the smoothed spring forecast should be multiplied by 1.3 to lift it 30 per cent above the trend.

The sales of many if not most products and services are affected to some extent by seasonality of demand. It will show through clearly for ice cream in summer, and toys just before Christmas, but may be insignificant for other products, for which trend changes and random effects are predominant.

Where seasonality is noticeable, there are two absolute rules for next-period forecasts: never use a weighted average, and always average over a whole year – that is, use four quarters, 12 months or 52 weeks in the moving average. Then you will ensure that you always have a representative cross-section of equally weighted seasons in each year of data that you average. Then when you chart the moving average for the next period, it will be entirely free of any seasonal influence, which must of course be re-introduced before it can be used as a sales forecast.

Moving averages to flag trend reversals

Trends are obviously important in arriving at accurate next-period forecasts. But trends don't last forever. Sooner or later a trend levels off or reverses. This does not matter too much for re-ordering photocopier paper or ball-point pens for the office – a correctly designed moving average should take it in its stride. There will only be a short lag before the forecast adjusts to the new trend.

But most businesses need to look further ahead than next month if they are to avoid getting caught by an economic down-turn. Some types of business are particularly sensitive to the irregular stop-go business cycles which dominate company fortunes. Retailers that order in advance non-essential or postponable products and services can suddenly find their customers staying away in droves when unemployment or interest rates start to rise. Unless they scale down their plans before a recession arrives, they can get badly caught with unsaleable products. Similarly they must increase their orders before the feel-good factor returns, to keep pace with accelerating demand.

Another example is the package holiday industry. Seven or eight years of good times may be followed by three or four thin years which will bring some less well-managed operators close to the brink. Often too close for some: the recession will have so depleted their reserves that when the bookings start flooding in again, rising costs and poor financial management lead to a cash crisis and failure. It used to happen so regularly in the UK that eventually the government stepped in and required holiday tour operators jointly to maintain a fund for reimbursing customers who lost their money when an operator went bust.

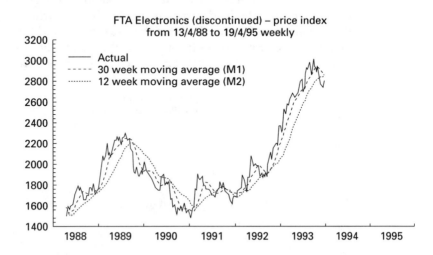

Figure 9.8   *The electronics sector share price index reveals a trade cycle. Source: Datastream*

Manufacturers face the same problem too, and some industrial sectors are particularly vulnerable. The electronics sector is notorious for being affected by trade cycles – as graphically revealed by the stock market electronics sector index, Figure 9.8. Companies making TVs, stereos and PCs enjoy burgeoning sales in the good times but languish when money is tight – and their share prices track their fluctuating fortunes. Silicon chips are a basic commodity in the industry. There are longish lead-times for scaling chip supply up or down, so, not surprisingly, the industrial market for chips is characterized by shortages and gluts which dramatically affect prices. This causes real problems for manufacturers of consumer electronics. In times of chip shortage and high market prices, there is the temptation to stock up – only to see the market turn a few months later. The manufacturer is then overstocked with high-price chips which, to make matters worse, have suddenly become cheap and abundant in the market.

Obviously therefore, trend reversals offer great potential for saving or making money. And nowhere is this more true than in the stock market. In fact there is a breed of analysts who spend all their time studying share price charts, watching trends and looking for reversals. They are called technical analysts, to distinguish them from the fundamental analysts who study the business of companies to form an opinion on their longer-term viability and profitability. Technical analysts are mostly highly skilled computer scientists and mathematicians, and many of them originally came to the financial sector from the aerospace industry – which explains why they are often referred to as rocket scientists. One method they use is to calculate two simple moving average forecasts of a share price, a 30-day and an 80-day perhaps. Of course the 30-day average is less smooth, but responds quicker than the 80-day average. On a rising trend therefore, the 80-day lags below the 30-day, which lags below the actual price, Figure 9.9. But if the price peaks and then begins to fall, the share price crosses through the 30-day, and the 30-day crosses down through the 80-day average, which takes longer to respond fully

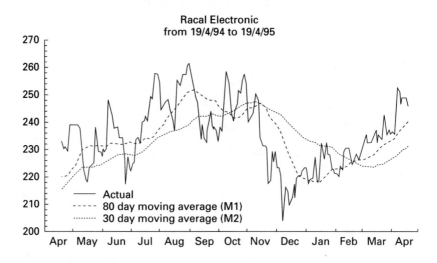

Figure 9.9   *How to use moving averages to flag share price trend reversals. Source: Datastream*

to the new trend. These cross-over points are seen by technical analysts as 'sell' signals. There are also corresponding 'buy' signals which occur soon after a trough in the share price. When a short average crosses up through a longer average, it is called a golden cross, and when it crosses down through the longer average, it is called a dead cross.

Computer programs can be written to trigger orders to buy and sell based on rules such as these, but if it was that easy, we'd all be rich. The problem is the share price can move sideways via a series of short up and down oscillations. Then the program will trigger a series of buy and sell commands, racking up dealing costs each time, but not making any appreciable capital gain. Nevertheless, the technique is still useful. It is another perspective on the data, which along with other background information, may help the knowledge worker to make more timely purchasing and selling decisions.

I have tried to explain moving averages in a non-mathematical way, to help your understanding of the techniques and help you form an opinion on their usefulness. But it's a bit like reading a book on ice skating, or brain surgery. Just reading such books is not enough. You may know in theory what to do, but you wouldn't be able to do much in the ice rink or operating theatre without practising first. It's the same with moving averages and the other numerical techniques. If you really want to know how they behave, get a computer spreadsheet such as Microsoft Excel and play around with the different methods. Remember Kolb's learning cycle: doing is essential to learning. Get some real sales figures from your company, or some real share prices and see if you can develop a useful method of forecasting for the next period. There are some suggestions below for you to practice with, before we move on to the next chapter in which we will see how sales forecasts are used as the basis for cash-flow forecasting and investment appraisal.

Pause for thought

1   How good is your next-period forecasting at work? Do you monitor the forecast error? Is there room for improvement? What method do you currently use to generate next-period forecasts? Is your data seasonal?

2   Is your business affected by cycles in trade, or business confidence, or interest rates? How do you know when to start gearing up after a slack period? Do you use moving averages to help confirm trend reversals? Do you know anyone who seems to have an uncanny knack of knowing whether sales will be up or down by the end of the month? Have you asked them how they do it? Is it a quality of leadership to be right more often than wrong about the future?

References and further reading

Gleick, J. (1987) *Chaos. Making a new science.* Abacus.

Fairtlough, G. (1994) *Creative Compartments – A design for future organisation.* Adamantine Press.

Morris, C. (1993) *Quantitative Approaches in Business Studies* (3rd edn). Pitman.

Curwin, J. and Slater, R. (1994) *Quantitative Methods for Business Decisions.* Chapman and Hall

10 When will the money come in?

Why read this chapter?

You can run a business unprofitably for months – or years if it is not haemorrhaging cash. But run out of cash and you'll be stopped dead in your tracks, instantly. Without cash, you cannot pay your employees, your rent, or bills for essential materials and services. Just as scuba divers monitor their air supply, self-managing teams operating as business units must monitor their cash position to know in advance if the cash is running out. Knowing six months in advance that you might be short by £100,000 is a solvable problem, but being surprised by the discovery that you are already short by that amount may be fatal.

In this chapter we will see how a sales forecast, perhaps produced with the techniques in Chapter 9, can be converted into a cash forecast. This is done by taking the current value of the cash balance on hand, and updating it month by month into the future, according to the positive flows of sales revenue which might be expected if the sales forecast holds good, and the negative flows of costs which might similarly be expected. You can read elsewhere how an aggregate cash-flow forecast is routinely produced as part of the accounting function, but potential investors in a particular project also expect a separate cash-flow forecast just for that project. This makes it possible to estimate how soon the project will pay back the original investment, and what profit the project will then start to generate beyond the payback period. When funds are limited, as they always are, investors use this analysis to choose between alternative proposals for their funds.

A cash-flow forecast is therefore an essential part of any project proposal or business plan, and all team members must know how to construct one if they are to contribute to the self-management of the team.

How to persuade investors to lend you money

Do you want to borrow £10? I'll lend it to you any time.

Do you want to borrow £10,000? I'll gladly lend you that too. But I need to be sure I will get all my money back, plus enough interest too. So how are you going to convince me on those two counts? Offer me security for the loan if that's possible but if not, we must talk. Can I trust you? Are you are honest and capable? Or are you about to lose everything on a foolhardy venture?

Good, close communication is the key here. If you cannot offer security, an arms-length deal is unlikely to succeed unless you can find a rich, trusting gambler – and they are an endangered species. The lender must trust the borrower, and trust depends on free and open communication. You no doubt remember from Chapter 4 how openness and trust can form a self-reinforcing virtuous circle, an example of a Peter Senge positive feedback system. So if you are a team co-ordinator in an inform-and-entrust environment and you need money for a project, put yourself in the lender's shoes. Ask yourself 'What would I need to know before I would be prepared to lend to this team?' Then set out to deliver in full the information any lender needs. The big lenders – banks, investors and the like – need the same information you would do: information to estimate the risk and return on the proposal. Initially the business plan is the medium for this. Lenders also need to be kept informed on progress throughout the life of the project – a subject we will return to later. But for now, let us concentrate on the business plan, and in particular that key element, the cash-flow forecast.

Cash-flow forecasting

Business plans which require external funding usually look more than a year into the future, because projects often take longer than that to pay back the original investment. But we have already seen that the business environment, like the weather, is inherently unpredictable, which make forecasting impossible beyond the short term. However despite the weather, ships ply the oceans of the world year-in and year-out, sometimes delayed but seldom failing to reach their objectives. So apparently even in a chaotic and unpredictable environment it is still possible to reach specific objectives which lie beyond the forecasting horizon. Taking the shipping analogy a stage further, we should remember it is only recently that sailing the oceans has become less risky, partly because today's powered ships are less vulnerable than the old wooden sailing ships. But short-term forecasts and longer-term plans are still important in estimating and controlling risk. And this is true for business as well as for shipping.

But exactly what is the purpose of the cash-flow forecast around which the business plan is constructed? And how can we justify a forecast which looks ahead more than a year, when we know it is impossible to predict with any accuracy what will happen that far into the future? Its purpose is to set a heading to steer by – both initially and also later when we get blown off course. So is it a forecast, or would it be more accurate to describe it as a plan? It certainly contains elements of both, and perhaps it would be more appropriate to call it a plan, because it has more in common with materials requirement planning for instance, than it does with weather forecasting. Materials requirement planning (MRP) is a computer routine for ordering the materials and parts needed to keep an assembly line running at the right speed to match demand. The routine requires an agreed schedule of how many finished products should be assembled each week for the next six or nine months, based on the sales forecast. Then the computer works backwards in time from this final assembly schedule, to make sure the materials and parts are ordered early enough to be ready for assembly in each future week.

The purpose of the cash-flow forecast is to do the same thing for cash that MRP does for materials. MRP makes sure we don't run out of materials, and cash-flow forecasting makes sure we don't run out of cash. It works backwards from the sales forecast to find what cash outflow is likely each month through paying wages and the other costs of delivering these sales to customers. It also estimates what cash inflow is likely from these customers when they pay for their purchases. Then it subtracts the outflow from the inflow to calculate the net cash flow each month. And finally it adjusts the amount in the current account by the net cash flow each month to make sure the borrowing limit will not be exceeded, Figure 10.1.

Cash-flow projection for new product launch

Assumptions:
Unit sales price: £100.
Payment received for sales: one month in arrears.
Interest rate on negative balance: 1% per month, quarterly in arrears.
Borrowing limit: £15,000.

Month	Jan	Feb	Mar	April	May
Sales volume in units			20	50	100
INCOME:					
Sales revenue				2,000	5,000
Other income	200	300	400	400	500
TOTAL INCOME	200	300	400	2,400	5,500
EXPENDITURE:					
Raw materials	5,000				
Wages	2,000	2,000	2,000	2,000	2,200
Other costs	300	300	300	300	300
Interest charges				272	
TOTAL EXPENDITURE	7,300	2,300	2,300	2,572	2,500
NET CASH FLOW	(7,100)	(2,000)	(1,900)	(172)	3,000
Opening balance	0	(7,100)	(9,100)	(11,000)	(11,172)
Closing balance	(7,100)	(9,100)	(11,000)	(11,172)	(8,172)

NB: Negative flows and balances shown in brackets.

Figure 10.1 *Example of a cash-flow forecast*

But isn't this exactly the kind of detailed forecasting that chaos theory suggests is impossible? Well yes it is – and that is why MRP computer routines are re-run every week to take account of the latest changes in demand. In fact the re-run is unlikely to change the plans for next week by much, but further ahead the plans become less reliable, and susceptible to change each time the routine is re-run. Thus as we look further ahead, reliable short-term plans gradually merge into less reliable, longer-term forecasts. But if MRP must be re-run each week, by the same token the cash-flow forecast should also be regularly re-run. So why include a cash-flow forecast in a business plan if it will be seriously out of date only a few months after the start of the project?

The answer is that cash is so important to the survival of even the soundest of projects that it would be foolhardy to ignore it in the planning process. Before a new project starts, we may have little experience to go on, and the projected cash flow will not be a forecast we can have much faith in. It should just show what we might realistically expect the cash situation to be, in each of the months ahead.

Cash is important to the success of any business, as lack of it will kill a business quicker than lack of profits. Clearly the cash-flow projection is fundamental to the business plan, and it can be used in a variety of ways throughout the life of a project:

● to simulate different scenarios while initially developing the project proposal,
● to communicate the project proposal as an investment opportunity, and
● to monitor and control the cash position during the life of the project.

Simulating different scenarios

We have already discussed in Chapter 7 how writing down a proposal in the form of a business plan helps to focus and refine initial ideas. The cash-flow plan forces difficult decisions into the open. Exactly how much cash is needed, and exactly how and when will it be spent? What sales revenue is expected, and when will it be likely to come in? Usually the outflows are easier to pin down: they are up-front and certain. The inflows are just the reverse – delayed and less certain in size and timing. By preparing the cash-plan as a computer spreadsheet, it is easy to try 'what-if' games. What if interest rates go up a couple of percentage points? Or three? Or five? What if sales demand is twice that expected? Or half? What effects will these changes make to the bottom line, individually or in combination? In other words, the spreadsheet makes it possible to gauge the sensitivity of the proposal to uncontrollable factors in the environment. The cash-flow plan is a model of the proposal, which can be subjected to different simulated conditions, so the proposers can develop a feel for how the proposal may work out in reality. If they find it too sensitive to interest rate changes, they can modify the proposed funding to make it less sensitive. The business plan could contain more than one cash-flow plan: a most likely scenario, together with a pessimistic and an optimistic scenario, complete with contingency plans to cover these less likely alternative scenarios. Used in this way, the cash-flow plan helps the proposers develop a better quality plan, one with improved chances of success.

Communicating with lenders

In communicating the proposal to a potential lender, the cash-flow plan can be the key medium for convincing financial specialists, and can be a focus for discussion. An enlightened lender will certainly not expect the cash-flow plan to work out exactly as specified in the proposal. The lender will probably look for the results of any spreadsheet sensitivity analysis performed on the cash-flow plan, and will be reassured by evidence that such analysis has been performed, and alternative scenarios considered.

If a lender wishes to monitor a big project more closely, it may be appropriate for the borrower to send revised cash-flow plans to keep the lender up to date on progress. It is much better to maintain close links with lenders, so each can trust the other side. This is especially important when things start to go wrong. If a lender saves up the bad news until it cannot be hidden any more, the news will come as an unpleasant shock at a time when it may be too late to do much about the situation. In any event, whoever is responsible for monitoring the project financially, they will certainly use the cash-flow plan as a standard against which to judge progress.

It is important to remember that borrowers and lenders have different perspectives. Borrowers want the money so they can do something practical with it – make a new product or sell a new service – whereas lenders just want somewhere to put their money so it will bring an adequate return, without too much risk involved. Each is looking at a different end of the value chain, so for trust to develop it is important for each to try to see the proposal from the other's perspective. Lenders always have more than one proposal to consider for the use of their money, and it is important for a borrower to understand how lenders choose between different alternatives. Then the borrower can adjust the whole proposal – not just the cash flow – to a form which will compare favourably with other competing proposals, and thus be more likely to attract funding.

One method very widely used by financial professionals for comparing different investment opportunities is a technique called 'discounting'. This is an extremely versatile method which produces a single-figure measure of the value of any project to an investor. Discounting makes it possible for lenders to compare widely differing types of investment opportunity.

Discounting techniques for comparing investments

For every borrower, there must be a lender. The purpose of this section is to help you understand the perspective of lenders, so you gain an insight into what they look for in an investment proposal.

As a reader of this book, you are unlikely to have much experience of lending large amounts of spare cash. You are more likely to be a net borrower, with a family and a mortgage. You probably have insurance cover for emergencies, a credit card for short-term borrowing, and a savings account for your holidays or a new car. But apart from your pension, you probably haven't the need to do much financial planning beyond the next year or two. When you put money aside for a holiday, you probably put it in your savings account, and in effect, you are lending it to the bank or building society that operates the account. To get the best value, you simply lend to the account which offers the highest interest rate. But banks and other professional lenders in the money markets face rather more difficult choices than this, because they lend money to business people who put forward a business plan and cash-flow projection instead of quoting an interest rate.

The money markets

Open a copy of the *Financial Times*, and you will be presented with a bewildering array of opportunities to borrow and to lend. There are long- and short-term opportunities, high and low interest rates, large and small sums, and risky or safe investments. But for all of these, the one common criterion which can be used for comparing them is the interest rate. When any loan is made, it is expected there will be a repayment of rather more than the amount loaned. Otherwise, who would bother lending? In theory this extra amount is payment in recompense for three things: for loss of access to the money, for loss of value of the money due to inflation, and for the expected loss from exposure to risk.

For loss of access to the money, the lender should receive a percentage at least equal to the interest the money would have earned if instead it had been stored safely and accessibly on deposit – for instance with a major clearing bank.

For loss of value due to inflation, the lender should also receive a percentage to make up for the loss in buying power expected during the period of the loan.

For loss due to exposure to risk, the lender should additionally receive a percentage based on the probability and size of the risk. This is often impossible to calculate with any degree of accuracy, but the greater the perceived risk, the higher the interest payment which will be needed to persuade lenders to part with their money.

In practice however, the setting of interest rates is not nearly so clear cut. Rates are influenced by supply and demand in the money markets, and the levels of risk perceived by the markets can be quite volatile. However, it can be useful to compare the interest rate on a risky investment against the rate offered on risk-free investments such as deposit accounts. The difference between the two is the risk premium – the extra interest paid to compensate for the risk. But to compare investments like this, the interest rate must be calculated the same way in each case. The method used throughout the money markets is based on discounting, which allows for the time value of money.

The time value of money

'In the long-run, we are all dead.' These unforgettable words from John Maynard Keynes, the economist, vividly captured the idea of the time value of money – that a benefit postponed is worth less than the same benefit enjoyed now. If you were offered the choice of £100 now, or £100,000 eighty years from now, you would take the £100 – right?

But less extreme choices can be awkward to resolve. Suppose the choice is between £100 now, or £120 two years from now. Remember, we are talking about investment money here, so choose only on the basis of efficiency. Your changing personal needs now and in the future must not affect the decision, so forget that your washing machine has finally given up the ghost and you need the money now more than you will in a couple of years when your son will have left home. And you don't need to consider risk either. The figures are guaranteed.

A logical approach would be to see how much £100 will be worth if you invest it for two years. Let's suppose you can put the money on deposit at 10 per cent per annum, and you don't touch the interest payments but immediately reinvest them (10 per cent may be unrealistic for a deposit account, but it makes the figures easier to understand.) The £100 will be worth £110 after the first year. Then this £110 invested during the second year will earn a further £11 interest to become £121. It is that old compound interest calculation you learned at school – remember? It's easy using your calculator: just multiply by 1.10 a couple of times. The original £100 grows to become £121 after two years. So at an interest rate of 10 per cent, we can say that £100 now, is the same as, or is equivalent to £121 two years from now. So we can reason that two years from now, you will be £1 better off if you take the £100 now, rather than wait two years for the £120.

What we did here was to compound the £100 forwards in time, to find its future value two years from now. We are only able to assume that £100 now is the same as £121 in two years time because the money markets make it possible through risk-free deposit accounts for anyone to exchange the one for the other. The risk-free interest rate actually available at any time, plays a fundamental role: it determines the time value of money, and therefore provides the basis for appraising investments and assessing risk.

Compounding forwards to the future versus discounting backwards to the present

Compounding forwards is easy to understand, but raises some problems, especially if you need to compare two investments, one which matures in two years, say, and the other in five years. You could of course assume that the proceeds of the two-year investment will be put on deposit for a further three years. Then you could compound them forwards to the same point in time five years from now. The difficulty then is in understanding correctly the difference between the two investments, because it is measured in what amounts to a foreign currency – future pounds. If the difference is £50 five years from now, how many loaves of bread will that buy then?

It would be much better if we could work with the currency we are familiar with – our present-day pound. And that is what discounting is all about: it just puts the compounding calculation into reverse, to convert future pounds back into present-day pounds. When we compounded forward, we assumed a risk-free interest rate of 10 per cent, and so multiplied by a factor of 1.10 for each year. So, to discount we simply divide instead – it's just as easy to do with your calculator. For instance to discount back the sum of £121 to the present from two years in the future, all you do is divide by 1.10 a couple of times. So, dividing £121 by 1.10 once, reduces it to £110. Then dividing it by 1.10 again, reduces it to £100. Each time we divide by 1.10 we bring the value back a year. Dividing by 1.10 has the effect of removing interest payments at the rate of 10 per cent per annum, a year at a time until we get back to the present day.

As well as being easier to understand, working with present values has another big advantage. Because all amounts are in the same currency so to speak, future receipts can be totalled along with present expenditure, to calculate the net present value of an investment.

Net present value of an investment

Investing means paying money now, to secure more money in the future. If you get the chance to put £100 in an investment which grows to £150 in two years, you might be tempted to say you will make £50 on the deal. But that would not be right, would it? It makes no more sense to subtract present pounds from future pounds than it does to subtract Deutschmarks from Lire. We should work in the currency of today's pounds and subtract the present price of £100 from the present value of £150 two years hence. If we once again assume a base-line rate of 10 per cent interest available on deposit accounts, we can discount the £150 two years hence, back to present value by dividing it by 1.10 a couple of times. We find that it has a present value of £124 (give or take a few pence). Now we can subtract the present cost of the investment, to conclude the investment opportunity has a net present value (NPV) of £24.

So how should we interpret this £24? There are several ways:

- in this simple example, it is the amount you must add to your original £100 on deposit in order to have £150 two years from now, or more generally –
- it is the present value of the future difference between £150 two years from now and what £100 on deposit will grow to by then. We found earlier that £100 at 10 per cent grows to £121 in two years, which is less than £150 by £29. Discount this future £29 back to present value by dividing by 1.10 a couple of times, and what do you get? That's right, £24.
- it is the present value of the extra return you hope to get for putting your money at risk, instead of keeping it safely earning the risk-free interest rate offered by a deposit account.

Whichever way you look at it, the net present value of £24 is the extra value in today's pounds of the £150 opportunity, over what anyone can get, risk free, by putting their money on deposit. Which allows us to address the next issue: what is the risk involved with the £150 opportunity? And is the premium of £24 enough to make it worth carrying this risk? But this is a whole new can of worms which you can read about in specialist books on investment, under the heading of portfolio theory.

Calculating net present value for practical projects

This is where we bring together the different elements of the project or business plan, and reduce them to a single-figure measure of the return on the venture. From the sales forecast we develop a cash-flow forecast, from which we can then calculate the net present value of the project. This is useful information for potential investors, because it is the extra value that the project offers, measured in present-day pounds, beyond what is available from leaving the money on deposit, where it is safe. Alternatively instead of working out the NPV it can often be more appropriate to present the return as a percentage. Later we will see how to do this, but first let us see how to calculate the NPV for a typical project which requires an initial down-payment or outflow, followed by a stream of future returns or inflows.

For example, Hardnfast Ltd are toolmakers who heat-treat tools for the engineering industry. Their ovens are heated by electricity, and are expensive to run. Hardnfast realize they can make savings by converting them to gas. They prepare a project proposal with a detailed cash-flow projection which shows the total cost of the project will be £10,000 all told, including indirect costs such as loss of profit while the ovens are out of service. The net savings in operating costs from using cheaper fuel, including indirect savings which arise from the project, such as a quicker oven cycle-time, come to £4,000 per annum for the next four years, after which the ovens will be worthless and will be scrapped and replaced.

The cashflows at the end of each year are therefore expected to be as shown in Figure 10.2.

End of year	0	1	2	3	4
Actual cash flows	−10,000	+4,000	+4,000	+4,000	+4,000

Figure 10.2   *The cash-flow forecast*

The figures in this annual cash flow projection are derived from the monthly cash flow forecast in the project proposal. When the Technical Representative from the supplier of the gas conversion kits sees the figures he is enthusiastic, and quickly points out that the project will break even in two and a half years, and from the £16,000 total revenue produces a profit of £6,000. However, the managing director of Hardnfast understands the time value of money on deposit at 10 per cent per annum. He adds some extra working to the table and discounts each of the future savings back to present value, Figure 10.3.

End of year	0	1	2	3	4	
Actual cash flows	−10,000	+4,000	+4,000	+4,000	+4,000	
Cash flows discounted to present value at 10% p.a.	−10,000	$+\dfrac{4{,}000}{1.10}$	$+\dfrac{4{,}000}{(1.10)^2}$	$+\dfrac{4{,}000}{(1.10)^3}$	$+\dfrac{4{,}000}{(1.10)^4}$	
NPV	−10,000	+3,636	+3,306	+3,005	+2,732	= 2,680

Figure 10.3   *The cash-flow for the Hardnfast project discounted at 10 per cent p.a.*

Using present values for the future cash flows, he finds the savings from the first three years come to £9,948 and are not quite enough to cover the original cost of the project. The payback period therefore, is just over three years, not two and a half years.

Also, the net present value for the project only comes to £2,680, not £6,000. Putting £10,000 on the project brings only £2,680 more present value than leaving it on deposit – not such a big reward for exposing it to risk for three years. What if interest rates go up and thus further devalue future savings? What if gas prices go up, reducing the cost advantage of gas over electricity? And above all, can he justify spending the valuable knowledge, creativity and problem-solving skills of his production and engineering teams on this unrewarding and potentially risky project? He decides to put the project on hold for a week, to investigate alternative projects for the limited finance and knowledge resources at his disposal.

He realizes it would be useful to express the return on this and other projects as a percentage rate, to compare them directly with each other and with the rate for money on deposit.

The discounted cash flow, or DCF rate of return

The return on a project may be expressed as a single net present value in pounds, but the NPV figure is not nearly so widely understood as the plain old percentage return on capital invested, which is the usual way that banks and money markets gauge investment opportunities. And this is the main disadvantage of the NPV – it does not allow us immediately to compare our internal project with any other external opportunity which will usually be expressed as a percentage return.

So how can we calculate the percentage return on the capital invested in our project? The problem is the cash flow for the Hardnfast project does not follow the usual pattern, in which interest payments are more clearly separated from the capital invested. When you put money on deposit, you invest your £10,000, say, and then collect interest payments regularly during the investment period, and then at the end you get your £10,000 back again. Under these circumstances, it is easy to calculate the percentage return each year. But in common with most practical projects, for the Hardnfast project the capital employed is not a fixed amount. It drops from £10,000 at the beginning of the first year, to zero near the end of the third year. And during the fourth year after the capital has all been paid back, there is still a substantial income from the project, and so in theory the return on capital is infinite for most of that year! Under these circumstances the normal way of calculating the percentage return won't work. So what we do instead is figure out what fixed annual rate of return would be needed on an external deposit account to produce over four years the same net present value from £10,000 as the internal Hardnfast project does. This figure is known as the discounted cash flow (DCF) return, or the internal rate of return (IRR) , to distinguish it from the return available on external investment opportunities.

How to calculate the DCF rate of return

The whole point of interest rates is to make it possible to compare the promised returns on different investments. And the base-line criterion against which all investments are judged is the risk-free interest rate available at the time, such as that offered by deposit accounts with the major clearing banks. And as you know, their interest rates are controlled by the rate charged by the Bank of England, which changes from time to time. When the Bank of England changes the base rate, it changes the time value of money, and there have been periods in the last century when base rates were very low – just two or three percent. Now imagine this scenario. Suppose interest rates fell to zero, so the clearing banks simply guaranteed the safekeeping of your money on deposit, without offering any interest. Money would have no time value, and £100 in the future would be worth the same as £100 now. Under these circumstances, the NPV for the Hardnfast project would be the full £6,000 difference between the future positive cash flows, and the initial negative flow of £10,000 put into the project. In other words all future sums are discounted by dividing by a factor of 1.00, which of course does not reduce their value at all when they are discounted back to the present.

But of course the risk-free interest rate is always greater than zero, and the greater it is, the smaller the present value of future sums. If interest rates continue to rise, the present value of the future cash flows for the Hardnfast project will continue to fall until at some point they are just equal to the initial investment. Then of course, the NPV for the project would be zero, and there would be no point in taking the money out of the deposit account and risking it on the Hardnfast project. We can therefore reason that because the Hardnfast project offers no advantage over leaving the money on deposit, they must both represent the same rate of return on the capital invested. The DCF return for the Hardnfast project is therefore the same as the base-line rate of return which would reduce its NPV to zero.

And that is how the DCF or internal rate of return on any project is actually calculated. You just find by trial and error the discounting rate which will reduce the net present value of the project to zero. You can see in Figure 10.4 how this might be done long-hand for the Hardnfast project. But for more complicated projects it is much easier using a spreadsheet such as Microsoft Excel. Call up the menu option Solver, and in no more than a few key presses and a few seconds it will calculate the internal rate of return – to several decimal places if that's what you want. However it is hard to imagine when you might need that degree of accuracy, given the wide margins of error inevitably built into the input data, which is forecasted sales, revenue, costs and interest rates for several years into the future. The DCF return for the Hardnfast project is 22 per cent to the nearest percentage point, so how should we interpret that?

End of year	0	1	2	3	4	NPV
Actual cash flows	−10,000	+4,000	+4,000	+4,000	+4,000	
PVs @ 10%	−10,000	+3,636	+3,306	+3,005	+2,732	+2,680
PVs @ 15%	−10,000	+3,478	+3,024	+2,630	+2,287	+1,419
PVs @ 20%	−10,000	+3,333	+2,777	+2,315	+1,929	+354
PVs @ 25%	−10,000	+3,200	+2,560	+2,048	+1,638	−554
PVs @ 22%	−10,000	+3,279	+2,687	+2,203	+1,806	−25

So, to the nearest percentage point, the discount rate which reduces the cash flow to a present value of zero, is 22%.

Figure 10.4 *An easy-to-understand way of calculating the DCF return for the Hardnfast project*

The advantages and limitations of the DCF return

On the simplest level, the 22 per cent earned on the Hardnfast project is better than the 10 per cent available on deposit, so that is a justification for transferring the money from deposit and into the project. However, an advantage of the DCF return method is that it is the method used by the banks and money markets, and it can be used to compare the returns on widely different types of investment. So long as you can estimate the future cash flows for the project in the form of initial negative flows followed by subsequent positive flows, you can calculate the DCF return. When you compare the 22 per cent available on the Hardnfast project with the 10 per cent available on the deposit account, you are comparing like with like. The two per-centages are calculated the same way, using the discounting method which for many years has enjoyed the official approval of financial and accounting professionals. It is for instance the same way your building society or bank calculates your monthly mortgage repay-ment, to reduce the debt and meet the interest due on the balance. That is why you have to pay more when the bank rate goes up.

Another advantage of the DCF return is that it can be used by any investor, including net borrowers as well as net savers. It can be used by companies that don't have funds salted away in a deposit account like Hardnfast Ltd does. So if Hardnfast Ltd did not have any cash on deposit, they'd have to go to their bank and borrow the £10,000 at, say, 10 per cent. In theory it makes little difference who supplies the capital – the net result on Hardnfast is the same. If interest payments at 10 per cent during the first year come to say, £800, then either way Hardnfast's cash position is reduced by £800. Either they lose £800 interest from their bank deposit account, or they pay £800 interest to their bank loan account.

In practice of course there always is a difference between borrowing from the bank and lending to the bank. The rates the banks charge on loans are always a little higher than the rates they offer on deposits – that's the way they earn their crust. But for secured loans the difference cannot be more than two or three percentage points, because the banks operate in a competitive market, and if the gap gets too big, a more efficient operator will take business away from them, by borrowing at the lower rate and immediately lending on at a smaller margin. So Hardnfast should use a discounting rate equal to the actual rate it costs them to fund the project, depending on whether they need to borrow or not. If the cost of capital to Hardnfast is 13% when borrowed, instead of 10% when taken from their deposit account, discounting back at 13% the NPV would come to £1,898 instead of £2,680. Thus when borrowing at 13% Hardnfast must ask whether the premium of 9% which the project offers over the 13% rate, is still sufficient to cover the risks involved.

One risk which is always with us, is inflation. The DCF return may be calculated from a cash-flow projection which takes no account of inflation, in which case an estimated average annual percentage rate of inflation must be subtracted from the premium which the project offers. Or alternatively a more detailed approach can be used. Separate inflation rates can be estimated for labour costs, sales revenue and so on, and their cash values adjusted for each year of the project. This produces a rather lower inflation-adjusted DCF percentage, the premium for which is not expected to cover the cost of inflation, but which must still cover the risk that inflation actually runs ahead of the percentage allowed for in the projection.

As you can now begin to see, there is potential for developing the DCF calculations in great – and perhaps too much – detail. In fact there are so many variables and so many estimates involved, that almost any desired value of DCF return can be arranged by massaging the figures a little. There was a time when many big corporations had a minimum DCF hurdle which any project had to clear before it would be considered by the finance department. But eventually some corporations realized that proposals were simply being adjusted to produce the required minimum DCF return. Amongst these was Union Carbide who abandoned the DCF return as a means of appraising internal projects in favour of more qualitative criteria.

Another problem with the DCF return is that some unusual cash-flow patterns can produce more than one DCF return. Imagine a big project which, in addition to the initial funding and revenue stream, will need a second, larger injection of funding about mid-term in the life of the project, followed by a larger revenue stream. Thus it looks a bit like two separate projects joined together – a smaller one first and then a larger one following straight on after it. However let us suppose it cannot be treated as two separate projects, perhaps because the second part cannot be done without the first part being done first. Under these circumstances a strange effect can occur which is caused by the discounting calculations. You know that at low discounting rates, the future values are scarcely reduced, so the larger, later part of the project will dominate the results. However, at high discounting rates, later values are very substantially reduced, sometimes to insignificance. Thus for high discount rates, the larger, later part of the cash-flow projection will no longer dominate, and the earlier part will take over. So as you start increasing the trial discount rate, the NPV for the whole project starts off positive, then quickly falls to zero at a particular discount rate, indicating a DCF return for the project. But if you carry on increasing the trial discount rate, the NPV can rise and become positive before once again falling back to zero – thus indicating two further values of the DCF return. Now this sounds complicated and difficult to interpret, but all it means is that the project will be profitable with interest rates up to the first calculated DCF return, and will be not far from breaking even for a range of interest rates up to and a little way beyond the third calculated interest rate calculated. Thus in contrast to a more conventional project in which all the funding is up-front, the NPV will not plunge ever deeper into the red as interest rates climb above the first-calculated DCF return, but will stay close to breaking even, Figure 10.5.

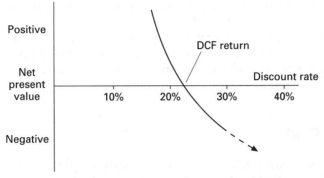

The pattern when the negative cash flows come first, as in the Hardnfast project.

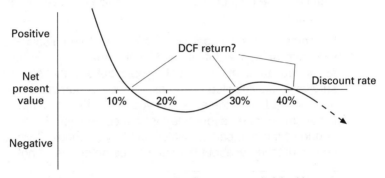

The pattern when negative flows are sandwiched between positive flows.

Figure 10.5 *How the NPV changes as the discount rate increases*

So in winding up this section and this chapter, let us remember that discounting methods have their strengths and weaknesses, just as most other methods do. But it is easy to fall into the trap of giving disproportionate attention to numbers which can be measured, and to profit in particular, so that other factors are not given proper consideration. Beware of always giving priority to the project with the highest NPV and DCF return, along with the lowest risk. Such projects are only likely to appear so attractive because you have completed similar projects before, so how much will you learn from repeating them yet again? New projects are bound to be more risky, but your organization will learn more from them. At the beginning new projects require new knowledge to be brought to bear, or invested in them, but there will be a payback in new knowledge later. We cannot measure knowledge, so constructing a knowledge-flow projection is out of the question, but such a notion is helpful. The source of today's cash is the competitive advantage you gain from today's knowledge, but your competitors are learning fast and reducing that advantage. Next year, today's knowledge will not gain you much advantage, or much cash. Next year you will need new knowledge, and that will only come from starting to learn now. So as well as examining the cash risks and returns, take a look at the knowledge risks and returns too. And favour projects which promise high knowledge returns as well as high cash returns. Take care of the knowledge and in the longer term, profits will more than take care of themselves.

Pause for thought

1   If you were presented with the Hardnfast project proposal right now, what discount rate would you choose in order to calculate the net present value? How might present and future interest rates during the lifetime of the project influence your choice of discount rate?

2   Hardnfast has a competitor in the area called Tools-R-Us, which is very similar to Hardnfast, except the managing director is an old-fashioned autocrat and most people believe the company owes its survival to his knowledge and experience. A number of new customers have started up in the area and you believe the tool hardening market is becoming more favourable for both companies. If you want to invest in one of the companies, which would you choose? What else would you want to know about the companies before deciding?

3   You need to increase your work force and there are two contenders on the short list. They are similar except one has recently gained a Certificate in Management Studies, and the other has no management qualification, but an authenticated record of involvement with a number of differing but successful projects. How would you gauge the knowledge you would be buying if you were to invest in one of these candidates by employing one or other of them?

Further reading

Mott, G. (1987) *Investment Appraisal. A guide to profit planning* (2nd edn). Pan Books.
Rutterford, J. (1993) *Introduction to Stock Exchange Investment* (2nd edn). Macmillan.

Part IV: Conclusion, scope and potential

Businessmen go down with their businesses because they like the old way so well they cannot bring themselves to change.

Henry Ford

The preceding chapters examined from the organizational point of view the reasons for, and the methods of changing to, the knowledge management approach. However, your individual organization is just part of wider national and global economic systems. The way you and your organization act out your roles will play a small part in determining the shape of the future. Part IV sets the knowledge management approach in the broader context of the world today, and suggests it as an appropriate way to address the emerging problems of the new millennium.

In Chapter 11 we examine the wider view to see what conclusions we can draw, concerning the economic and social effects of many organizations interacting freely in a single global competitive market. We also examine the effects that organizations can have on our individual behaviour.

In Chapter 12 we look briefly to the future, to imagine possible scenarios which may face us in the post-industrial era. Hence we construct the basis of an agenda for decision.

11 The wider context: how organizations affect people

Why read this chapter?

The purpose of this chapter is to allow us a chance to reflect for a while on the bigger, longer-term implications of the changes we see all around us. As managers and as human beings we do not live in isolation. We learn from, and interact with our environment, which partly consists of other managers and human beings. They in turn also learn from and interact with their environment – of which we are part. These feedback loops can create virtuous upward spirals capable of lifting us all to new heights, but they can also start a vicious downward spin to disintegration. With insight, we can influence which way it goes, but for how long will we have the chance to choose?

Organizations affect psychologically and economically the people who work inside them, and also to some extent everyone else in the economy outside. In this chapter you can learn from some fascinating studies which cast light on the odd ways people sometimes behave at work. This is essential knowledge for modern managers.

Knowledge management: a review

After the detail of the preceding chapters, let us regain a holistic perspective. The overall conclusion we seem to be converging on in the developed world is that the old, profit-motivated, command-and-control approach is too crude and simplistic. The world today presents new, complex opportunities and threats which require a new response – a more sophisticated response than can be achieved by organizations driven by fear and focused primarily on shareholder profit.

Before the Industrial Revolution, the threat of violence was the basis for power. In those days if you displeased your superiors, you were likely to end up on the rack or in the dungeon. However, violence has never been very satisfactory in controlling what people think: the socially skilled conceal what they think, and there will always be a few martyrs who are prepared to suffer rather than abandon their beliefs. The fundamental weakness of fear however, is that it can only be used to discourage by punishing wrong behaviour. It cannot be used to encourage right behaviour. That is why, according to Alvin Toffler (1990), money began to replace violence as the basis for power during the Industrial Revolution, and why knowledge may eventually eclipse both violence and money in the information age.

One of the fourteen rules in the Deming management method (1986) is 'drive out fear', and rightly so, because although fear may stop people from doing things they shouldn't be doing, it also inhibits creativity and stops people from trying new things, which is what they should be doing. We have machines to do the routine work, and they get cheaper and more powerful every year. The ongoing threat of layoffs can create fear, but providing extra automation without layoffs will just add to costs unless the time it frees up for people is put to creative use. And that will not happen while people play safe and stick to the old rules because of fear.

As motivating forces, the threat of punishment is too crude and the primacy of profit is too cynical for many people today. The old rules of management assumed that business was run purely for profit, and that people behaved according to the characteristics of 'economic man', who sought to maximize personal gain and was entirely self-interested. Maslow's hierarchy of needs supports this rather one-sided view of people as being entirely self-interested. His hierarchy rightly shows we must satisfy our short-term, physical survival needs before we can concentrate on longer-term, more cerebral needs, but even the highest levels of the hierarchy focus on self – self-fulfilment and self-actualization. Self-interest lies at the core of the old paradigm which is blind to everyday acts of charity and self-denial performed by ordinary people at home and at work, let alone the ultimate act of self-sacrifice which some people through the ages have consistently shown themselves willing to make for their cause or their country. Certainly self-interest comes first, but self-denial is also a normal part of human nature which should not be entirely ignored. We have ample evidence to suggest that Maslow's hierarchy is incomplete: an extra topmost level should be added, which looks beyond the concept of self, to reflect the ethical, humanitarian, spiritual needs and motivations of people. Sooner or later personal gain is not enough for most people: what is the point in spending a third of a lifetime in pursuit of profit, only to leave it all behind when we finally depart?

Fear and money will of course continue to influence our behaviour, but as people and organizations develop, and as civilization itself advances, so the lower, more obvious short-term physical needs in Maslow's hierarchy become less important as motivators. For brain workers it is often the highest, least obvious, long-term cerebral needs which eventually become the most important motivators. In Western developed nations the influence of the church is minor compared with its all-pervading influence in many eastern nations, and people here seldom evangelize and are reluctant to moralize – especially at work. It is therefore easy for us to overlook this ethical, spiritual aspect of human nature and its hidden influence on people's behaviour. There are signs however that progressive managers intuitively recognize the importance of these highest needs. For instance there is growing recognition of the importance of shared values in organizations.

To conclude this short review then, the knowledge-based, inform-and-entrust approach being tried out by a growing band of organizations shows every sign of being an appropriate alternative, capable of a suitably sophisticated response to the business problems we face today. Not only is it superior at achieving the old goals of command-and-control organizations, it also promises solutions to human and ethical problems which were never addressed by the old approach. It is a truism to say that knowledge will always ultimately prevail, but if there is such a thing as a general, unifying theory of management, then the knowledge-based approach may be as near as we have ever come to it.

Economics of a brave new world?

Our old management paradigm came from the industrial age, when a little knowledge went a long way, and knowledge was only required at the top of an organization. For instance, Henry Ford and a few close associates did all the thinking to create and run his company. They embedded their ideas in an enduring structure of machinery and systems for producing cars – a huge car-making machine which ran continuously for sixteen years converting raw materials such as steel and rubber into a simple, standard product – the Model T. Everything depended on simplifying, standardizing and endlessly repeating the same short tasks. Tasks were so simple that when more direct labour was needed, farm labourers from the fields could operate the machinery, and work on the assembly line with virtually no training. Henry Ford's River Rouge car plant was a rigid system for co-ordinating the physical effort of thousands of labourers to mass-produce a simple product for a mass market.

River Rouge made Henry Ford rich and powerful, but it did so while raising the standard of living of all Americans – by providing jobs and incomes for local workers, and by providing a convenient new form of transport for customers across the USA. The plant generated wealth in the closed system of the American economy by improving transport and communication, by re-cycling money and returning most of the revenue to American workers and shareholders, and by paying taxes which the government spent on improving infrastructure and services.

From the knowledge perspective, Henry Ford became rich by using his knowledge to build a system which leveraged the physical labour of workers. Ford's knowledge enabled them to produce a valuable new product which they could not have produced on their own. You could argue that Ford exploited his workers by forcing them into inhuman, mind-numbingly repetitive jobs, but at that time the world knew of no other more humane way of advancing the lot of humankind. And most Americans did not begrudge Ford his wealth, because they could see the benefits they too were enjoying.

Meantime the same phenomenon was occurring in Europe. For instance in the UK, William Henry Morris used the assembly line to produce cars at Cowley near Oxford. He too made a fortune, and like Henry Ford, returned much of it to the nation through wages, taxes and dividends. He also set up a university college, a trust and a foundation. In recognition of service to the community he was raised to the peerage as First Viscount Lord Nuffield.

That was the situation during the first half of this century, but now as we approach the millennium, things are very different. Harvard Professor Robert Reich, one of America's foremost political economists, has identified (1991) several fundamental global changes which have transformed the economics of production since the 1960s. Three major shifts which have affected the American economy must also apply to the UK and the rest of the developed world.

The shift from high-volume to high-value production

This is an obvious shift. Prior to the 1960s there was little global competition. Demand exceeded supply for most products, and so organizations concentrated more on maximizing supply, and less on quality and service. The reverse is true today. You can buy a Ford in any colour including black, and including a wide choice of optional features. We have already discussed in earlier chapters how this change complicates production and calls for knowledge to be deployed throughout the organization.

The shift from national ownership to global ownership of businesses

This has changed the relationship that businesses have with the nations within which they operate. Prior to the 1960s organizations were owned and controlled by shareholders who were almost exclusively the nationals of the country in which the organization was formed and had its headquarters. This is no longer true for larger organizations, whose shares are dispersed across a complex international web of private and institutional investors. In the UK Rover has an alliance with Honda who hold 20 per cent of their shares, but BMW is the controlling shareholder. And Nissan and Toyota have car plants and research centres in the UK. In America General Motors still has its headquarters in Detroit, but trades and has shareholders all around the world.

The shift from physical work to knowledge work as the basis for creating value

This fundamental shift is already having a profound effect on employment opportunities and the types of work available. There are now few jobs of the type which were most plentiful at River Rouge. In fact there are fewer jobs in total, and the remaining jobs nearly all require some knowledge or skills. In the developed world, the chance of getting a factory job if you are an unskilled worker are almost zero, and even if you have a degree that is no guarantee of employment. What should be done about the growing proportion of citizens who are becoming unemployable because they lack the new skills needed today? On its own within individual nations this shift from physical to knowledge work has major repercussions, which are made more severe by the competitive demands of free world markets. The divisive effects of growing inequality could eventually pose a real threat to civilized society.

The rise of the symbolic analyst

Reich categorizes American workers into three groups exposed to global competition, and one sheltered group of agricultural and government workers. The three exposed groups are:

- routine producers, who perform repetitive operations such as assembly line work,
- in-person servers, who deliver services in person to the customer such as hairdressers, and
- symbolic analysts, who use coded information to identify and solve problems.

This last group covers all knowledge workers and includes lawyers, designers and computer programmers. Prior to the 1960s symbolic analysts, though well-rewarded, constituted only a small part of the economy, which was dominated by routine producers and in-person servers. However, by 1990 in the USA, symbolic analysts formed one-fifth of the nation's work force. A separate analysis showed that at the same time, the top fifth of the nation's work force received about half the nation's total income. Although the two studies were not looking at exactly the same fifth of the population, it is likely there is substantial overlap, Figure 11.1. Routine production work is offered

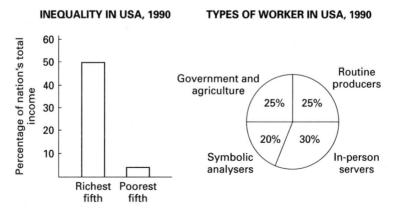

Figure 11.1   *Types of work, and distribution of incomes in USA. Source: Reich, 1991*

more cheaply abroad where labour rates are a fraction of those in America, and in-person service can often be delivered better and cheaper by automated services such as coffee machines and hole-in-the-wall cash dispensers at banks. But world demand for problem solvers and identifiers – the symbolic analysts – continues to outstrip supply. This group – only 20 per cent of the work force – continues to grow in importance to the American economy, at the expense of the other groups.

In the context of these three changes, Reich concludes it is no longer true that, in the words of Charles E. Wilson, president of General Motors in 1953, 'what was good for our country was good for General Motors, and vice versa.' In those days, GM provided dividends to American shareholders, wages to American workers and payments to American suppliers. But now, ownership of GM shares is no longer exclusively American, and GM buys goods and services from sources around the world, wherever the best value can be found. This certainly benefits symbolic analysts working for GM, many of whom are American, but not the much reduced and decreasing number of American routine producers. When an American customer pays $10,000 to GM for a Pontiac Le Mans, only about $3,800 goes to American workers and shareholders. By far the larger part of the total leaves the country to pay for routine goods and services purchased elsewhere in the world. Reich's America today is clearly a very different place from the one Henry Ford knew, back in the 1920s.

As Reich points out, national governments are slow in responding to these shifts in the economic landscape, and sometimes when they do, they reveal an out-dated mindset. For instance, US government development grants for factories in America were still being restricted to American companies, when it made more sense to award these grants on the basis of potential to generate jobs, wages and tax revenue, regardless of who owns the factory. The new economic reality today is that the standard of living of a nation's people depends not so much on the success of a nation's big corporations, but increasingly on the knowledge contribution the workers in that nation make to the world economy – on the value of their skills and insights – regardless of which company they work for. These skills improve with experience, because people and organizations learn by doing. So for instance in the UK, Nissan building and operating a factory may contribute more to our people and our economy than a British company might do by building and operating a similar factory abroad.

National governments are in danger of losing the initiative. Transnational corporations open factories in countries where taxes and wages are lowest, and where grants are highest. Global finance scarcely notices national borders any more. Electronic tidal waves of cash surge around the globe chasing the best interest rates, and national governments seem powerless to resist the erosion of their authority by the forces of free world markets. What fiscal control can national governments exercise, when taxes must be low to keep home production costs down, and the base rate and exchange rate are held hostage by international currency speculators? From the knowledge perspective, what should national governments now do? The embedded, tacit knowledge and skills of a nation's citizens are the only remaining national resource which cannot be diminished rapidly by flowing out across its borders – unless the citizens themselves emigrate en masse. The message is clear: for an improved standard of living, national governments should develop an environment in which citizens are enabled and encouraged to improve their knowledge.

Global civilization – or technical jungle?

Civilization advances in fits and starts, and sometimes it slips back a few decades. Some command-and-control organizations may still be driven by fear, but when we look back over the centuries we can see that we have advanced.

All Crimes in England that touch the Life of Man, are either High-Treason, Rape, Buggery, Murder, or Felony.

Altho' some High-Treasons are much more heinous and odious than others, yet the Punishment by Law is the same for all sorts, (except Clipping and Coining of Money) and that is, that the Traytor laid upon a Hurdle or Sledge, be drawn to the Gallows, there hanged by the Neck, presently cut down alive, his Entrails to be suddenly pulled out of his Belly, and burnt before the Face of the Criminal; then his Head to be cut off his Body to be divided into four Parts; and lastly, that the Head and Body be hung up, or impailed where the King shall command.

If a Criminal indicted of Petty-Treason ... refuseth to answer ... he is ... to be sent back to the Prison from whence he came, and there laid in some low dark Room, upon the bare Ground, on his Back, all naked besides his Privy-Parts, his Arms and Legs drawn with Cords, fastened to the several Quarters of the Room; then shall be laid upon his Body, Iron and Stone, so much as he may bear ... the next Day he shall have ... Bread, without Drink, and the third Day shall have Drink ... without Bread; and this shall be his Diet till he die.

But tho' the Law continues, yet we so abhor Cruelty, that of late they are suffered to be so over-charged with Weight laid upon them, that they expire presently.

An extract from *The Present State of Great Britain* (1708) by John Chamberlayne, Esq; FRS. Book II. Chapter VIII. Of Vices & Punishments.

Today in Britain, life is less brutal than it was three centuries ago, though even then it seems we were beginning to realize that cruelty was wrong.

To civilize means to lift out of barbarism, to enlighten, refine, educate. To become civilized we must adopt values which favour knowledge rather than ignorance, beauty before ugliness, and humanity in place of brutishness. Civilization is a quality of society rather than of an individual. And as illustrated by the boxed Chamberlayne quote, it is a relative characteristic, not an absolute state of grace which we have now reached. The process of civilization is a process of cultural and intellectual development, encompassing art and technology, religion and politics, business and leisure. Civilization is the on-going process of evolution towards higher quality in all aspects of human society – and as we know, there is always room for quality improvement.

These fine words open up a subject large enough to fill a book, but we only have time here to consider briefly the ethics of our decisions as managers, and how they might affect society. The problem is we seem capable of supporting dual ethical standards – one standard at home and another at work.

Ethics at home and at work

On the simplest level, at home we impress upon our children how important it is to be honest and truthful. Yet at work we frequently yield to the demands of the situation and find ourselves being economical with the truth, and sometimes downright deceitful. Perhaps we have always had dual standards for home and work, ever since prehistoric times when stone age man loved and cared for his family in the sanctuary of the tribe, but went out with the other warriors to cut and slash mercilessly at predators and prey. Are these dual standards learnt – or the remnants of race memory once necessary for the survival of the species? Or perhaps we should ask: is dishonest and uncivilized behaviour an inherent human tendency, or is it in some way encouraged by the work environment?

Human beings on the whole are more good than bad, or civilization would not have developed as far as it has. The average person will tend to do the right thing more often than not – other things being equal. But other things such as work environment do influence behaviour, and as in all human attributes, there is wide variation between individuals. A few people are saintly, and at the other end of the spectrum, a few are evil. Here is a quick, selective review of the work of social psychologists who have studied moral reasoning and behaviour in humans, and also the effects on behaviour of group situations that people find themselves in, as provided by Rita Atkinson et al. (1993). Let us see if there are any conclusions we might draw, if we are interested in promoting a civilized society as well as advancing corporate objectives.

Moral reasoning and human behaviour

According to one of the century's most influential thinkers, the Swiss psychologist Jean Piaget, we are not born with the higher intellectual capacity for moral reasoning. It is an ability children acquire as they grow and develop. Piaget's work has been extended beyond childhood into adolescence and adulthood by the American psychologist Lawrence Kohlberg, who believes that moral judgement develops with age through three main stages:

● **Level I.** Pre conventional morality. Up to the age of about ten, children don't think too much about what is right or wrong – they just obey rules to avoid punishment or obtain favours.
● **Level II.** Conventional morality. By the age of thirteen, most children are capable of reasoning and abstract thought. They uphold laws and conform to social rules in order to avoid disapproval of others and the censure of authorities, but now also to avoid internal feelings of guilt.
● **Level III.** Post-conventional morality. By adulthood, many though not all adults will be capable of formulating their own abstract ethical principles. Most adults will be capable of guiding their actions without referring to rules, but instead to principles commonly agreed with their peers for public welfare. Kohlberg believes that a minority of less than 10 per cent will develop even further to a point where they can guide their actions according to self-chosen ethical principles which value justice, dignity and equality. Adults who reach this final stage of development are driven more to avoid self-condemnation than condemnation by others.

Clearly the scientific view is that we do know right from wrong, but there is also evidence that we often don't behave according to our principles. It seems our internal disposition is often at odds with our external situation. In fact according to Fritz Heider, the founder of modern attribution theory, we are more likely to behave according to the demands of the situation than follow our own natural inclinations. Ross in 1977 confirmed Heider's observation and showed we are wrong to believe that behaviour tells us about the person, when a person's ethical behaviour is so heavily influenced by the situation. Ross coined the term 'fundamental attribution error' for the very common error of believing that behaviour results from the person's disposition, when it is largely governed by the situation.

The Astroten case: when the situation prevails over ethics

Nurses are unlikely to be attracted to the profession because of the pay or conditions of employment, so presumably many of them will have an internal disposition towards altruism. But Hofling et al. in 1966 showed that even nurses may encounter situations at work which pressure them to act contrary to their internal disposition – pressure they seem powerless to resist.

Researchers conducted trials in hospitals with nurses on regular duty who knew nothing about the trials. A nurse would receive a phone call from a doctor she knew to be on the staff, but had not met:

> This is Dr. Smith from Psychiatry calling ... I'm going to have to see Mr Jones again tonight. I'd like him to have had some medication by the time I get to the ward.

The doctor asked the nurse to check the medicine cabinet, and she saw a pillbox labelled 'ASTROTEN – Usual dose: 5 mg. Maximum daily dose: 10 mg.' After reporting she had found the drug, the doctor continued:

> Now will you please give Mr Jones a dose of 20 mg of Astroten. I'll be up within ten minutes: I'll sign the order then, but I'd like the drug to have started taking effect.

This order violated hospital rules and professional nursing practice: phoned orders were not allowed, the dose was excessive, and the medication was not on the authorized stock list. Yet 95 per cent of the nurses started to give the medication – actually a harmless placebo – at which point the trial would be terminated.

Such is the power of situational forces. But you wouldn't give in to them, would you? Don't be so sure. When other nurses were told the full circumstances of the situation and asked how they would react, 83 per cent said they wouldn't give the medication, most thought a majority of nurses would also refuse, and 100 per cent of student nurses said they would refuse.

There is a really important lesson here: we must all guard against under-estimating the power of situational forces. Unless you are truly exceptional, you too will be subject to Ross's fundamental attribution error.

So when we behave unethically at work, Ross has given us an excuse to blame it on the organization! There are many social effects which make our work group and the hierarchy such a pervading influence. There is only time to touch on them briefly here, but they are described in more detail by Atkinson et al.

Pressures to conform in groups

De-individuation, pluralistic ignorance and diffusion of responsibility

The concept of de-individuation was proposed by Festinger, Pepitone and Newcomb in 1952, and extended by Zimbardo, and then Diener in the 1970s. It is the feeling of losing your personal identity and merging anonymously into a group, so you no longer feel restrained from immoral or mob behaviour.

Pluralistic ignorance is where everybody in a group misleads everybody else into ignoring or misinterpreting danger signals. The herd instinct can cause crowds to panic, but also to remain calm in danger when each person postpones displaying alarm because they don't want to be the first to do so. It is related to diffusion of responsibility, in which each person knows that others are present and so the burden of responsibility does not fall solely on him or her. Studies were conducted in the late 1960s by Darley, Latane, Piliavin and Rodin.

The majority view, group polarization and group think

No one likes to be the odd one out. Even when you are sure you are right and the group you are in is wrong, there is great pressure to conform. Solomon Asch's classic studies in the 1950s produced striking results. In a series of trials supposedly investigating visual judgement, a subject is put in a group, all of who have secretly agreed beforehand to give the same wrong answer, even though the correct answer is obvious. Subjects conformed to the incorrect group consensus on about one occasion in three on average, and about three-quarters of subjects conformed at least once. Atkinson et al. (1993) describe the work of seven other researchers who have added to the studies on conformity pressure.

In a separate series of studies also in the 1950s, James Stoner overturned earlier conventional wisdom that groups are more cautious than individuals in their decision-making. He showed that on the contrary they are more extreme in their attitude to risk. If members are initially inclined to be cautious, then after discussion, the group will be even more cautious. However, if members are initially inclined to take risk, then discussions will lead to even riskier decisions. This phenomenon, known as group polarization, extends beyond risk and caution into other judgements concerning opinions and values. By 1990 other researchers had added more than 300 studies to extend the work started by Stoner.

Group think is a theory proposed in 1982 by the social psychologist, Irving Janis, who used historical studies rather than laboratory experiments to study group conformity pressure. Janis found that group think can lead members to suppress their own dissent in the interests of group consensus. The example which triggered the study was J. F. Kennedy's advisory group which planned the disastrous Bay of Pigs invasion of Cuba in 1961. A cohesive, isolated group under a strong leader who favours a particular course of action can lead to illusions of invulnerability, morality and unanimity through collective rationalization. The desire to achieve consensus and avoid dissent can lead to disastrously flawed decisions. Group think allows incomplete information to be inadequately analysed because of self-censorship of dissent. Laboratory experiments in the 1970s and 1980s to help understand the complex processes resulting in group think have produced mixed results.

In group think, the leader has a big influence on the group. Let us now review other studies of authority and its effects, which Atkinson et al. describe in more detail.

Pressures to obey in hierarchies

The hierarchy is a system for amplifying the influence of the person at the top. It depends on people throughout the structure obeying orders given both explicitly and implicitly through job descriptions, procedures and accepted practice. When we work in hierarchies, there is immense pressure to obey orders, not only because of enforcement sanctions, but also because of situational pressures. In fact the combined pressure can make it practically impossible for us to disobey, even if we know what we are being ordered to do is wrong. If an evil person gets to power at the top, the ethical standards of everyone else in the hierarchy can prove to be entirely ineffective in preventing the amplification of the power for evil. With Adolf Hitler in charge of Nazi Germany millions of innocent people were systematically put to death, not because the disposition of Germans is less ethical or more evil than that of other nations, but because the evil of Hitler was amplified without any effective counterbalancing checks, as orders were passed down through the chain of command.

Hierarchies are amoral, uncaring systems which are effective because they force the people who work in them to subordinate their own desires to some common purpose. Unfortunately however, the same enforcement can also cause people to subordinate their moral consciences as well. Thus it is not uncommon to see stories in the press of an employee who after many years of loyal service is sacked for infringing some minor procedure – a disproportionate penalty for an insignificant crime. There is a procedure, a procedure for enforcing the procedure, and a procedure for enforcing the enforcement – and no one feels responsible, or has any incentive to risk breaking the chain.

This anecdotal evidence is supported by the important but controversial experimental studies conducted by Stanley Milgram at Yale University in 1963. The subjects of the study – ordinary men and women – were paid expenses to participate in what they thought was a study of memory. The experimenter told the subjects they would play the role of teacher in the study, in which a learner was to learn word pairs. The subject, as teacher, was to read a series of word pairs to a learner, and then to test his learning by asking him to choose the right second word when given the first word. However the circumstances of the learning were most unusual. The subject saw through a window into the next room, where men in laboratory coats strapped the learner into a chair, and attached an electrode to his wrist. The subject was seated at a shock generator near the window, and required to administer a 15 volt shock when the learner made an error. After each error the experimenter who was sitting near the subject, instructed the subject to increase the voltage of the shock. In fact the learner did not receive any shocks, but acted out his role. At first he could be heard protesting through the wall, and as the shocks got stronger he began to shout and curse. At 300 volts he began kicking the wall, and beyond that up to 450 volts he no longer answered the questions or made any noise.

Naturally many subjects objected and pleaded with the experimenter to stop the experiment, but the experimenter just replied: 'The experiment requires that you continue'; or 'You have no other choice – you must go on.' The measure of obedience to authority was the voltage level the subject administered just before refusing to continue.

And the results? Not one subject stopped before 300 volts, and 65 per cent went all the way to 450 volts. How about that for obedience? Ethically motivated disobedience is clearly not easy for an isolated individual. Atkinson et al. list some factors illustrated by the Milgram experiments which cause individuals to subordinate their ethics to become agents of an immoral system:

Social norms and surveillance

We don't like to go back on our word. It is really very difficult to break an agreement and violate this strong social norm. The subjects in the Milgram experiments had agreed, and received payment to participate, and there was no natural stopping point once the experiment had begun. The subjects are just asked to carry on doing what they are already doing.

Also we don't like to accuse people of wrong-doing. And quitting early would be tantamount to accusing the experimenter of being immoral. These influences were intensified by the presence and surveillance of the experimenter in the same room as the subject. Later experiments in which the experimenter issued instructions by phone, obedience dropped from 65 per cent to 21 per cent.

Buffers

We don't like to experience too directly the suffering of fellow human beings. Milgram reported that obedience fell when the learner was in the same room as the subject, and fell even further when the subject was asked to hold the electrode on the arm of the learner. However, when the subject was only required to close a switch in advance of another teacher administering the shock, obedience soared to 93 per cent. Modern technology buffers the button-pusher from the suffering that can be unleashed by such a simple act as pushing a button or pulling a trigger.

Ideology

We are much more likely to subordinate voluntarily our own moral beliefs if we can accept we are supporting a higher set of beliefs that legitimize the authority of the person in charge. In Milgram's experiments the legitimizing ideology was the importance of science. In Nazi Germany it was the primacy of the Fatherland.

Ideologies strengthen the calls of those in authority for those beneath them to subordinate their individual interests in support of the common good. But as we saw in earlier chapters, meaning is lost as jobs are divided up, so those near the bottom of a hierarchy cannot assess for themselves whether those above them are better-placed to decide and are acting in good faith – or are misinformed, miscalculating and misappropriating.

Simple, imposed ideology smacks of propaganda, brain-washing and political correctness. It is a crude instrument which can do more harm than good. Even the apparently benign ideology of the primacy of knowledge could be used to support malign instructions – to conduct medical experiments on healthy prisoners, for instance. In place of ideology we need more complex sets of shared values and beliefs which strike a balance between society, group and individual well-being.

Conclusion

It is clear that organizations have a powerful influence on the thoughts and behaviour of those who work in them. It also seems clear that different types of organization influence people in different ways, with some types of organizations operating in more benign ways than others. Until recently, most organizations were constructed to concentrate power at the top and control what people did. This resulted in a conflict of interest between the managers and the managed, with the pay and conditions of those at lower levels in the hierarchy held down by those at the top. However the age-old hierarchical organization no longer seems to be the best way of organizing people, particularly those doing brain work. New forms of organization are proving more competitive in today's business environment, and for the first time in history there is a convergence of interest: what is right for the organization and its shareholders is getting closer to what is right too for employees and most other stakeholders in the organization, including, suppliers, customers and the local community. This has all the potential for constructing a virtuous circle in which everyone with a stake in the organization gains to some extent, like they did at Henry Ford's River Rouge plant.

It seems that viewing knowledge as the ultimate resource might provide the beginnings of a vigorous new profitable phase in our development which has the potential to bring benefits to the whole of society. Just as Henry Ford created River Rouge to leverage the manual work of his labourers and thus benefit all Americans, we must now create new organizations to leverage the brain work of knowledge workers in such a way as to benefit all citizens. However there is a cloud on the horizon: not all citizens are benefiting at present. Trends are emerging towards higher unemployment and greater inequality between those in secure jobs and those with no permanent jobs or security. Those with stakes in successful organizations are benefiting, while those whose main ability is for repetitive manual work and those with no significant stake, are losing out. The trick that society must now learn to pull is how to share out the work and the spoils more fairly while continuing the war against wasted time, effort and materials. The case for intelligentsia oblige may require us, as Dr Deming taught the Japanese in the 1950s, to replace the fundamental objective of maximum profit with that of 'jobs and more jobs', Figure 11.2.

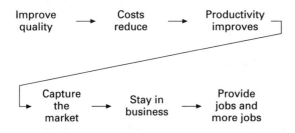

Figure 11.2   *The Deming Chain Reaction. Source: Deming, 1986*

We will discuss these issues further in Chapter 12.

Pause for thought

1   'Businesses should not adopt an ethical standpoint. They should simply make sure they operate within the law.' Jot down two arguments to support this statement, and two to refute it, for a business operating in global markets. On balance do you agree or disagree with the statement?

2   Can you think of two separate occasions when you felt uneasy at work because there was the potential for, or actual conflict with your personal ethical standards? For each, write down a line or two to indicate the occasion.

3   Write down the name of three recent cases in which there has been a public outcry and reaction against something a business has done. In

each case say whether the public reaction had any effect on the business.

4 Write down two main reasons for supporting and two for opposing free global trade in goods and services.

5 On balance, would you feel happy or unhappy about a foreign company coming to your home country and,
(a) building a factory, employing local people and selling the products world wide?
(b) taking over and operating one of the private electricity, gas or water utilities?
(c) taking over and operating one of the country's top four banks?

6 Do you believe that different types of organization favour different types of behaviour, and therefore different types of leader?

References and further reading

Atkinson, R. L., Atkinson, R. G., Smith, E. E. and Bem, D. J. (1993) *Introduction to Psychology* (11th edn). Harcourt Brace.

Chamberlayne, J. (1708) *Magna Britannia Notitia or, The Present State of Great-Britain, with Divers Remarks Upon the Antient State Thereof.* Goodwin, Wotton, Tooke, Midwinter and Wells.

Deming, W. E. (1986) *Out of the Crisis.* Cambridge University Press

Reich, R. B. (1991) *The Work of Nations. A Blueprint for the Future.* Simon and Schuster.

Toffler, A. (1990) *Powershift – Knowledge wealth and violence at the edge of the 21st century.* Bantam.

12 Anxieties for the new millennium

Why read this chapter?

Knowledge is changing the world. There is nothing new about that except the rate of change – which has been accelerating for so long it will soon reach escape velocity. Where are we headed, and do we really want to go there? Is there any point in asking these questions, or have we unleashed forces we can no longer control? So many things are changing so rapidly the combined effects may already be beyond our ability to comprehend.

Knowledge is power: never before has that been so true, especially when shared and leveraged by teams. Teams have used knowledge to eradicate diseases – and also to wreak mass destruction. What teams will we need in business, in government and in society to ensure this power is used to improve the lot of all humankind and not just concentrate wealth in the hands of a minority at great cost to the majority?

The information revolution

The information revolution, although as yet bloodless, is nevertheless creating confusion and social upheaval on a scale similar to that of other, more violent revolutions. The old order is being torn down and swept away, and during this period of rapid change, it is not yet clear what new scheme will be established in its place. We are fortunate that technology can now supply many of our material needs and it is no longer necessary for us to toil from dawn to dusk. We should be entering a new utopian age, but unemployment and inequality is beginning to spoil it for all but a privileged few. Are we just passing through a necessary transitional period of adjustment and renewal, or are we entering a new period of lasting disorder? For the time being, everything is up for grabs: there are big opportunities and big threats. As managers in organizations, what can we do to encourage a favourable outcome?

The nightmare scenario

Which is better: free markets and democracy, or centralized planning and totalitarianism? Many Western managers may have reservations about operating in totally free markets, but most would choose free markets and democracy rather than the alternative. They might give as an example the failure of the communist system in the USSR, compared with the success of the American free enterprise system. But total freedom is not far removed from total anarchy, and even in Western democracies our freedom is partially constrained by the requirements of a civilized society. However, the economic effects described by Robert Reich have none the less shifted markets significantly towards the freedom/anarchy end of the spectrum, resulting in inequality, unemployment, wasted lives and social tension. Will Hutton (1995) describes our 30/30/40 society in the UK as consisting of 30 per cent disadvantaged, 30 per cent marginalized and insecure, and 40 per cent privileged. The disadvantaged are those without jobs, and the marginalized are those in temporary or part-time employment and who have no employment protection. The privileged are those in full-time employment with a secure income, and can therefore get a mortgage and raise a family with some degree of confidence in their future. According to Hutton, more than half of UK citizens now lack these benefits.

As we usher in the new millennium the futurologists are in full cry. Books and TV documentaries predict heaven and hell, a new utopia and a new period of lasting disorder, similar to the dark six-century medieval period after the fall of the Roman empire. The opportunities are real, but so are the threats. Totalitarianism cannot survive in the glare of free and open information provided by satellite TV and the Internet. Indeed this technology is a democratizing force which could eventually provide the basis for a new global democracy. But the bastions of civilization – the family, the church and the state – are all in decline. Divorce and unemployment have undermined the authority of parents in the family environment where children first learn to socialize. Only a tiny minority of the UK population are regular church-goers. And the authority of the state is waning as tax revenues decline, and fiscal control becomes more and more constrained by market forces. Yet with an ageing population and burgeoning unemployment, demands on the state for increased spending on health care, social security and education continue to grow.

There are lawless no-go areas in many European cities now. For the disadvantaged there are the semi-derelict tower block estates where the drug barons rule, and for the privileged there are high wealth, high security middle-class ghettos with private security guards at the gates. The nation state is being overwhelmed by global competition, leaving a vacuum waiting to be filled. Will the state fight back, or will we descend into a kind of Mad Max feudalism?

The dream ticket

Throughout history, elites have always controlled a disproportionate amount of the wealth of the societies they lived in. Vilfredo Pareto, the nineteenth-century social economist, showed that inequality is impossible to eradicate, and indeed most people would agree that some inequality is a desirable feature of society, but civilized societies always find ways of containing inequality within reasonable limits. Yet the twin forces of the information revolution – free markets and computer technology – are conspiring to increase inequality, an influence Western governments have so far shown little capacity or inclination to resist. And the revolution has further – much further to run. For instance at the end of the 1980s, the UK banking sector had a total payroll of close on half a million managers, secretaries and clerks. By the mid 1990s more than one in five of these jobs had been cut because of automation, telephone banking and increased competition. And it is predicted that one in five of the remaining jobs will also disappear by the year 2000. During one decade, three in eight banking jobs will have gone – a pattern which may well be repeated in other information and knowledge-based sectors of the economy. Will learning process re-engineering (LPR) cut a swathe through UK schools, colleges and universities? Will our 30/30/40 society become a 40/40/20 society in which the 20 per cent become even more privileged at the expense of the 80 per cent?

We are on the brink of achieving the utopian vision of a society in which the majority enjoy prosperous, fulfilling lives without having to toil every waking hour. It is within our grasp, yet it still eludes us, not because we are short of the material or technical means, but because we have not yet learned how to make the necessary social adjustments. In round figures we have a quarter of the working population with plenty of money, but very little time to spend it, and another quarter of the population who have no discretionary money, but more time than they know what to do with. How supremely ironic.

If there is such a thing as a panacea for all our troubles, it must surely be abundant, shared knowledge, and a willingness to share the benefits of knowledge. But with the family, the church and the state in retreat, where can the process be started? Is there a role for business organizations to play here? And what are the implications for other organizations in society?

A unifying paradigm: exploiting the knowledge resource ...

It is easy to confuse the knowledge and abilities which groups of people possess, with the people themselves. Knowledge is a resource which it is right and proper to exploit: knowledge breeds more and better knowledge when it is exploited. People on the other hand are diminished when they are exploited. It is wrong to view, or describe people as a resource. They are not commodities to be used efficiently – perhaps conserved for a while, but ultimately to be exploited and replaced. It is wrong to exploit people, and we should try to avoid language that implies that it is OK to do so. People are human beings, not a human resource, or human capital, or a labour market. On the contrary, people should be the beneficiaries, not the victims of knowledge.

If you are able to subscribe to this viewpoint, it may transform your view of the world. It can reveal insights, and suggest policies which will seldom instantly, but often ultimately, be richly rewarding. Let us see what the implications are, for different sections of society.

... in business organizations

A growing number of businesses around the world now see the enormous importance of knowledge as the basis for their competitive advantage. In fact because they are so acutely conscious of it, a growing list of companies don't wish to rely just on what the state provides, and are establishing their own internal 'universities'. The list includes Unipart, IBM, AT&T, Ericsson, McDonald's and Motorola in the Western hemisphere, and Tatung in the East. But whereas the Western company universities are tiny in comparison to their parent organizations, the Tatung model is more of an equal partner. In Taiwan, Dr T. S. Lin is President of the Tatung Group of 20 factories and 20,000 employees, which produces over half of all the computer monitors sold in the world. He is also President of the Tatung Institute which produces 2,400 PhDs each year, about a fifth of whom stay on to work in the Tatung Group. Clearly the Tatung Institute is in a different league from the Western company universities; it is not just a larger than average training department. It is an example of something quite remarkable going on at Tatung and in Taiwan – a clue to the fundamentally different attitude towards knowledge in that country. They see knowledge as the well-spring of their prosperity, dignity and standing in the world – the foundation for everything they are building, and therefore fundamentally, supremely important. This almost reverent attitude is enshrined in their constitution: at least 15 per cent of the national budget must be invested (not 'spent') on education. That's three times the rate in the UK.

There are similarities between Taiwan and Japan. Both are small island nations with no natural resources, off the coast of powerful neighbouring nations. Both have come from nowhere in the space of a few decades to become major influences in world markets. And both initially got started by learning from Western businesses to build up their manufacturing and banking sectors, but now look set to continue out-running their erstwhile economic superiors.

Taiwan, a country the size of Wales with £90 billion of currency reserves, is now the fourteenth richest trading nation in the world. Their industrial rebirth began two decades after that of Japan and there are still some environmental problems, but their economy is growing at 6 per cent per year and already their skilled workers earn about the same as their equivalents in Western economies. How can we account for this phenomenal success? Clearly there must be several influences, but could it be that their attitude to knowledge and education has played a major role? If you believe this to be the case, what should we do back here in our Western companies? If you have read as far as this I scarcely need spell it out to you, but if you want a basis for drawing up your plans, there's a draft manifesto supplied in Appendix II to this book.

The rifts in society between the knowledge-rich and the knowledge-poor can only be healed by making knowledge more abundant and sharing it and its benefits more widely. The responsibility for basic education has slipped from the shoulders of the family and the church and looks in danger of partly slipping from the state. If the concept of the nation state is to survive, the education of its nationals must again become one of the prime responsibilities of the state, but who should pick up the mantle in the meantime? The company university can simultaneously make a contribution and create a competitive edge, but so too can smaller initiatives such as those of Ricardo Semler. When people are treated as human partners rather than as a resource to be owned and exploited, they can grow in stature with their company to become unbeatable in their chosen markets. There are more similarities than differences between races and nations: what can be done in Taiwan and Brazil can also be done in the UK.

But if it takes weeks for individuals to begin changing their attitudes and beliefs, it takes months for organizations and years for governments.

... in government

When the bombs were falling on London and Coventry during World War II, the UK was politically united in a way we have not experienced since. We had a coalition government and we depended on each other for our very survival. But as soon as the war was over, we reverted to bi-partisan confrontational politics, with labour and capital competing for power. And it seemed to work for a while, after a fashion, with the responsibility for government alternating between the two main parties, and each curbing the worst excesses of the other. But that was at a time when the borders of the UK as a nation state were still intact, and we had to provide for ourselves our own labour and our own capital, and both were important to industry and the wealth of the nation as a whole. But industry no longer needs much manual labour. The balance of power has permanently shifted, excesses are no longer being curbed, and inequality is higher than it has ever been in living memory. And while we squabble internally, the Asian Tigers of the Pacific Rim continue to grow in stature.

Our political systems in the West no longer seem appropriate in the modern world. At a time when customers are offered a bewildering variety of options to choose from, voters can only choose between two main political parties. As voters in the present system we cannot support individual policies. All we can do is vote for the package of policies in a party manifesto, even though we may strongly disagree with some policies. As a result, politicians rather than policies compete, attacking each other personally. It is another example of the undesirable situation described in Chapter 4 in which people instead of ideas compete. Meanwhile, voters look on with growing cynicism as jobs become less secure and manual workers are marginalized by the twin forces of global markets and information technology. But whatever may happen in the immediate future, the fundamental problem is that few political parties in Western nations fully represent all their citizens. Generally speaking, parties on the right represent those with money, and parties on the left those with jobs, while the growing number of people with no job security and little money are very poorly represented. The politics of confrontation prevail, with crude ideological win-lose battles between politicians, at a time when the politics of dialogue and win-win competition between ideas is needed.

So what's the solution? Are the problems of running UK plc conceptually similar to the problems of running any other organization? Political debates in Westminster often centre on the same issues fought over in industrial disputes, and the solutions may be conceptually similar too. If this is so, we need the principles of TQM and the learning organization in Westminster, together with all that entails – less top-down control and more local empowerment, less emphasis on financial measures and more emphasis on the quality of life. To succeed in world markets, we need to feel we are one nation, united behind political leaders whose values and beliefs we can all broadly share. With the whole nation thinking and working together, we can regain our self-respect and start making a proper contribution to the world once again.

If this sounds starry eyed and idealistic, consider the alternatives. Further loss of faith in our politicians, and further erosion of the authority of the state? We should not underestimate the consequences: eventually democracy itself could perhaps be threatened. But what can be done? Where to start, and how to overcome resistance from vested interests? In the absence of a written constitution we might benefit from a written statement of values, safe from modification by party politicians, which we can all subscribe to. Perhaps a new Bill of Rights enshrining the values of shared knowledge, full employment and equality of opportunity might be a suitable start.

... in life

Knowledge is the key to any, and every problem, from the simplest question of a child to the grandest, most all-encompassing questions we have about the universe and the meaning of life itself. Learning can be difficult, painful and dangerous, but it can also be exhilarating, fulfilling and rewarding. To seek to learn is part of what it means to be human, but we share this individual ability with other animals. What sets us apart from other species is our much greater capacity to learn, both as individuals and as groups, and to pass on this learning from generation to generation. In fact this is the mechanism by which civilization progresses, but when hate is passed on and learned, it can hold back civilization, or even put it into reverse. We have seen in Bosnia the appalling things that humans are capable of doing to each other, and assume we could never behave like that, but can you be sure? The studies in Chapter 11 have shown how immensely powerful situational pressures can be.

For our own and our children's sakes we must try to build structures at every level in society in which the situational pressures encourage dialogue and support learning. Then the problems we face will surely yield to the leveraged brain power of millions of minds. This is perhaps the key challenge we face as we plunge deeper into the information revolution: how to promote self-managed group learning in families and communities, in organizations and the nation, which encourage us to value the ultimate resource – knowledge – and to develop it, share it and exploit it for our common benefit.

Pause for thought

1   In your judgement how accurate a view does this chapter put forward? Do you regard it as a true or distorted perspective on a developing situation? Which parts do you accept as probably true, and which parts do you have difficulty in accepting? Go back to the text and mark in the margin any issues you would like to find out more about.

2   Do you view this chapter as party political and partisan? Or do you see it as a mainly dispassionate and impartial commentary on the possible effects of social and technical changes? Which issues affect the whole of society, and not just a particular group, which you may or may not belong to? Mark in the text any issues which do not, and never will affect you and your family.

3   Jot down two or three observable good effects of free markets. Do the same for observable bad effects. Might it be possible in theory to limit some of the bad effects without curtailing the good effects? Under what circumstances might this be possible?

4   How has this book influenced you? Has it helped you develop your view of the changes taking place in the world? In what way might you behave differently at work as a result of reading this book? Jot down two or three practical measures you will probably now take. Jot down any changes in your values as a result of thinking about the topics covered, which may affect your decision-making at work.

References

Hutton, W. (1995) *The State We're In*. Jonathan Cape.

Appendix I: Metaphors for promoting shared values

What keeps an organization on track in the absence of a command-and-control structure? The answer is consensus, leadership, communications and shared values – or in other words, a firmly held shared vision. Of course people will always disagree about the details, and so it is important to allow some ambiguity in constructing the vision. When we are allowed this freedom to supply the details – to help construct the vision – we buy in to it and commit ourselves to its achievement. A powerful device for constructing a vision, as Gareth Morgan has pointed out, is the metaphor.

The organization as ship

Ships have a captain who is in charge, a crew who sign up for the voyage, and perhaps passengers. All have a common objective – to arrive safely. All at times must trust and depend for their safety on just one person – like for instance the helmsperson at night when everyone else is asleep. Sometimes the ship is tossed around by a storm, and may get blown off course. The speed and safety of the ship depend not only on the skill and effort of the captain and crew, but also on the cargo being carried, design of the hull and the navigational equipment installed.

The organization as feudal manor

The feudal manor is run by the baron, who allocates land to knights so they can afford the expenses of a horse, a sword, armour and a squire. In return the knights owe homage and allegiance to their baron, and through him to their king. Knights throughout Europe obeyed a common code of chivalry, which developed from the rules of jousting.

Knights also go on crusades to spread the word, and to bring back trophies. They must defend their baron and their king in battle when called on to do so.

The organization as brain

A brain receives information through eyes and ears, processes it, stores it, and transmits it verbally by mouth, or in writing by hand. The brain may also direct the fists to fight or the legs to flight. Different parts of the brain, or groups of brain cells, perform different types of thinking task: the left side mostly for logical, analytical tasks, and the right side for creative, integrative tasks. The brain controls the body through the nervous system. Some bodily functions are automatic, some semi-automatic and some entirely voluntary.

Thinking takes place by adjacent brain cells connecting through synapses and thus communicating.

The organization as sports team

Teams have a captain. They are in competition with other teams. The purpose of the team is to out-perform other teams within the rules of competition. Teams usually display esprit de corps. They enjoy competition, and recognize that each player has a particular role which they must be relied upon to fulfil. Players must not let the side down. Teams members must practise together regularly, and they get to know each other very well. The performance of the team as a whole depends very much on members knowing the strengths and weaknesses of each other. Teams enjoy each other's company and have fun together.

The organization as organism

Organisms monitor their environment for predators and prey. They respond to stimuli and depend for their survival on quick and appropriate reactions. They require a constant supply of air, water and food. They consume these inputs, and eject waste products. Some simple organisms live on the waste products of other larger organisms.

The organization as chess pieces

The players deploy their pieces in combat. A player may sacrifice a piece in order to gain a strategic advantage. Pawns are the most numerous and least valued pieces. Needless to say, the pieces do not think or feel for themselves: the player does the thinking and the pieces are just manipulated by the player.

The organization as machine

The owner of the machine can speed it up or slow it down, switch it on or off at will. The machine is an inflexible assembly of cogs, wheels, spindles and belts which must all turn at the same speed. When a part wears out, it is usually thrown out and replaced by a new part. Oil is needed to reduce friction between the parts, and to keep it running smoothly.

The organization as farm

Good farmers think of themselves as temporary custodians of the farm land, even when they own and intend to keep the land. At some stage the land will pass to someone else, either a family member or a purchaser, but the condition of the land will continue to bear witness to the custodianship of earlier farmers. Trees planted now may not reach maturity until many years after the farmer who planted them is gone. A good farmer will never sell off any parcels of land, unless compelled to do so.

The soil must be prepared for sowing. The seed is sown, nurtured and protected, then harvested and sold. Crops should be rotated to prevent the soil being exhausted. The farmer should experiment with new crops from time to time.

Appendix II: A draft manifesto for the knowledge-based organization

1. Knowledge is the prime resource of our company – more important than all other resources, including capital. All our decisions on improving the products and services of our company will be guided by this principle.
2. Our employees are not a resource – we are all members of the company. We jointly commit to develop, share and use knowledge for our common benefit.
3. We expect to be rewarded by our company in proportion to our individual and joint knowledge contribution, but never at the expense of other members.
4. We will exploit our knowledge to our benefit, and to the benefit and well-being of all other stakeholders, in the following order: customers, shareholders and creditors, the local community, all other fellow nationals, all global citizens.
5. To achieve these ends we will strive for excellent communications amongst our members and with our external stakeholders. We will also strive to promote and maintain a balance between the following values: responsibility, freedom, commitment, truth, self-criticism, openness, trust and respect for the individual.

Glossary

Batch size – This is the number of items or orders which are dealt with together as a batch to be ordered, processed, transferred or delivered. Individual items in a batch have to wait for all other items to be ready before the batch as a whole can move on to the next stage. Thus the bigger the batch size, the longer the lead time, and the longer the external or internal customer has to wait.

BPR – business process re-engineering. A business improvement technique popularized in 1990 by Mike Hammer of MIT, and James Champy of CSC Index. It calls for businesses to be fundamentally redesigned around the latest digital technology, rather than just using it to automate existing business processes. In many cases it has yielded closer to ten-fold productivity improvements in place of the usual ten percent increases achieved by simply automating existing processes. Layoffs frequently follow BPR projects, though it was never Hammer's intention that this should be the result.

Chaos theory – the new science of complexity and unstable systems. In this context, chaos does not mean utter formlessness and confusion, but does suggest that some aspects of the world are much more complex than we previously thought, and may in fact be entirely unpredictable beyond the short-term.

Client/server – a database structure in which database software in several client desktop computers works with files stored in a single server database on a larger central computer.

CNC – computer numerical control. A computer system attached to production machinery, dedicated to the task of controlling the tool paths, speeds and feed rates used in cutting and forming the materials being processed. A CNC machine can hold several different programs, and can switch from one to another almost instantaneously. Very high standards of quality can be achieved, and changeover times are almost non-existent.

CSCW – computer support for co-operative work. A general term to cover networked computers equipped with software specifically designed to support team working.

DCF – discounted cash flow. The financial markets make it possible for a larger future amount of money to be exchanged for a smaller present amount. The size of the larger future amount is found by compound interest – compounding the present amount forward into the future. Discounting is simply the reverse of this calculation, and a discounted cash flow is the values of future payoffs from an investment, discounted back to present time.

Division of labour – a principle first proposed in the eighteenth century by the economist Adam Smith in his book *The Wealth of*

Nations. He was the first to explain the big improvements in productivity which could be achieved by dividing up a manufacturing process into a series of simple tasks in a production line, with each performed by a different worker.

Economic batch size – There is a constant ordering or set-up cost when purchasing or authorizing production of a batch of product. The smaller the batch, the more often this is incurred, and the larger the total cost. However, very large batches require large amounts to be stored to meet demand for the product during the longer periods between orders, so storage costs are heavy. The economic batch size is the one which produces the lowest cost compromise between these two extremes.

Empowerment – the process of passing the authority and responsibility traditionally held by middle management down to lower levels in the organization, so they may act in a more timely and responsive manner to problems and customer requests as they arise.

Gantt chart – a horizontal bar chart with calendar dates along the top. The length of each bar represents the duration of something, such as a project activity or a holiday period. Several activities or people can be listed down the left side of the chart, each with their activities or holidays shown on the same row.

Groupware – software such as Lotus Notes, and Microsoft Windows for Workgroups, which is specifically designed to support team working. It facilitates sharing of files, email, conferencing, scheduling and planning of group activities, and automation of work flow.

HRM – human resource management. A new approach to managing people, more suited to the flatter, team-based organization. It represents a distinct break from the traditional personnel function which was more suited to bureaucratic organizations. The HRM approach seeks to coach rather than train, empower rather than control, devolve rather than centralize, and maximize the use of peoples' skills rather than minimize their cost.

IRR – internal rate of return. This is an alternative name for the discounted cash flow rate of return, the method used to calculate rates of interest for building society and bank loans. It is called the internal rate of return because by using the same calculations as the banks, it is possible to compare internal investment projects directly with external opportunities for investing the money.

JIT – just-in-time. A system of production where products are transferred from process to process in transfer batches of one, with almost no buffer stocks between processes. When a process somewhere in the middle of the production routing finishes its processing and passes an item to the next process downstream, it should receive another item from the process upstream 'just in time' to keep it busy. The system depends on tight scheduling, and the highest levels of manufacturing quality.

Kaizen – the Japanese word for continual improvement. It is also the name given to the management philosophy which in the west we refer to as total quality management (TQM).

Kanban – the Japanese word for visible record. It is a way of ensuring the minimum of work-in-process is held between stages of manufacturing, and is a key element of just-in-time manufacturing.

Lead time – the time which elapses between placing an order and receiving the goods or services. It applies to internal Works Orders, and to external Purchase Orders. Lead times in both cases must be as short as possible for maximum flexibility and customer satisfaction.

MPS – master production schedule. A statement of the total requirements of finished prodcts to be produced week by week for the next six months or so. It is the schedule of production which the production planning department is aiming to achieve, and is derived from sales forecasts and orders received.

MRP – materials requirement planning. Computer software first developed in the 1960s for working out when parts should be made, and when materials should be ordered. It takes the master production schedule which is a statement of the weekly requirements of finished goods, and works backwards in time to find out when the parts and materials should be scheduled to be delivered, to allow time for processing and assembly.

MRP 2 – manufacturing resource planning. MRP software which has been further developed and enhanced to take in the scheduling of all manufacturing resources for a given MPS, not just materials and parts, but also the acquisition of finance, machinery, personnel, etc.

Multimedia – a free intermix of a wide variety of audio-visual effects. Originally, computers could only handle alphanumeric characters. Now they can handle a combination of text, graphics, animation, video, music, voice and stereo sound effects. Interactive multimedia presentations can be a powerful form of communication.

NPV – net present value. This is the net return on an investment, calculated by finding the sum of all the future positive cash flows, each discounted back to the present day, and then subtracting the initial amount invested. It may be thought of as the value of an idea implemented as a project, using finance borrowed at the going rate.

OO systems – object-oriented systems, which store records as objects, instead of in hierarchies of tables. In traditional databases the data and the procedures are kept separate, but objects contain procedures along with the data. OO systems are more flexible and easier to modify to suit the changing business needs of an organization than the traditional monolithic systems based upon relational databases.

Paradigm – the fundamental beliefs or mindset which exerts a powerful influence on decision-making. These beliefs are acquired as part of initiation to membership of a particular scientific or professional community. They are held at a deep level, and are seldom brought to the surface for re-examination.

PERT – programme evaluation and review technique. A method for planning, analysing, co-ordinating and controlling the activities which make up a project. The method makes it possible to identify the few critical activities which determine the project duration from amongst the many other non-critical activities which have more time available than is required for their completion.

Quality circles – groups of workers who meet outside normal working hours to discuss ways of improving the way things are done at work. The groups, also known as quality improvement teams, are paid for the extra efforts and encouraged by management to study and acquire any skills they may need. These groups of up to ten workers are often led by a supervisor, who acts as coach, mentor and advisor.

Scientific management – a school of management or set of beliefs associated with F. W. Taylor, in which workers are assumed to share some of the characteristics of machinery. For the highest productivity, workers are to be provided with the best methods, the right food (fuel), rest periods, levels of heat and light in the work place and so forth – all of which should be determined by scientific experimentation.

TQM – total quality management. A management philosophy which trains, encourages and empowers everyone in the organization to work in teams, to apply a systematic approach to manage their own work and to solve their own problems – especially quality problems. Quality is determined by the expectations of the customer, that is the next person to receive the work, whether inside or outside the organization. The aim for everyone is to exceed the expectations of their customers.

WIP – work in process, or work in progress. It consists of partly completed work, temporarily stored, or in transit between stages of manufacture. It includes partly processed materials, sub-assemblies, and partly assembled finished goods.

Index